Communing with Nature

A Guidebook for Enhancing Your Relationship with the Living Earth

JOHN L. SWANSON, Ph.D.

ILLAHEE PRESS • CORVALLIS, OREGON

Illahee Press
460 SW Madison, Suite #12
Corvallis, OR 97333-4795

Cover Design by Jan Weir

Cover Photograph by Christopher Speakman

ISBN: 0-75963-661-3

This book is printed on acid free paper.

Library of Congress Control Number: 2001091195

Permissions and Acknowledgments
I'm grateful for receiving permission to include the following poems and quotations from the following works: Excerpt from article "I Can Sing of Death, But I'm Obsessed with Life" by Dotson Rader reprinted with permission from *Parade*, Copyright © 1995. Pattiann Rogers, "The Determinations of the Scene," in *Song of the World Becoming: New and collected Poems 1981-2001* (Minneapolis: Milkweed Editions, 2001) Copyright © 2001 by Pattiann Rogers. Reprinted with Permission from Milkweed Editions. "Return", copyright 1935 & renewed 1963 by Donnan Jeffers and Garth Jeffers, from THE SELECTED POEMS OF ROBINSON JEFFERS by Robinson Jeffers. Used by permission of Random House, Inc. "Force of Gravity", from RILKE ON LOVE AND OTHER DIFFICULTIES: Translations and considerations, translated by John J. L. Mood. Copyright © 1975 by W. W. Norton & Company, Inc. Used by permission of W. W. Norton & Company, Inc.

1stBooks - rev. 08/28/01

PRAISE FOR COMMUNING WITH NATURE

"John Swanson is that rare guide who not only shows us the terrain, but also sharpens our lenses, deepens our presence. In his company we can learn to merge with the natural world – our larger body – and experience the delight, reverence, and renewal that is our birthright."

---- Joanna Macy, author *Coming Back to Life: Practices to Reconnect Our Lives, Our World*

"*Communing with Nature* is an intelligent and deeply inspiring journey into the heart of the human-nature relationship. In a time when so much is at stake in our world, this ecopsychological guide for reconnecting with nature is a valuable resource for educators, therapists, wilderness guides and anyone who loves the earth. This wonderful book is filled with insightful theory, practical exercises, suggestions for using the exercises and examples of how the author has successfully applied them in his own teaching. I highly recommend this book.

---- Jed Swift, Director of the Center for Ecopsychology Naropa University, Boulder, Colorado

From the rejection letters of major publishers:

"*I was impressed by the author's vision for this project and his lovely writing style.*"

---- Mark Chimsky, Rodale Press

"*Communing with Nature is a terrific, accessible, practical, sensible proposal but I don't see a wide readership for it, much as I wish I did.*"

---- Leslie Meredith, Executive Editor Ballantine Publishing Group

Nature, (if we may combine a billion interlocking miracles into one word) is the ultimate teacher. Never for a single moment are we out from under her influence. From the moment of our birth until our planet reclaims us we are locked into a web of incredible happenings. Our breathing is a miraculous (and extremely complicated) natural event, and so is every sound we hear, every flash of color our eyes relay to our brains. In every touch, be it soft or rough or hard or smooth, our bodies in their every part are receivers of information—and nature is always the sender.

There is no real place for any of us unless we at least begin to understand that we belong to something larger than ourselves—the cosmos. There is no real peace for any of us unless we at least know that we can fit in. The greatest hope any of us can have for getting along with each other is to know that we are part of one design. That design is nature, the natural systems that control everything around us . . . No lesson is greater than this—we are a part of it all . . .

Every time we look up and see a cloud and understand it, we are closer to understanding ourselves. When we pick up a rock and admire it instead of heaving it at something, we are closer to some ultimate truth. When we hear a bird and stop for the sheer pleasure of that sound, we are far nearer to real life than we were before. When we acknowledge beauty, we benefit from it most. When we feel the texture of the world around us, we are closer to accepting with grace the best it can offer us."

Roger Caras (Introduction to *Enjoying Nature with Your Family* by Michael Chinery, Roxby Press 1977)

Acknowledgments

An old sociology professor of mine, Dr. Robert McNair, liked the quote, "Creativity is the result of lost sources." By remembering this quote and forgetting its author, I add credence to its message. In trying to formulate this book's message, I did much background reading. I found that many others had already barked up this tree before and had articulated parts of my message very well. I picked up a good phrase here, another there, modifying them to fit my own biases. I have quoted many sources in this book, but many of the tiny bits-and-pieces contributors will go unrecognized. I didn't want the book to read like a piece of scholarly research by citing every phrase and idea. I'll start then by thanking my teachers, many of whom are listed in the bibliography and the many others who are now forgotten sources.

More close to home, I'd like to thank those who were more personally involved, those who previewed the manuscript and shared their ideas: Pat Korb, Chris Anderson, Matt Yurdana for helping me see the big picture. To Allison Clement for helping me trash unneeded words, editing out my over-doings. To Michael Mielke for engaging me in stimulating dialogue which kept me working on these ideas. To Wolfgang Dengler and my other nature companions.

On the home front, I'd like to thank my wife, Jeanne, whose own success as a writer helped show me the way; who helped not only with encouragement but with editing out polysyllabic obfuscations and word-clutter. My son, Andy, and daughter, Anna Marie, also contributed to the loving family support that nurtured me along the way.

And finally and most importantly to my beloved teacher and primary resource, Mother Earth and her many emissaries. To otter, osprey, hawk, butterfly, sacred rock and waterfall, sunrise and sunset, moonrise and moonset, wind, rain, snow, and the star-filled heavens. Without the many awe-filled moments brought by these emissaries, I would never have been inspired to write this guidebook.

Table of Contents

Part I: Participating In Nature

Part II: Exploring the What, Where, and When of Nature

Part III: Experiencing the Sacred in Nature

My Story

Even though I have been a nature-lover for as long as I can remember, my experiences, as wonderful as they were, remained limited by the blinders of our culture's commonly held assumptions about nature. Not until I was over forty did my experience of nature change in profound ways.

In 1987, I arranged to take a five-day backpack for personal rejuvenation. Through a series of remarkable coincidences, this trip evolved into a self-styled vision quest experience, the first of my annual pilgrimages into the woods that have had an unexpectedly powerful transforming effect on my life. Until then, outdoors was for recreating, especially for fishing.

My grandma introduced me to fishing at age five. My nature outings revolved around my passion for catching bluegill, bass, trout, or whatever else I could entice onto my hook. On my first vision quest, that summer of '87, I became hooked on "cosmic fishing," a metaphor that emerged for catching epiphanies in nature. My passion had shifted. No longer was nature in the background, the wonderful setting where I went fishing. Being in nature became the primary focus. I began to delight more in seeing fish dance on the surface of the lake than putting them in my creel. An ever-deepening commitment grew as I consciously explored and cultivated my relationship with nature.

Now, nature speaks to me and I listen. I enter into relationship with Mother Nature, a relationship which is so intimate that I experience her as the very ground of my being. My nature experiences now serve as primary guiding forces in the way I live my life.

For all my adult years, the exploration of personal growth and helping others has been my passion. As a mental health counselor and counselor educator I devoted myself to mastering relationship skills to help people heal and grow. My two greatest passions, being with clients in my office and being with nature in the great outdoors remained separate until my vision quest experiences brought them together. I began wondering how these kinds of nature experiences, which had been so powerfully transforming for me personally, might also apply to mental health practices in general.

This book reflects my efforts to integrate these two devotions of my life. What has been remarkable to me in this process is how much of what I've learned about creating healthy human relationships also applies to creating healthy relationships with the rest of nature. In retrospect, it seems so obvious that I wonder how I, along with most everyone else, have remained so entrenched in our habitual worldview of nature as inanimate object rather than living subject. It's time to climb out of this entrenched position and take a fresh look. The activities in this book have helped catapult myself and others into the adventure of rediscovering nature anew. Now it's your turn.

Introduction

"Thousands of tired, nerve shaken, over-civilized people are beginning to find out that going to the mountains is going home; that wildness is a necessity; and that mountain parks and reservations are useful not only as fountains of lumber and irrigating rivers, but as fountains of life."

John Muir

I'll bet, like me, you've had some special moments in nature: childhood memories of playing in the creek, a special family vacation spot, a beautiful sunrise or sunset, or maybe a close encounter with a wild animal. When I ask people, I hear amazing stories. They tell them to me with passion and nostalgia. These experiences are priceless gifts; and if you know how to be open to them, they need not be rare. This book will help you learn how to cultivate these precious experiences so that they become ongoing formative influences in your life.

To better cultivate these experiences, we must first understand that the ways we typically approach nature frustrate rather than foster their emergence. Our culture invites us to recreate the same way we work. When recreating in nature, we're usually busy doing something. As someone once said, we might better be called "human doings" rather than "human beings." Go into a bookstore and nature guidebooks abound: how to bird-watch, hunt and fish, mountain climb, explore caves, hike, camp, backpack, track, use a compass, rock climb, kayak, raft, sail, hang-glide, scuba dive, bicycle, identify wildflowers, collect shells, and so on. While these outdoor activities are valuable, my purpose, however, is not to tell you more about doing, but to help you explore how "to be" in nature.

The Challenge to Change Our Relationship with Nature:

"The world today is sick for lack of elemental things, for fire before the hands, for water welling from the earth, for air, for the dear earth itself underfoot."

Henry Beston

Our environmental crisis may be the greatest challenge ever to confront humankind. As most of us now recognize that our physical survival depends on saving our endangered planet, growing numbers of us are also beginning to realize that our environmental problems cannot be resolved without a change in consciousness. Unfortunately, while eloquently advocating the need for this change, few environmental experts address in any depth the challenge of how to achieve this life-preserving goal.

A growing number of us are beginning to realize that our physical survival is not all that is at stake. Our psychological and spiritual survival also depends upon changing our relationship with nature. In this book I offer you practical guidance for transforming your relationship with nature in ways that will help you explore and enhance the psychological and spiritual dimensions of your life. As these explorations are not wedded to any religious dogma or spiritual tradition, you will find ways to enrich yourself spiritually, whatever your religious persuasion.

The many books on environmental issues and ecology fall into the "natural sciences" category of knowledge. Psychology and self-help books fall into the "human sciences" category. Helping people change their consciousness, their perceptions, their feelings and behavior is in the province of the human sciences. The growing edge is at the interface between these two traditionally separate areas. This book attempts to blaze a trail linking the two.

Bringing together the ecological, the psychological and the spiritual, *Communing with Nature* invites you to explore the psycho-spiritual dimensions of the universe. It beckons you to awaken to your own identity as one that is inextricably embedded in your relationship to your environment, our planet and ultimately the universe.

We need to review our habitual ways of using the environment and explore new ways of moving into a more balanced participation with the ecosystems that make up our earth. Only then we will begin to know what it really means to be harmoniously attuned with nature.

In our culture, we typically view nature as inert material, as natural resource, object of scientific inquiry, pretty scenery, outdoor playground and jungle gym; as something separate from us that needs our conquering, domesticating, and civilizing. Yet, we may very well be living in the midst of a transformation that rivals the Copernican revolution in magnitude. This revolution involves a paradigm shift from a mechanistic to an ecological worldview, a shift in which nature will come to be experienced as "thou," a living presence. As such, we enter into an I-thou relationship with nature, rather than merely use it as we see fit. When we tune in to the expressions of nature, entering into dialogue with it, the psychological and spiritual, as well as the material, dimensions of our experience are activated. From this new emerging worldview, communing rather than consuming becomes the dominant focus of our interactions with nature. As expressed in the Eucharist, when we deeply know that our bread and wine come from the body of the divine, consumption itself becomes a communion experience.

The time for a fundamental change in the way we relate to nature is now. Our very survival depends on it. I believe this book will help us build the bridge needed for saving our planet, and our psyches and souls in the process.

When we experience nature as a living presence, the radiant beauty of the planet touches us in ways that intellectual information never can. We become more than scholars of nature. We become nature connoisseurs. Taking an experiential path we learn to develop our powers of awareness to enhance our knowing of nature in intimate personal ways. Even beautiful photographs of nature at the heights of its glory are only two-dimensional visual representations, satisfying to the eye but lacking the transformative impact of sight, sound, touch, smell that an experience of complete sensual immersion in nature provides. The printed page is not the place to experience the vitality of the earth. That's why I present experiential activities for exploring your relationship with nature.

Just being in nature is not sufficient. The wisdom and teachings of nature do not come automatically. When a pickpocket meets a saint he sees only pockets, just as a person working for the timber industry may see only board feet of lumber when looking at a forest. We must concern ourselves with *how* we relate to nature. With what goals, attitudes, fears, and preconceptions do we approach nature? In what ways are we blocked from experiencing nature? How do we avoid intimate contact with nature?

In this guidebook, I invite you to examine your own states of awareness and responses as you enter into special ways of relating to nature. With guidance, you can learn to have experiences that increase your love for the wild, unfettered, vibrant abundance of nature, converting yourself into a devotee of the vast repository of wisdom inherent in the earth. New concepts reframe our understandings leading us into different realms of experience. Yet we must do much more than change our minds about nature. We must immerse ourselves in a transformative series of experiences that change us in heart, mind, body, and soul.

The primary purpose of this guidebook is not to provide you with answers, but rather to plunge you deeper into the mysteries of existence, to provide you with navigational tools for discovering and developing your own unique relationship with nature. Through this book, I pass on to you the gift of relating to nature in healthier ways with all its wonderful benefits. By following the nature prescriptions in this book, you will discover and develop your capacity for entering, dwelling, and reveling in the community of life.

Prescribing Nature

"Is it possible, then, that every nature poet since Wordsworth has been right in telling us our sanity depends upon access to wilderness and natural wonders, upon the companionship of trees and beasts, and above

all upon the reverence we experience in the presence of the inhumanly magnificent? If so, then healing the wounded psyche may require that we find ways to 'prescribe nature.'"
Theodore Roszak "Beyond the Reality Principle"

As an alternative to prescribing medications to help us adapt to unhealthy lifestyles in inhospitable environments, we can prescribe what John Muir called "the tonic of wilderness." Medications are necessary and beneficial in some cases. In others, however, adding chemicals to medicate away distressing feelings further complicates matters by disrupting and distorting the body's natural self-regulating processes. In small doses or large, nature activities provide drug-free revitalizers, energizers, and tranquilizers, whether a five-minute meditation in a local park on the way to work or a weeklong retreat.

Bay Area psychologist James Swan prescribes nature. "My prescription for inner turmoil is spending a minimum of four hours alone in a natural area, with no activities or distractions. Just sitting quietly in that atmosphere allows most people to process a lot of emotions and issues they haven't been dealing with." Swan also recommends keeping track of natural symbols, such as plants or animals, that appear in dreams and, when practical, reinforcing them by bringing them into our daily lives. If you dream of the seashore, you might arrange a trip to the coast, for example.

Therapist Evelyn Bassoff advises her clients to establish a relationship with nature. To do this she suggests solitary walks, hiking along a creek, planting and tending a small garden, sitting under the stars at night, filling a room with plants and flowers, caring for an animal, absorbing the warmth of sunlight, watching birds and squirrels, or buying a bouquet of flowers.

In her book *The Shelter of Each Other,* psychologist and author Mary Pipher shares the prescription she frequently gives to families in therapy, "I'm going to make a couple of radical suggestions here. One is that you turn off the television and computer for at least a couple nights a week, and two, that the family do something out of doors every week. Watch a sunset, go for a walk or take a trip to a wilderness area."

Nature can be a source of solace for those struggling with the pain of loss. That's why giving flowers to the bereaved is such a longstanding and widespread custom. For those whose distrust of others makes nurturing by other people problematic, nature can be a nurturer. Many have experienced the soothing effects of listening to the rippling water of a stream or watching clouds drift overhead.

Client after client of mine report special places in nature that comforted them, giving them sanctuary from the demands of their troubled lives. Judy, who was severely abused by her first husband, told me how she would often go to the seashore. "Without these times walking on the beach, staring out at the ocean waves, watching the seagulls, I don't think I would have been able to survive. When I started thinking about suicide, I knew it was time to get myself to the coast."

Nature writer Gretel Ehrlich describes how nature supported her grieving, "I had a sense that the best place for me to grieve for David was with animals and out on the land. There were many things at play. When you're sick, the instinct is to go to bed. When you're grieving, the same instinct makes you want to find a place that is uncomplicated, accepting, and tolerant. I wanted to hook up with whatever it is that makes things live and die, and I wanted to be with people who weren't going to talk it into the ground."

In addition to providing comfort and solace for healing, and sanctuary from the stresses of modern day living, nature, when woven into the fabric of everyday life, provides nourishment for vibrant healthy living. The idea that time in nature is especially beneficial for mental health can be found throughout recorded history. The pervasiveness of testimonials by renowned environmentalists, naturalists, philosophers, theologians, essayists, and poets provides strong anecdotal support for the idea that nature is good for what ails you. For example, Frederick Law Olmsted, one of the first landscape architects in the United States and designer of New York City's Central Park, stated it this way back in 1865, "the occasional contemplation of natural scenes of an impressive character, particularly if this contemplation occurs in connection with relief from ordinary cares, change of air and change of habits, is favorable to the health and vigor of men . . . beyond any other conditions which can be offered them, that it not only gives pleasure for the time being, but increases the subsequent capacity for happiness . . . The want of such occasional recreation where men and women are habitually pressed by their business or household cares often results in a class of disorders the characteristic quality of which is mental disability, sometimes taking the severe forms of . . . insanity, but more frequently of mental and nervous excitability, moroseness, melancholy or irascibility, incapacitating the subject for the proper exercise of the intellectual and moral forces."

The profusions of nature are nurturing, aesthetically pleasing, physically invigorating, stimulating of the imagination, even spiritually profound. There is plenty of evidence that human nature and mother nature resonate to a common order that is physically, psychologically, and spiritually whole-some. Reconnecting with nature reawakens us to pleasure and beauty that feed us in body, mind, and soul. In the words of John Muir, "Climb the mountains and get their good tidings; Nature's peace will flow into you as sunshine into flowers; the winds will blow their freshness into you and the storms their energy, and cares will drop off like autumn leaves."

Understanding the therapeutic value of nature is the focus of a new movement in mental health called ecopsychology and ecotherapy. An ecological approach to personal growth includes exploring people's responsiveness to the vitality and toxicity of their environments. How does commuting between work and home effect them? What is their response to their work environment? How much beauty and comfort do they find in their own home? How much time do they spend in man-made vs. natural environments? What links are there between people's environmental problems and their psychological problems and symptoms?

We can become aware of how, for better or for worse, we are embedded in a complex web of interrelating systems within the bioregions in which we choose to live. We are in relationship not merely with other humans, but also with the plants and animals, with the landscape and its climate, with the sun and the moon, with all of it. We are continuously shaping and being shaped by "all our relations." We will be healthy to the extent that these relationships are healthy.

How to Use this Book

This book is not meant for reading once from cover to cover. Rather, it is a guidebook, a reference for you to refer to when your situation calls for it, when you go on a camping trip, plan a retreat, or when you're in the mood to explore your day-to-day relationship with nature. The nature activities provide you with over eighty "recipes" for creating special experiences in nature. When you consider all of the possible permutations of taking these activities into a wide variety of natural settings, the opportunities for growth become endless.

The book is divided into three parts. Part I begins with a chapter that introduces the nature activities. *Chapter 1 is a must read before you begin experimenting with the activities.* It outlines the types of activities and gives you guidelines and tips on how to implement them. If the activities are like recipes in a cookbook, this chapter is like a brief overview in the fundamentals of cooking.

I recommend scanning or a light reading of the book to obtain an overview of its contents. The activities in Part I provide the basic building-block activities that are elaborated upon in Parts II and III. Start with learning some of these basic activities. Then move on to Parts II and III. Part II introduces the many manifestations of nature that can be explored in a wide variety of ecosystems at different times of day and seasons of the year. Part III provides guidance for exploring the sacred dimensions of nature. It concludes with a chapter that helps you plan extended stays in nature.

Part I

Participating In Nature

1

Introduction to the Activities

"Nature seemed to me full of wonders,
and I wanted to steep myself in them.
Every stone, every plant, every single thing
seemed alive and indescribably marvelous.
I immersed myself in nature
crawled, as it were,
into the very essence of nature."

C.G. Jung *Memories, Dreams, Reflections*

Making Tea

March 16, 1997. My plan for this particular morning is to prepare for my upcoming "Nature and Psyche" workshop in Florida. I wake up early with the following dream: I'm observing an outdoor nature workshop. The participants are standing in a circle in an open grassy area which is itself encircled by majestic old oak trees. In silent ceremony, the workshop leader goes around placing what appears to be a medicine bag, a pouch in which talismans are placed, around the neck of each participant. I'm startled when I recognize that the pouches are actually tea bags. At that startled moment of recognition, I wake up feeling bewildered. Reflecting on the dream, I remain mystified until my thoughts land on what you do with tea bags. Ah ha! I go to my copy of *Webster's Encyclopedic Unabridged Dictionary* and look up the word steep.

From the dictionary, I read the following definitions of the word steep: **1.** to soak in, to soften, to cleanse, to extract some constituent. **2.** to drench, saturate, imbue (to impregnate or inspire). **3.** to immerse in with some pervading, absorbing or stupefying (the power to overwhelm with amazement, astound, astonish) influence or agency: *an incident steeped in mystery.*

By exploring the definitions of the word steep, the message of the dream became amazingly clear. My dream had given me a wonderful metaphor for participating in nature activities. You, the participant, are the tea bag. Your skin is the permeable membrane. You are to be immersed in nature and soak it in. You will be softened, cleansed. You will become imbued, impregnated, and inspired by Mother Nature. Immersing yourself in the all-pervading presence of nature serves as the catalyzing power to influence you in astounding ways, to overwhelm you with amazement. You will have incidents of being steeped in mystery.

The making of tea is a process of physical transformation. Unless the teabag is immersed in water, nothing happens. Without participating in the activities, without immersing yourself in the physical presence of nature, nothing will happen. There will be no transformation. You may learn about the process, you may have read the cookbook, but you will produce no meals. I myself have read self-help books and skipped over the activities.

To be transformed, you must take yourself in your permeable membrane outdoors and soak it in. You will need to plan special occasions to go outside and do the activities. Experiment with them. Repeat the ones that work for you. Try them in many combinations, in many seasons, in many places, in many moods, in small doses and large. My greatest hope would be that the essence of these activities becomes habitual, enabling you to benefit from a more harmonious relationship with nature. Immersed in the fluid presence of nature, you will become affluent, enriched by her many gifts. You will awaken into the fullness of Life. So be it.

The Activities

My background in gestalt therapy strongly influenced me in designing the self-directed activities in this book. I have studied and practiced it for over thirty years. The gestalt perspective, originating in the 50's, popularized in the 60's, and maturing into a well-established form of therapy in the 70's, is uniquely suited to guide us in relating to nature. This orientation informs both the conceptual framework and nature activities presented in this book.

Gestalt therapy is grounded in the belief that discovery is the most powerful form of learning. Awareness is the primary tool for change and growth.

Discovery is the "ah ha!" of recognition when gestalts are formed, when things come together in integrated wholes. More than mere intellectual insight, the discovery involves not just your mind but your feelings and perceptions. Understanding through discovery occurs when your experiences literally come together in ways that "make sense." Rather than try to change yourself, your developing awareness is the catalyst for change.

Gestalt is an experimental as well as experiential approach. Fundamental change comes about by experiencing yourself and your world differently. Rather than be passive, I invite you to become actively engaged in experiential activities that are designed to facilitate your growth. These little experiments in living interrupt your habitual ways and invite you to try something new and different, something that probably would not occur without the guidance provided by the activity.

One of the great strengths of the gestalt approach is that it provides methods for exploring and enhancing awareness. Throughout its history, gestaltists have been developing experiential activities designed with this in mind.

Well-designed activities invite and challenge you to change. New flexibility and possibilities emerge from what before were rigid, stuck patterns. Experiential activities support exploration, elaboration, and discovery.

While certain underlying assumptions and beliefs guided me in writing this book, I tried to avoid presenting you with a new dogma for acceptance as the latest gospel. There is no Right Way to do these activities. This is not to deny that I have some hunches about what may emerge. The activities are genuine experiments for learning about life and how it works. What's required of you is a curious exploratory attitude that is powerful enough to overcome fears of the unknown. Rather than trying to prove a point or manipulate for a certain outcome, I trust that your own unique experience is the valid one for you and is to be honored as your evolving truth. Learning to trust your own experience is much more important than attachment to any particular results. So, if your personal experience does not match with some of the ideas and beliefs presented, or if your personal response to some of the activities is quite different than the responses used to illustrate how the activities worked for others, trust your own experience. Remain open to the teachings of whatever emerges from the activity. Here's the most challenging part: When your experience contradicts long-held beliefs about yourself and nature, be open to revising them. The focus is on "what is," not on "what should be."

The activities in this book will: (1) increase the range, clarity, and fullness of your awareness; (2) help you experience yourself and your surroundings more fully; (3) guide you to explore intimate I-Thou relating with nature; and (4) help you explore and expand your self-boundaries. All four of these paths for personal growth are directed toward enhancing the quality of your relationship with nature.

Types of Activities:

The activities roughly fall into six types:

(1) *Directed Awareness Activities* invite you to pay attention to the environment or to a particular aspect of your behavior. Practicing these awareness techniques add depth, clarity and immediacy to your experience. Introduced in Chapter 2.

(2) *Foundational Activities* help prepare you for optimal communing with nature. Like tuning an instrument, these activities invite a state of relaxed alertness for resonant responding to nature's messages. Introduced in Chapter 3.

(3) *Sensory Awareness Activities* help you explore and develop your sense of hearing, seeing, taste, smell, and touch for enhancing the quality of your direct contact with nature. Introduced in Chapter 4.

(4) *Language and Experiencing Activities* help you explore how your use of language can block or enhance your experiencing of nature. Introduced in Chapter 5.

(5) *Nature Exploration & Dialogue Activities* invite you to explore I-thou relating with nature, experiencing it as a living presence rather than inanimate object. Introduced in Chapters 7 and 8.

(6) *Identification Activities* help you develop empathy for nature by inviting you to experience yourself as part of nature. Introduced at the end of Chapter 7 and reintroduced as a catalyst for peak experiences in Chapter 14.

Selecting the Activities

I recommend you treat the nature activities in this book much the same way you would recipes in a cookbook. Most people I know don't approach a cookbook by trying all the recipes in the order presented. More commonly, they first familiarize themselves with the recipes in the various sections of the cookbook.

After familiarizing yourself with the nature activities, try out one or two that interest you most. Then plan an outing that includes a variety of activities selecting ones that fit your personal needs, the landscape to be explored, and weather for that particular day. Set aside plenty of time so you won't be rushed. The last chapter covers extended stays in nature helping you to plan nature activities for several days or weeks at a time. The index of activities in the back of the book will come in handy when planning your nature outings.

Tailoring the Activities:

To be effective, each activity needs to be a good match for you, your interests, your experience and comfort in various nature settings, your available time, internal state, the circumstances available to you, and so on. The activities often present a number of variations to consider. I encourage you to adapt them to best fit you and your own unique situation. This includes "grading the activity" to be the right amount of challenge for you. If the activity is too easy, it is likely to fall flat, to lack energy and seem old hat. On the other hand, if an activity is too difficult, then you are more likely to avoid trying it in the first place, tighten up with too much anxiety, become overwhelmed, confused, or in other ways interrupt the process in ways that reduce or even eliminate learning and growth. So, I recommend that you actively and creatively tailor these activities to make them a good fit for you.

Rather than take the guidebook outdoors, exposing it to wind, rain, and soil, consider copying the activities onto 3 X 5 cards, modifying them with personal notations. Laminating the cards protects them from the elements. You might also consider making a tape recording of the instructions for some of the more detailed activities, choosing words and phrases that would best fit you and the unique circumstances of your nature outing.

General Guidelines for the Activities:

1. After tailoring the activity to your unique circumstances, read it over several times to get familiar enough with it so you won't have to go back to read it over while doing the activity.
2. Do the activities outdoors, in your yard, a park, or other natural setting that appeals to you. Once in awhile, for comparison and contrast, you

might try the same activity indoors in a man-made environment that isolates you from nature.

3.   Explore and be curious.
4.   Do them as if for the first time. Try to let go of your preconceptions about how the world operates.
5.   Take time to savor. Don't rush. Let the reality of your experiencing sink in.
6.   Trust and follow your own pace.
7.   Pay attention to what attracts and repels you. (For practice, see Attractions and Repulsions Activity, p. 32)
8.   Notice your tendencies to distract, interrupt, or tune out. When your mind wanders, gently bring it back to your immediate awareness of what is before you. (For practice see Duration and Flow Activity, p.33)
9.   Accept "what is" without judgment and trying to do what you should.
10. Pause along the way. Take time to digest your response to the experience before you move on to the next.
11. In finishing the activity, review to see how these sensations fuse and blend into a total experience. Look for common threads, themes, and lessons that tie it all together.
12. Write down your experience in a (nature activity) journal. (I would very much enjoy receiving accounts of one or two of your nature experiences. I also welcome your ideas for improving the activities and your suggestions for new ones. Send them to the address at the end of the book.)

One of the most challenging aspects of engaging in these activities will be learning the discipline of staying with the moment-to-moment flow of your experiencing. For example, when we think to ourselves, "What's next?" we interrupt our ongoing concrete connection with the emerging experience and move to the mental realm of anticipation. In meeting this challenge, you first become aware of the myriad of ways in which you interrupt, distract, block, close down, lull yourself to sleep, numb out or otherwise reduce the full impact of your ongoing experiencing. Next, you learn to observe these disruptions without blame. Then, by letting go of them, you can return to your on-going awareness in ways that deepen your experiencing. Learning to gracefully recover from our many mis-takes along the way is most helpful. Sometimes serendipitously and sometimes as a result of hard earned practice, we get "in the flow" of ongoing experiencing. It's delightful while it lasts. Though this approach is not especially difficult to grasp intellectually, each little step along the way can be quite challenging. So, be gentle and patient with yourself. It's a lifelong discipline that is probably never fully mastered.

When participating in the activities, it is very helpful to put yourself in the frame of mind of experiencing your world as if for the very first time. Pretend you are a newborn infant or a first-time visitor from another planet. The idea is to break out of habitual ways of experiencing that make for dullness so that you will experience with fresh fascination the dynamic dance of life.

> *"In the beginner's mind there are many possibilities but in the expert's there are few."*
>
> **Suzuki-roshi**, *Zen Mind, Beginner's Mind*

The Practical Business of Getting along with Nature

The activities are adaptable to a wide variety of settings. You can explore nature close to home, contemplating a vase of flowers in the comfort of your own living room; or you can rough it in a remote jungle, miles from the nearest convenience store. When you do choose to leave the comforts of home and get off the beaten path, the practical business of knowing how to protect yourself from nature's harshness is a sensible necessity. "City Slickers" need to learn the ropes. *The Complete Walker*, a classic by Colin Fletcher, has been called the "hiker's bible." It gives the complete practical compilation of all the equipment needed for a comfortable excursion into the backcountry. Books and resources for overcoming phobias and for learning wilderness survival skills, first aid, backpacking and hiking etiquette can benefit you in learning to live in modern day harmony with nature. Books on survival, orienteering, tracking, snow camping, and many others of this genre abound. One lighthearted book sports the title: *How to Shit in the Wilderness.* These books are of value not only for protecting you from the wilderness, but also for protecting the wilderness from you. I strongly urge you to read books that teach you how to leave the wilderness as you found it—undisturbed, unpolluted, undefiled. Select the resources that are relevant to you and your unique situation. The scout motto "be prepared" applies.

By participating in the activities in the chapters that follow, you will enter into an exploratory journey of transforming your relationship with nature into something more alive, more growth enhancing, and more wonder-full. I believe you will find this journey both challenging and fulfilling.

2

Enhancing Your Awareness

"Only that day dawns to which we are awake."

Henry David Thoreau
(closing message in *Walden Pond*)

Awareness Practice

You can learn to use your awareness in the service of your own personal growth. Enhanced awareness will serve you in creating healthy encounters with nature.

It is incredible how much you can realize about your existence by simply paying attention to your ongoing awareness process. Buddhists call this the practice of "mindfulness." Through awareness activities you can learn to open yourself to the depths of your own experiencing.

The first activity of this book, while deceptively simple, may be the most important of all. Originally developed as a gestalt therapy technique, this activity invites you to WAKE UP to the fact of your own existence. I first experienced this simple activity over thirty years ago and I continue to return to it over and over again.

Activity One ➢ Basic Awareness

Begin to explore your awareness by silently saying to yourself, "Right now, I'm aware of . . . " and finish each sentence with what you are aware of at this very moment. Begin each sentence with this introductory phrase, over and over, as you continue to state to yourself each emerging awareness. Pay attention to the flow of your awareness. Where does your awareness go? "Right now, I'm aware of . . . " . . . repeat . . . After completing this activity, do you feel any different than you did before? How?

This exercise invites you to be aware of the flashlight of your own awareness and how you use it in the present moment. To the extent that you can make this activity work for you, the resulting enhanced awareness will make you feel more alive, charged up with a new sense of vitality. The next activities will help you become savvier about how rich meaningful experiences are created.

Because we are finite rather than omniscient beings, much of life's unfolding happens out of our awareness. We can't swallow life in a single gulp. Healthy awareness, like the beam of a flashlight, is limited and selective. What is within the beam's light of our direct attention is called "figure," while everything else fades into the "background." Psychologists have found that the inability to ignore the many stimuli bombarding us every second is characteristic of certain severe mental disorders.

The awareness activities in this chapter, like the first one above, invite you to pay attention to the segments of experience captured by your "right now I'm aware of" statements. Each segment of awareness, by itself, may seem disjointed, even arbitrary. But collectively, like brush strokes on a canvass, they most often coalesce into a meaningful picture. This peculiar procedure brings you into the present moment to directly explore the concrete ways that your experiences are created.

There are three zones toward which the flashlight of awareness can be directed: the outside zone, the inside zone, and the fantasy zone. Awareness can be directed outward toward the external world. Our senses (seeing, hearing, touching, tasting, and smelling) can be directed toward people and things in our external environment. Awareness can also be directed inward toward the self, toward one's feelings and bodily sensations (proprioceptions). And third, it can be directed toward the midzone of fantasy, toward one's thoughts and imaginings.

Activity Two ➤ Zones of Awareness

Repeat the previous "Right now, I'm aware of . . . " activity, only this time note which of the three awareness zones you are in each time your awareness shifts. After completing this variation, did you notice what kinds of things and events you became aware of? Did you notice colors, shapes, textures, sounds, tensions, smells, movements in the external zone? Your ideas, imaginings, rememberings, anticipatings, fantasies in the midzone? Your breathing, muscle tone, lightness or heaviness, passions, and other feeling tones in the internal zone? Was there a full range of these varied kinds of experiencing? What kinds were included? What kinds were ignored? Out of the immense number of possible experiences, you select out a very small number for your attention

Next, explore the ways you experience being in each zone of awareness by doing the three variations of the basic awareness activity described below.

Activity Three ➤ Inside Zone

Explore the inside zone of your feelings and internal sensations. When you find yourself shifting to either of the other two zones, just gently bring yourself back into the inside zone. For example, "Right now, I feel light, expansive and joyous . . . tension in my neck . . . Now, I feel anger as I clench my fists . . . " and so on.

Activity Four ➤ Midzone

Explore the way you experience being in the midzone of thoughts and imaginings. For example, "Now, I'm thinking about going for a hike . . . imagining what this waterfall would look like in wintertime . . . trying to figure out why there are so few butterflies this year . . . " and so on. Note how being in this zone moves you away from the concrete and specific and into the world of abstractions and generalities. Also, it can remove you from your immediate present situation. To illustrate, try "Right now, I'm remembering . . . " or "Now, I'm anticipating . . . " Our present moments may entail rehashing and analyzing the past or planning and rehearsing for the future. Note how these rememberings and anticipatings can be emotionally charged and engaging, closely connected to the past or future horizons of your current situation; or be stale and detached, dreamworlds away from the significance of your present life.

Activity Five ➢ External Zone

Explore the way you attend to the external environment. For example, "Now, I'm watching the sky gradually change color as the sun sets . . . hearing the sharp cries of a bird overhead . . . " and so on. Remember, when you find yourself shifting to either of the other two zones, just gently bring yourself back into the external zone.

Is one of the three zones more foreign or familiar to you? Do you tend to gravitate towards one and have a hard time staying in another? Repeating these "Zones of Awareness Activities" helps you find out more about your natural tendencies. You can add much clarity to your life by learning to distinguish between the three zones, knowing when and how your internal sensations, your midzone fantasy material, and your sensing of the external environment are informing you.

The external zone activity and many of the activities in the upcoming chapters help you develop clearer seeing, hearing, and touching which are so essential to healthy functioning. Becoming overly self-absorbed with midzone thoughts and imaginings or inside zone feelings and sensations cuts you off from your external environment. The external zone activity teaches you about being out there more, strengthening your capacity for taking in nature. Photography or sketching in nature can support being out there visually. In general, healthy awareness involves a lively dance among all three zones that converge to provide rich meaningful experiences.

Out of the vast number of possible objects upon which we might focus our attention, what tends to draw our interest often reflects our current needs. For example, a hungry guest coming to a party might immediately zero in on the table of drinks and hors d'oeuvres. After snacking for awhile, her attention might shift to someone who reminds her of an old friend. An artist guest, on the other hand, might focus on the host's paintings. The next variation of the Basic

Awareness Activity helps you explore how your awareness tends to naturally gravitate towards perceptions that reflect your current needs, wants, desires, or interests.

Activity Six ➢ Awareness Selectivity Activity:

Repeat the Basic Awareness Activity: "Right now, I'm aware of . . . " As you go along repeating this phrase to yourself, note with each area your flashlight of awareness lands on, how the content may reflect your current needs, wants, desires, or interests.

Generally, what is perceived as nurturing or pleasant in the environment attracts us, and what is perceived as toxic, unpleasant, or threatening repels us. Freud called the basic dynamics of attraction and repulsion, positive and negative cathexis. Behaviorists call them positive and negative reinforcers. These attractions and repulsions are often linked to what brings us pleasure and pain.

Things perceived as irrelevant to meeting our needs fail to hold our attention as we scan the environment. Forced attention to the non-nurturing often results in feelings of restlessness or boredom. What attracts our attention in the world is most often a reflection of our own inner state. As you try these activities, see if you experience this as true for you.

Activity Seven ➢ Attractions and Repulsions

As you scan your environment with your awareness, see if you can sense whether you feel an attraction or a pulling back response. Try starting sentences with the phrases, "Right now, I'm attracted to . . . " or, "Right now, I'm repelled by . . . "

When we disengage prematurely from our developing contact with the environment, we interrupt and dilute the quality of our experiencing. Gestaltists call this disturbance of healthy contact "deflecting." Satisfying contact and deeper intimate relating is cut off. The following activity explores this process.

Activity Eight ➢ Duration and Flow

Begin by paying attention to your flow of awareness. "Right now, I'm aware of . . . " Don't interfere or change anything. Let it spontaneously and naturally move from one to the next. Notice how fast or slow the flow of your awareness is. Experiment with speeding it up and slowing it down. Notice how this changes the quality of your experiencing. Again return to simply observing your awareness as it freely flows. Does your awareness tend to jump quickly from one thing to another? Be aware of how some experiences last longer than others. Which ones do you dwell on and which ones do you pass over quickly? Notice when your flow of awareness is interrupted. When it shifts abruptly, try returning for awhile to what you were aware of just before the interruption. As your awareness moves from one to the next, how are these experiences related to each other? Follow your flow to learn about its direction. What are the themes connecting the successive things you become aware of? Do you find your awareness returning back again to certain kinds of things? Do you find your flow alternating between one kind of experiencing and another? Pay attention to transitions or abrupt interruptions that create a feeling of discontinuity and incompleteness. See if you can stay with your unfolding awareness so that you have a sense of full engagement and completion before moving on to the next.

Awareness can be directed to suspected "blind spots," to areas that are blocked, avoided, diminished, or distorted in some way. Nature itself can be a blind spot, remaining in the background of our experiencing, habitually ignored or even avoided, for a variety of reasons. The following activity helps break up habitual patterns and leads you to new insights.

Activity Nine ➢ Breakthrough Awareness

Begin this awareness activity like the others with the phrase, "Right now I'm aware of . . . " When you notice your awareness shifting to something else try, "and I left out . . . " or "and I skipped over . . . " or "and I interrupted . . . " Then try, "Right now, I am avoiding . . . " Many find this activity weird and awkward, especially when the phrases often are not in sync with their emerging awareness. Yet on the occasions when they are, most find that they make some interesting and sometimes powerful discoveries.

Don't give up on this activity too soon. With a little perseverance, it can give you a better sense of what your experiencing is like when you are avoiding something. With this enhanced sensitivity, you will, with increased frequency, spontaneously discover yourself avoiding when doing other activities.

The next activity highlights the relationship between our awareness of the external world and how we respond to that connection. In this "shuttling" activity you shift your awareness back and forth between outside and inside zones, between contacting the environment and withdrawing back into self-awareness of your organismic response.

Activity Ten ➤ Awareness Shuttling Activity

Begin with, "Now, I'm aware of . . . (something in your external environment) . . . and then say, "and my response to this is . . . (and finish this sentence with whatever you become aware of inside your body whether it be a feeling or bodily sensation). For example, "Now, I see the clouds drift slowly overhead. And my response to this is to feel my body lighten and slowly sway in sympathy." Continue this shifting back and forth between the external environment and your internal response for awhile. See what you can discover about how your awareness of inside events is related to your experience of your outside surroundings.

This awareness shuttling activity invites the openness and responsiveness needed for healthy engagement with your environment. Healthy engagement is flexible rather than rigid and is characterized by a rhythmic movement between connecting (meeting and engaging the environment) and separating (withdrawing into self-awareness of your own needs). This healthy back and forth flow called "organismic self-regulation" is a natural process that needs to be regained if it has been disturbed. I have included awareness shuttling in many of the nature activities that follow to help foster this process which is so important for healthy functioning.

Doing and Being In the World

We define ourselves by what we do or what we've done. For example, "I'm a father, counselor, member of the school board, and . . . Last year, I published five professional articles, visited three countries, climbed the highest mountain in Peru, made seventy thousand dollars, and . . . "

Activity Eleven ➢ "Who Are You?"

Respond to the question, "Who are you?" with "I am . . . " Ask it over and over. Note your responses. How often do you respond by defining yourself in terms of a role or an accomplishment? Do you also respond in terms of an inner quality or personal trait? For example, "I am introspective, quick witted, catlike, . . . an indoor person, a lover of poetry . . . " These responses focus not so much on what you do in the world, but rather on your ways of being in the world.

Our culture emphasizes productivity and accomplishments as a primary way to evaluate self-worth. To be idle is to court the devil, to waste time, to be bored. No wonder we spend most of our time doing rather than being.

Our contact with the outside world comes in two types distinguished by whether or not the contact is goal-oriented. For example you are looking at the words on this page right now as you read. Your eyes are moving along for the purpose of extracting meaning from the page. Goal-oriented contact puts us in the doing mode.

Contact can also be *"for-its-own-sake"* when it is not in the service of another goal. If, for example, you were interested in calligraphy, you might be seeing these words in a *whole different light*. An aesthetic dimension is added which brings visual appreciation into the foreground of your experience. This type of contact puts us in the being mode.

A purely goal-oriented contact can reduce the quality, range, and depth of experiencing. In response to an urgent and highly focused goal, our stressed organisms often respond with tight tunnel vision. On the other hand, when the focus shifts from doing to being, perception often loosens and broadens. The energy used in acting on the environment can be made available for enhancing perception.

Goal-oriented contact is very pervasive in our culture and the emphasis on this way of orienting in our world invites I-It rather than I-Thou relating. For example, when we look at a tree as lumber for building a log house, it exists merely as an object in the service of our goal of house construction. I-It relating is characterized by treating the other as an object, a means to an end, instead of living subject as we do in I-thou relating. Rather than take a narrow utilitarian view, we can appreciate all of the inherent qualities of a tree when engaging it in the I-Thou mode.

Activity Twelve ➤ Doing and Being

Spend some time (10-50 minutes) in a nature setting in goal oriented activity (gardening, fishing, bird watching, etc.) and then an equal amount of time in the same setting just being, just appreciating and noticing nature for its own sake without any goals. Compare and contrast these two ways of living in the world. What is it like when you focus on goal-oriented doing? On process-oriented being?

The activities in this chapter were designed to increase, through your own personal experience, your understanding of different ways of living in this world by:

- Learning how to develop your awareness as a tool for personal growth
- Learning to be in the here and now
- Exploring and developing healthy organismic self-regulation
- Bringing nature and wilderness out of the background and into the foreground of our awareness, and
- Learning to leave the doing mode and enter into the being mode of living in the world.

These insights will support you as you cultivate I-Thou relating in general, and with nature in particular.

3

Opening To Your Inner Nature

"The rare moment is not the moment when there is something worth looking at, but the moment when we are capable of seeing."

Joseph Wood Krutch

There is a primordial, vital connection between the alive and aware human body and the body of the living earth. This connection can be recognized, honored, and refined or it can be ignored, devalued, and broken.

Alienation from the earth's body and the human body go hand in hand. The disowning and abuse of our earth is an outward manifestation of the disowning and abuse our bodies. This relationship exemplifies how outward behaviors are oftentimes manifestations of inward processes. We do unto others what we do unto ourselves. Conversely, reconnecting with our bodies leads us to reconnect with the earth. When we re-own and love ourselves as living organisms, we are much more likely to re-own and love the earth as a living organism. Re-awakening to the physical, sensing dimension of our experience opens us to an immediate concrete relationship with the living earth.

To get in touch with your own body is to connect with your inner nature, which is the primary focus of this chapter. Direct sensory contact with the earth awakens the human body, which is the primary focus of Chapter 4. These two approaches mirror and support each other. Lynda Wheelwright Schmidt describes her experience of this relationship in her book *The Long Shore: A Psychological Experience of the Wilderness*. "The more I was most natural, the more welcome I felt in nature. I became part of nature discovering both my capacity to hear and feel nature as it goes about its business and my capacity to hear and feel my own systems of breathing, sweating, cooling, hunger, and itching as I moved through grass, dust, shade, and water . . . This process is one way to find the self."

Opening to your inner nature prepares you for opening outwardly to receive nature-as-a-whole. Foundational activities, like the ones presented in this chapter, are sensory awareness activities directed toward your internal zone of awareness. These inwardly directed nature activities involve "listening" to your body language, getting in touch with your organismic self. With experience you learn to read the nonverbal messages of your body. Resensitizing to your embodied self gives you a solid and heightened sense of your own aliveness. Developing this awareness is essential for living fully as a sensual being.

By tuning your organism for heightened sensitivity, the foundational activities in this chapter help you enter into a state of receptivity that will enhance the quality of your nature experiences. They help get you out of the doing mode and into the being mode.

Begin your nature explorations with one or more of the following activities. They will prime you for receiving nature's wonders.

Breathing

Breathing is a matter of life and death. It is essential, forever joined with the animating energy of the living body. To cut off this our most regular and intimate relationship with the environment is to begin to die. Breathing is a relationship of intimate exchange and transformation in which the environment is taken in and made part of the organism. The oxygen extracted from the inhaled air is burned as fuel, and then carbon dioxide, a byproduct of breathing, is released from inside the organism back out into the environment. The oxygen that you and all other animals are taking in at this moment is a gift from green plants, a byproduct of photosynthesis, given off by them as they breathe in the gift of carbon dioxide that we and other animals have exhaled. Plants and animals are linked in this symbiotic life-giving exchange. This phenomenon powerfully illustrates how we partake in the interdependent web of life. We are participating in what geophysiologists call "the breathing of the biosphere." To cut down a rain forest is analogous to surgically removing part of the earth's lungs, to massively destroy one of nature's most amazing power-plants, a producer of vast quantities of life-giving oxygen for humanity and all other oxygen dependent life on earth.

Breathing is more than just a physiological process for fueling the body. Developing a conscious connection with your breathing gives you important information about your feelings. Breathing and emotions are linked. Respiration is altered reflexively in states of changing emotional tension. The rapid emergency hyperventilation of a panic attack is a dramatic example. On the other hand, people suppress feelings and mounting excitement when holding their breath. In doing so, they cut off their most basic source of physiological support.

Another important aspect of breathing is its close connection with both the voluntary and autonomic nervous systems. Breathing can work automatically or be consciously altered. This linkage has led to speculation that the process of breathing is an important connecting link between the conscious and subconscious mind. By paying attention to your breathing, you can observe this dual aspect of the self at work. The yoga practice of breathing techniques called pranayama provides a more systematic and in-depth method for learning how different ways of breathing create different states of awareness.

Most importantly, focusing on your breathing is one way to directly connect with the depths of your being. Observing your inspiration, you experience your body taking in life-giving air. You are being inspired, in-spirited, animated with life. The human body is the Temple of the Holy Spirit, the vehicle through which the soul can establish relation with the earth and the universe. No wonder mystics throughout the ages meditate on their own breathing as a way to enlightened being.

Healthy quiet breathing, which is most desirable for intimate connecting with nature, is consistently described as relaxed rather than tense, deep rather than shallow, slow rather than rapid, and rhythmic rather than irregular. In quiet breathing, inspiration occurs by the active contraction of only the inspiratory muscles; and expiration by relaxation of those same muscles. The diaphragm is the principle muscle involved: a large, dome-shaped sheet of muscle that separates the thoracic from the abdominal cavity. The contraction of the diaphragm pulls down its central part, much as a piston moves downward in a cylinder. The movement downward creates a vacuum in the lungs which air rushes in to fill. Healthy breathing is abdominal breathing using primarily the diaphragm. Zen practitioners call it "belly breathing."

Relaxation of the abdominal muscles is important during inspiration. Abdominal tension makes the diaphragm work harder and limits deep breathing. People who habitually breathe by raising the chest and shoulders are restrictively tense. This "chest breathing" fills only the upper and narrower part of the lungs resulting in faster, shallower breathing. Improper breathing caused by the tendency to tighten and restrict the diaphragm is one of the worst and most far-reaching consequences of chronic tension and anxiety. Chest breathing is strenuous, involving neck, shoulder, and costal muscles that are not designed for continuous work. With ongoing use, they become overstrained and chronically tense. Chest breathing is what we need in physically demanding emergency situations. It rapidly eliminates carbon dioxide from the bloodstream when it has become overloaded by bodily exertion.

For communing with nature, you want relaxed belly breathing. Learning to distinguish between chest breathing and abdominal breathing will help you cultivate relaxed belly breathing. The internal sensation of the body in chest breathing is upward on inhalation and downward on exhalation. With diaphragm breathing it is the opposite. With chest breathing the chest and shoulders lift up and out to create room for additional air in the upper body cavity. With belly breathing the diaphragm drops down creating room in the lower body cavity. The following activity will help you learn to experience the difference between these two types of breathing.

Activity Thirteen ➤ Chest and Abdominal Breathing

Loosen or remove any clothing that may constrict your breathing. Lie comfortably on your back and close your eyes. Place one hand on your chest and one on your belly. Start with chest breathing. Lift up with your shoulders and expand your chest muscles to draw air into the upper body cavity. Tighten your abdominal muscles to flatten your belly as you suck in air through your nose. The hand on your chest rises while the hand on your stomach stays the same or drops. Now try belly breathing. Relaxing your abdominal muscles, allow the diaphragm to drop down so that air rushes in to fill the resulting vacuum in your lower body cavity. Your hand on your belly will rise. See if you can experience the movement of your diaphragm. Notice how with abdominal breathing, the diaphragm's downward movement fills the belly first and only in the last stages of the inhalation in deep breathing does the chest expand if at all.

Healthy breathing is not achieved through breath control, but through a letting go process. The following activity teaches you how to concentrate on your breathing, observing its inner movement until the breath, left to itself, returns to its own rhythm.

Activity Fourteen ➤ Breathing Observation Activity

Loosen or remove any clothing that may constrict your breathing. Lie comfortably on your back and close your eyes. Observe the natural flow of your breathing. Don't try to change or control it. Simply observe your breathing as it is now. Feel the air enter and leave the nostrils of your nose. Feel the expansion sensations in the body as the lungs fill with air. Notice the sensations in the diaphragm, stomach and chest muscles. Notice the rhythm of your breathing. Notice the depth of your breathing. Notice spontaneous adjustments in your breathing that take place without effort, as you become aware of your breathing. As you continue to breathe, keep your attention alert to the details of each breath. Let your body breathe itself according to its own natural rhythm.

Breath and mind are linked. The state of one most often mirrors the other. Rapid shallow breathing fuels a restless mind. Anxious neurotic thinking activates rapid shallow breathing. A restless mind can be calmed down by consciously breathing deeply, slowly, and naturally. Zen Meditation, the practice of sitting motionless and concentrating on one's breathing, helps people learn to listen, accept what is, and be more fully present. All three are important supports for entering into the I-Thou way of relating.

Activity Fifteen ➤ Calm Breathing

Trying to follow these lengthy instructions and focus on your breathing at the same time may create frustration rather than relaxation. For the best results have a partner read the instructions to you or record them on a cassette tape. Once you learn the basic self-instructions for calming your breathing, you will be able to do the activity on your own.

Loosen or remove any clothing that may constrict your breathing. Sit or lie in a comfortable position and close your eyes. Begin as above, by simply observing your breathing. Breath through your nose. If you find yourself chest breathing, see if you can shift to abdominal breathing. Allow your abdominal muscles to relax. You don't need to use your chest and shoulder muscles to take a breath. Let them relax. Let yourself exhale completely before the start the each new breath. Notice how, without any deliberate effort on your part, each of your breaths begins with the plunging down of your diaphragm. Continue to breathe naturally, gradually allowing your breathing to become more relaxed. As you exhale, let go of any remaining tension you feel in your abdominal muscles. As you exhale, allow your neck, shoulder, and chest muscles to relax more fully. Continuing to relax, allowing your breathing to gradually slow down and deepen. With each inhalation, know that you are bringing in the life-giving oxygen that energizes every cell in your body. And with each exhalation, you can release tension. Breathe in energy. Breathe out tension. With each inhalation you become more energized and alert and with each exhalation you become more relaxed. Allow yourself to find your own comfortable, relaxed, slow, deep, rhythmic breathing pattern. With no effort, you can simply allow the wisdom of your organism to find its most optimal way of nourishing and supporting you at this moment. Continue to explore how you can allow your breathing to be comfortable, relaxed, slow, deep, rhythmic, and energizing. You may notice yourself blocking or interrupting this process. When this happens, simply let go and return to your relaxed abdominal breathing. Discover with each breath your own natural breathing pattern that best nourishes, supports, and energizes you.

The next activity invites you to explore how calm breathing effects the way you experience nature.

Activity Sixteen ➤ Breathing Meditation in Nature

Pick a special place in nature that is for you, quiet and serene. Find a comfortable place to sit with a straight back. If your back needs support, find a tree or some other source of support. Take a few moments to familiarize yourself with your surroundings and settle in comfortably. Then repeat the Calm Breathing Activity with your eyes closed, establishing your own natural breathing pattern that nourishes, supports, and energizes you. Continue to breathe and observe your breathing. If thoughts or sensations distract you, simply return to your breathing. After a period of time that feels comfortable to you (5-10 minutes), gently open your eyes. Open all your senses to drink in this special place. Continue to monitor your breathing as you open yourself to receive with full awareness whatever this place has to offer you.

Reducing Tension

When stressed and tense, we're less receptive to all that nature has to offer. Chronic tensing of the muscles dulls the senses and constricts the pathways of the circulatory system. Good circulation is essential for a healthy metabolism that energizes the body. Chronic muscle tension cuts us off from the body cues and responses that put us in touch with our feelings.

In this muscular way, we can constrict ourselves against the expressive motion of emotion. This turning of the energy back in toward the self, the energy of restraint, is called *retroflection* in gestalt therapy. When restraint becomes locked in as chronic tension, relaxation techniques help re-energize and resensitize the body.

Relaxation often begins paradoxically when we become aware of our tensions. The key to unlocking these tensions is to learn how we create and maintain them in our bodies by tensing our muscles. The next activity will help you with this important first step in learning how to let go and relax.

Activity Seventeen ➢ Tension Awareness Activity

Find a comfortable place to lie down on your back. Now focus your awareness on the physical sensations going on inside your body. Pay attention to any movements, tensions, discomforts, or other activities of your body. Express each new awareness as an ongoing activity. For example, notice your tightening, holding, pressing, pushing, stiffening, loosening, letting go, releasing . . . If you experience tension in your shoulder, tense it slightly more. If you discover a held in sensation, slightly increase this holding. Take responsibility for your muscular activity and its consequences by silently saying to yourself statements like, "I'm scrinching my shoulders up and making them sore." Continue the activity to strengthen your identification with the physical activities going on inside your organism.

Relaxation helps reduce unneeded tensions that block effective sensing, drain us of energy, and lead to our "tuning out." However, most of us associate relaxation with rest and sleep. Lying down will often enhance the likelihood that we will go limp and tune out. For our purposes, relaxation is in the service of heightened awareness, not resting or sleeping. I'm reminded of one of my group participants who fell asleep each time he tried to meditate. Working long hours on changing shifts as an emergency room physician no doubt contributed to this problem. When you're especially tired, relaxation will appropriately lead to sleep rather than heightened awareness.

Your posture will also effect your ability to achieve a state of relaxed alertness. Some people slump down when relaxing which can cause restricted breathing and back strain. Sitting or standing up with a straight back tends to support an alert state.

Finding and maintaining this state of relaxed alertness can be quite a challenge. You can't force yourself to relax. You *allow* yourself to relax.

Activity Eighteen ➤ Relaxation

This activity works best with a partner who gives the instructions, or by recording the instructions on a tape. Find a comfortable place to lie down on your back. Close your eyes. Begin with the "Calm Breathing Activity."

As you establish your calm breathing pattern, think of taking in energy with each inhalation, and letting go of tension with each exhalation. Continue to let yourself relax more with each breath for a few minutes. Then as you take in a deep breath, tense both legs by lifting your toes up as if you were trying to touch your knees with them. Tense all of the muscles in your feet and legs and hold your breath for the count three. Then let go, relax the muscles, and exhale completely. Repeat two more times. Next, as you take in a deep breath, tense your buttocks, abdominal and chest muscles, holding your breath as you tense them for the count of three. Then let go, relax the muscles, and exhale completely. Repeat two more times. Next raise both arms directly overhead. As you take in a deep breath, make tight fists with your hands, and stretch your arms as long as you can. Tense your hand, arm, and shoulder muscles for the count of three holding your breath. Then let go, relax, and exhale completely. Repeat two more times. Next tighten up the muscles of you face and neck. Scrinch up your forehead, squeeze your eyes shut, clench your jaw. Hold your breath and tense for the count of three. Then let go, relax, and exhale completely. Repeat two more times. Now put it all together; lifting both feet, tightening the buttocks, abdomen, and chest; stretching both arms; tightening face and neck. Tighten all the muscles of your body and hold your breath for the count of three. Then let go, relax, and exhale completely. Repeat two more times, each time squeezing out more tension, each time allowing yourself to relax more deeply. Now take a moment to survey from head to toe to see if areas of tension remain. When you come upon a part of your body that is not yet fully relaxed, inhale into that part of your body and tighten it just slightly. As you exhale just let go and release the tension. Continue to survey your body for other areas that have any remaining tension, repeating this procedure in each instance to obtain a more complete state of relaxation. When done, slowly and gently sit up, all the way up so you have a straight back rather than a slumping posture. Return your attention to your breathing, continuing to relax with each exhalation. If any distracting thoughts appear, simply allow them to pass through like birds in flight. Return to your breathing. Pay attention to how you feel in this state of alert relaxation. Now, you are ready to open yourself to nature.*

Centering

> **Force of Gravity**
> *Center, how you draw yourself out*
> *from all things, how you also reclaim yourself*
> *from flying things, center, you strongest.*
> **Rainer Maria Rilke**

Centering reduces internal static and strain so you can be more receptive to the environment. If you stand up and swiftly turn about, how does this effect your perceptions? Becoming centered involves bringing the body into balance, finding your center of gravity so that you are not straining against the force of gravity, but staying aligned so that your skeletal structure provides efficient support for your body mass.

Centering has a psychological as well as a physical dimension which involves quieting the mind, reducing mental agitation and activity. You can best attune yourself to nature by learning to find your inner stillpoint out of which

---

* The above activity is a version of the tension-release approach to relaxation which was originally developed by E. Jacobson *Progressive Relaxation* Chicago: Univ. of Chicago Press, 1938. This approach has been adopted for widespread use over the years in many therapeutic contexts.

clear awareness arises. Becoming centered is to become like a completely calm and clear lake on a sunny day that reflects its surroundings.

> *"'Mirror mind' is empty, clear, clean, reflecting what is."*
>
> **Lao Tsu** (Taoist Sage)

Activity Nineteen ➤ Centering

This activity works best with a partner who gives the instructions, or by recording the instructions on a tape.

Select a time and place where you will not be disturbed or distracted. Remove your shoes and loosen clothing so your breathing is not restricted. Sit in comfortable erect sitting position, back supported if needed. Begin with the calm breathing activity. After you have established a comfortable pattern of relaxed, deep, slow, rhythmic breathing, bring your attention to your belly area (solar plexus). See if you can locate physically what feels like your center of gravity, or psychologically what feels like the center of your being. Keep your attention there as you continue to breath calmly. Go deep into that center and see if you can find the stillpoint at its core. If you experience any upset or agitation in the area, breath energy into the area, tense it very gently, and then as you exhale let the tension go, allowing the area to relax and quiet with each exhalation. If your mind is agitated with thoughts of past or future, gently repeat to yourself the affirmation, "Nothing to do, nowhere to go, just be here now" Then return to your center, the serene stillpoint at the core of your being. Continue to deepen and develop this sense of serenity, allowing it to gradually spread throughout your body. Emanating from your center, let it spread in all directions. Let the calm from the depths of your inner lake spread to the surface so that there are no ripples. Calm and still, your surface is like a clear mirror ready and sensitive for receiving the sensations of nature.

> *"The still mind of a sage is a mirror of heaven and earth."*
>
> **Chuang Tzu**

Grounding

> *"The press of my foot to the earth springs a hundred affections."*
>
> **Walt Whitman**

Every child, every plant, and every animal reacts instinctively to the pull of the earth. Plants respond to the pulling down of the earth with reaching up towards the sunlight. The plant's metabolic energy draws it upward in response to the downward pull of the earth's gravity. Both the roots in the soil below and the sun above are sources of life energy for plants. This basic direction, "down," always means down to earth. The direction of this gravitational pull is certain and constant, always there for us to come to rest on. Perhaps this is one of the reasons why the earth has been called mother. There is a yearning to return to her. Upon death, according to custom in many cultures, we are returned to our final resting-place, mother earth, for burial.

Humans and earth have the same root, "humus" which means the good earth. Nature's seeds are planted and begin to grow in the fertile soil of the earth's body just as the human seed is planted and grows in the fertile body of the mother. We are born from the earth and to the earth we return.

Your body has special sensors for balance and movement located in the muscles, tendons, ligaments, and joints that respond to stimuli produced within the body. These sensors, called proprioceptors, tell you where you are in space, whether you are moving or standing still, balanced or unbalanced. The sensing of weight comes from these sensors. Proprioceptors of the inner ear, for example, are involved in balance, position of the head, changes in speed, and changes in gravitational force from going up or down. On the evolutionary timeline, proprioceptors belong with the systems of touch and temperature as the oldest general senses in animals.

We spend precious little time paying attention to and educating ourselves regarding these foundational upholders of life. Dancers and gymnasts are more likely to pay attention to these kinesthetic senses in order to develop their skills. However, their focus tends to be more task-oriented than contemplative and appreciative, more on the body's expressive motoric rather than receptive sensoric systems.

How aware are you of your own posture and muscle activity? How often do you pay attention to the ever-present pull of gravity? As I sit here at the keyboard writing this sentence, I can become aware of whether or not I am slumping or sitting erect, whether I am yielding to or fighting gravity, whether my position in life is open or constricting. As I do this, I find myself making spontaneous adjustments to feel more comfortable. As you read this sentence, be aware of your own posture, your relationship with gravity, and observe what happens for you . . . Explore the grounding process more by trying the next activity.

Activity Twenty ➤ Grounding

This activity works better with a partner who gives the instructions, or by recording the instructions on a tape.

Outside. Bare feet. Standing. Pay attention to your posture. Pay attention to the sensations of your feet on the ground. How is your weight distributed? on the heel or ball of your foot? on the inside or outside edge of your foot? Notice any differences between your feet. Rock slowly back and forth, spread your toes, shift weight left and right. Pay attention to your sense of balance. Feel the weight of your body as it is pulled to the ground by gravity. Feel the energy that holds your body upright, the vitality that gives you an uplifted feeling. Experiment with slumping down and stretching up high. Bend your knees and gently bounce. Feel the support of the ground beneath your feet. Be aware of how your feet contact the ground. Do your feet receive the ground, grip it, draw back from it? Note how the ground returns your touch on the soles of your feet. How do your legs feel? How do they support your upper body and connect you to your feet? Close your eyes and find out what happens to your sense of balance. Do you feel supported by the earth relying on proprioception for balance without the added support of visual orientation. Continue to experiment with both open and closed eyes. Find your center of gravity in your body, usually in the upper part of your abdomen near your solar plexus. Allow your body to gently sway from this center of gravity point, then to spiral in smaller and smaller concentric circles around this point of balance sensing your body coming more into vertical alignment. Continue to explore and experiment, making ongoing adjustments that increase your sense of solid contact with the ground so that you feel securely supported by the earth. As you explore these sensations see if you feel more solidly connected, even rooted to the earth. Take in your surroundings. Do you experience your environment differently now than before doing this activity?

We can study gravity, our relationship to the ground. We can learn to be better grounded in our life by paying attention to how we stand, lie down, carry bundles, lift and set down, climb and descend, dance and walk. Simply walking on uneven ground is often very effective. Charles Brooks reports in his book *Sensory Awareness*, "Our students have often learned more from the rough woodsy paths and rocky headlands" than from anything indoors. (See the Walking Meditation Activity on p.78)

In Yoga, the foundational standing pose is called "Tadasana" which means mountain pose. All of the other poses relate back to and support the enhancement of this primary pose. In Tadasana the body extends upward through the crown of the head and downward through the feet creating a firm base so that you can feel solid like a mountain. This grounding pose teaches balance and centering. You learn to experience the alignment of the spine that best supports the flow of metabolic energy and balances you in space so that your body is not unduly stressed by the pull of gravity. This postural alignment and flow of metabolic energy generate feelings of lightness and well being. Learning yoga is an excellent practice that helps develop proprioceptive sensory awareness. We can uncover chronic imbalances created by illness, injury, or poor training. With awareness, maladaptive habits are opened up for creative healthier responsiveness. Ongoing sensitivity to the messages coming from our bodies re-establishes the spontaneous organismic self-regulation of the body.

"And the world cannot be discovered by a journey of miles,
no matter how long
but only by a spiritual journey,
a journey of one inch, very arduous and humbling and joyful,
by which we arrive at the ground at our feet,
and learn to be at home."

Wendell Berry

4

Awakening Your Senses

*As I spoke, beneath my feet
The ground-pine curled its pretty wreath,
Running over the club-moss burrs;
I inhaled the violet's breath;
Around me stood the oaks and firs;
Pine-cones and acorns lay on the ground;
Over me soared the eternal sky,
Full of light and of deity;
Again I saw, again I heard,
The rolling river, the morning bird;
Beauty through my senses stole;
I yielded myself to the perfect whole.*

Ralph Waldo Emerson
closing lines of *"Each and All"*

Perception and Your Senses

The study of perception can be approached from many perspectives. Sight can be understood in terms of photons entering the retina of the eye. Hearing can be understood in terms of sound waves entering the ear and causing vibrations of its bones which in turn cause a movement of fluid in the inner ear. Next, the hair cells of the inner ear stimulate the auditory nerves which in turn transmit impulses to the brain.

The senses of taste and smell respond to chemical energy in the environment. Mechanical energy in the forms of light waves, sound waves, temperature and pressure are the mediums for the senses of sight, hearing, and touch. This scientific view is valuable and important, enabling physicians to restore sight to the blind and hearing to the deaf. The accomplishments of modern science are truly miraculous. The scientific approach, however, is not the only valid framework for understanding perception.

Perception can also be examined from a communications perspective. A more holistic ecological rather than atomistic mechanical view can be adopted. In this larger view, perception is understood not in terms of I-It, of material objects being sensed by the organs of human perception; but from an I-Thou perspective. The focus shifts from perceiving objects to perceiving relationships.

For example, you can examine the characteristics of water, such as its clarity and temperature; or you can expand your perspective to include water in the context of a river. Psychologist Laura Sewall takes this broader relational view describing the relationship between water and land. "Water flows all over rocks and sand. We can see water flow over, under, and around. We see water deflect, merge, lick, crash, and softly lap up against. We see water reflect like giant mirrors. We see it take away and give back, and we see all of this in relation to land. And we may notice the most essential and contrasted material relationship within our experience. It is the interface between elemental forces; ocean and land, river and mountain. It is where erosion meets resistance, hard meets soft, solid meets fluid, and where tawny-colored sand meets deep blue water." (in *Ecopsychology*)

For humans, perception, as a form of communication, is a nonverbal conversation between the person and the gesturing sounding landscape one inhabits. There is an ongoing constant primordial exchange, a reciprocal interaction between living presences. The person, like all living organisms, orients and responds to the active solicitations of the sensory world.

From this communications perspective, thoughts and images are understood as one level of responding to the messages being sent to us by the natural environment. This includes internal messages from within our bodies as well as those from the external environment. For example, sleeping people with full bladders may have dream images reflecting their condition. One night I dreamed that I was peeing in the in-box at my office. This dream was not only a reflection of the pressure in my bladder at the time but also symbolized the pressure I was feeling at work, not to mention my feelings about it!

The school of philosophy, called phenomenology, seeks to explore, describe, and understand sensation as we experience it. From this subjective perspective, the natural world is the vast, inexhaustible, forgotten source, the ground of our sensory experiencing; and communing with it is not merely an intellectual activity but a sensuous immersion invoking the whole play of the senses.

The Healthy Sense of Self

A basic premise of the gestalt approach is that the "self" is an embodied self. When we disown our embodied selves, we make our body an "it" rather than an expression of self. This body-mind split is not merely an abstract Descartian philosophical position, but a psychological reality. Healing the mind-body split involves bringing back into awareness the disowned aspects of the self, including the full range of sensations that put us in touch with our feelings and behaviors. Our *sense* of self comes from these bodily sensations. Without clear inner sensation, we lose touch with who we are and what we need, want, and desire. We need to be perceptually grounded in our sense of self as well as grounded with our physical environment in order to be well connected to and supported by the earth.

Desensitization: Losing a Healthy Sense of Self

"The deadening of our senses is at the heart of the environmental crisis and...reawakening them is an integral step toward renewing our bond with the Earth."

Laura Sewall, *Ecopsychology*

When exposed to toxic or impoverished environments that persist over time or are traumatic in impact, people disown aspects of the self in order to cope and survive chronic frustration, intolerable pain, suffering, and grief. Sensations signaling organismic needs become frustrating when they persist in a context in which meeting them is not possible. We often cope by diminishing our capacity for perception, by shutting down or numbing out. This eases the experience of discomfort, but at the price of a loss of capacity for aliveness and full sense of self. For example, when receiving a massage, the touch often awakens places of tension or soreness that surprise us.

Desensitization occurs by:
  (1) Selective attention, distracting away from and avoiding body experience;
  (2) Interference with breathing, since shallow, minimal, interrupted breathing limits sensation and flow of feeling; and
  (3) Chronic muscular contraction that squeezes off bodily sensations.

Resensitizing correspondingly involves:
  (1) Focused awareness on bodily experience;
  (2) Restoring natural unconstrained breathing; and
  (3) Enlivening body sensitivities by releasing chronic tensions in the body through relaxation, massage, yoga, dance and other forms of touch and movement.

The previous chapter, *Tuning the Organism for Enhanced Sensitivity,* is devoted to activities that promote resensitization. Having a full range of sensations accessible to awareness provides us with a more complete and accurate assessment of our situation which is necessary for more optimal functioning.

With resensitization, problems such as "image-pollution" and "noise-pollution" (sensory overload), "people-pollution" (spending too much time cramped together with others), and "wilderness-deprivation" (not spending enough time outside man-made environments) will be felt rather than accommodated without awareness.

Let's take "noise pollution" as an example. When there is harmony and rhythm, that's music to our ears. Sounds can have both therapeutic and damaging effects. Music therapists specialize in fostering the healing effects of music. On the other hand, we can be assaulted by the din and clatter of noise. When exposed to too much volume, whether 90-100 decibels of chainsaw noise or 120 decibels of music at a rock concert, we can permanently damage our hearing. In our culture, hearing loss comes with aging. The Mabaan, who live in Sudan, have sensitive hearing even in old age. Their world is a quiet one. But most of us, swamped by the cacophony of modern life, can look forward to a loss of hearing. We adjust to a noisy world, become accustomed to it, even seek it out. When noise pollution becomes normal, we may experience silence as strange and unsettling. By continuously exposing ourselves to unhealthy levels of noise, we become desensitized. Writer Milan Kundera warns us of the consequences, "If beauty is to be perceptible, it needs a certain minimal degree of silence. Beauty has long since disappeared. It has slipped beneath the surface of the noise—the noise of words, cars, music, signs—we live in constantly."

On the other hand, we can selectively expose ourselves to the beautiful sounds of nature and music in ways that cultivate our sensitivities. Rather than becoming desensitized, you can develop your sense of hearing to become more finely tuned, more discriminating, able to distinguish subtle nuances of sound, able to identify the direction a sound is coming from, and so on. The "sensory awareness" activities in this book help you enhance rather than bombard your senses. They are designed to promote a healthy sensuous engagement with the world.

Coming to our Senses

"Everything is alive, not supernaturally, but naturally alive. There are only deeper streams of life, vibrations of life more and more vast . . . For the whole life-effort of humans is to get into direct contact with the elemental life of the cosmos, mountain-life, cloud-life, thunder-life, air-life, earth-life, sun-life."

D. H. Lawrence

We can awaken into life via the senses. Such a life is not dull; it's sensational. On the other hand, we dilute our present experiencing when we withdraw into our heads and get caught up in thoughts, fantasies, obsessive worries about the future or futile ruminations about the past that are disconnected from our present life situation.

Here's a soliloquy I made up to illustrate how we can get caught up in mental machinations. "I look at the cherry tree and notice the many blossoms. Looks like there will be a good crop this year, many more than last year. I wonder why? I can hardly wait to make a cherry pie. The one I made for the church potluck last year was delicious and I got lots of compliments. Oh, the birdfeeder is empty. I need to get it refilled. No wonder the birds haven't been around much lately. The grass looks a little brown. Time to water again. That's an unusual looking bee flying into that blossom, not your ordinary honeybee. I wonder what kind it is? I'll have to look it up . . . "

Solid contact with ourselves and our environment is maintained through full use of our senses. The focus in sensory awareness is on direct experience, undiluted contact with what is going on.

A more sensuous engagement with the world might go like this: "My cherry tree is so beautiful this year, just loaded with white blossoms. They shimmer in the bright sunlight and vibrate with the gentle breeze. I lift my head into the branches and stick my nose into a clump of blossoms to inhale their fragrance. The blossoms tickle the tip of my nose. Then, I hear the bright cheerful song of a bird chirping in the branches high up in the tree. I look up into the canopy in the direction of the sound and see a black and yellow bumble bee hovering about the blossoms on the next limb up . . . "

Sensory awareness involves emptying the mind so one can be receptive. If your awareness is full of words, there is no room for new input. We also need to understand and notice how we objectify our worlds. When we do, process becomes object, thou becomes it. We can distance ourselves from our world by labeling it. Labeling can create the illusion that the world is made up of static fixed entities rather than ongoing processes. Thinking when disconnected from perceiving creates a kind of hypnotic conditioning where expectations of what we think is there replace the actuality of experiencing what is there. We develop preconceptions that cut short, distort, and close down our senses to new input. For example, when urgently goal oriented, we tend to adopt an exclusively instrumental approach to the world. We tag ongoing phenomena with functional labels and move on to the next. The labeling of an object often marks an end to curiosity and exploration.

Mary came to me for counseling because her "life was empty." She was lonely and isolated. Poised, expressionless, her gaze often was directed toward the carpet. In one of our sessions, I asked her to tell me what she noticed about my office. Although puzzled by my request, she complied. Her response was something like this: "There are two chairs with an end table between them, a lamp on the table, and a vase of flowers, a desk over there, a bookcase to the right of it . . . " I commented matter-of-factly that her description sounded like an inventory. I asked her to continue, but to describe what she noticed in more detail. With some minimal prompting on my part, she began to notice color, shade, texture. She leaned over to smell of the flowers, stroked the metal vase that held them. She became more animated. Smiling now, she said she couldn't believe how much she closed herself off from the world. "I usually just stare at the ground in front of me when I walk to my classes." In our next session, she reported how our little experiment had helped. Looking around on the way to class right after our session, she had met the gaze of a fellow student who spoke to her and . . .

Rather than focus on the facts of what we think we know, we can benefit by learning how to live in a world of phenomena rather than a world of objects. Living out on the edge of our knowing, letting our curiosity draw us into exploring the unknown makes life a phenomenal experience. To be fully alive is to be tuned in to the energies of the continuously changing processes of life. We can learn to be resonant and responsive, to be in harmony with this unfolding dance of life. This dynamic way of experiencing our world will escape us if we get habitually locked into a hurried, overly pragmatic orientation.

Sensory experience is like a root support system that feeds our higher levels of consciousness. Our perceptions are the concrete and specific building blocks from which we generalize about our experience. Sensory awakening can become an integral part of our lives, making them more substantial, enriching our experience with more active ingredients. Whatever the activity or experience, whether it be eating, walking, painting, playing, or breathing; sensory awareness activities can be an enhancing addition. They are like meditations in everyday living, paying attention to what we are constantly doing anyway. Being mindful of our senses helps restore and develop our interior sensibilities.

These basic sensibilities of life are rarely the central focus of our attention. We look elsewhere for excitement and meaning. Entering into this realm of experiencing is often prematurely interrupted by our impatience for drama and desire for instant gratification. On the other hand, full awareness of these fundamental life processes may plunge us into experiencing the miracle of "I am in this world."

"Linking what is at hand with what is in the heart can recall us into communing with the wonder and gift of the Presence in the present."
Gunilla Norris, *Being Home*

Sensory Awareness Activities

"Experience is not what happens to you. It is what you do with what happens to you."
Aldous Huxley

Sensory awareness, while it involves receptivity, is not a passive process. There is an active seeking, a reaching out to discover and take in the environment. My senses don't passively pick up everything; they actively search. Full-unbridled curiosity brings energy to the activity. On the other hand, there are experiences when nature captures my attention. In those instances, I'm not seeking but am being called. There are deep forces at work in each encounter with nature twisting their way into the perceiver's thoughts, drawing the attention here, then there, activating desires. Identifying who is seeking whom isn't always obvious.

Sensory awareness activities involve paying attention to and exploring what comes through the senses. Relaxed alertness is the desirable state for these activities, which are spoiled by rushing and enhanced when time is taken for savoring. We can come to our senses most fully to the extent that we can learn to let go of our tendency to focus on and be distracted by the chatter of our minds, our inner dialogues, self-talk, thoughts, labeling with words. Letting go of these word games and trusting the nonverbal dimensions of our experiencing is an ongoing challenge that can easily slip away unnoticed. Most of these nature activities exclude talking because of this tendency for words to detract from our sensing.

One of my more powerful early experiences in nature took place back in my college days when a friend and I decided not to talk during a backpacking trip into the Sierra Nevada Mountains. My friend's suggestion that we try not talking for awhile, casually presented as we hiked down the trail, lasted several days! We became so involved in this spontaneous experiment that we just kept it going.

Eliminating words seemed to have an almost magical effect, taking us into a different realm of experiencing. Great spaces opened up for uninterrupted experiencing. The greens seemed greener, the birdcalls crisper, the smell of pine fresher. My world became much more vivid.

One night eating together by the campfire, we shared an unforgettable experience. We had just prepared a meal together. It all went so smoothly as we danced around each other in our outdoor kitchen. I fried the trout. He cooked the rice. We were just sitting there eating when he glanced up at me; and without hesitation or thought of any kind, I handed him the salt. A moment later in the midst of his applying the salt, we simultaneously burst into laughter when we recognized what had just happened. This moment epitomized the kind of sensitive attunement that we were able to achieve.

Ever since, I have coveted my silent times in nature. When there's a conversation going on, I will often walk ahead or drop behind my hiking companions so I can enter this silent world of vivid impressions. I often feel a poignant loss when I resume talking after dwelling in this wordless realm for an extended period of time.

Nonverbal activities help us quiet the overly dominant, verbal preoccupations of the mind. In gestalt terms, we become more "fully present" to our experiencing. This involves learning to stay with the continuous ongoing flow of incoming sensations. Yet, it is so easy to become *distracted*. As the word suggests, we lose traction, lose our ground—which is precisely what happens when we lose our connection with being fully present.

Paradoxically, this desired state is not a goal to be achieved. By trying to do it right, the desired state eludes us. We arrive by focusing on what *is* happening rather than on doing it right. We can't make it happen. Rather, we learn to allow it to happen. We don't change by trying to change, but by fully accepting "what is." The process of becoming emerges from fully entering into being. Change is not made to happen, it is a given. Awareness of your immersion in these life processes invites spontaneous creative adjustments to both internal and external conditions. Sailing rather than manufacturing is a better image for understanding how we can guide the inevitable ongoing change in our lives in a healthy direction.

Exploring Each of Your Senses

"To perceive freshly, with fresh senses, is to be inspired . . . My body is all sentient . . . the age of miracles is each moment thus returned.
Henry David Thoreau

In everyday life, the senses are blended and intertwined. We don't go around deciding whether to perceive something by seeing, hearing, or touching. Perception operates as an integrated whole. Yet, the following activities, by singling them out for individual attention, give us an experience of the incredible depth, subtlety, complexity, and powers of our sensing organisms.

Perceptual powers can be developed and enhanced by learning about them, paying conscious attention to them, and participating in activities that exercise them. The saying, "use it or lose it" applies. Skillful perception can be approached as a devotional practice.

Our standard educational curriculums emphasize reading, writing, and math. Perception as a field of study in curriculum development is most often absent or plays only a minor role. As a culture we place great emphasis on developing our language skills, but show little concern for our perceptual literacy. We focus on the verbal and abstract, rather than the nonverbal and concrete.

In the sensory awareness activities that follow, pay attention to what happens when you explore nature from different aspects (such as size, aroma, and texture) through different modes of sensing (sight, smell and touch). Note how your body makes internal adjustments (eyes, nose and skin) when you shift modes. Just paying attention to the oftentimes-subtle shifts in the way we engage our world can powerfully effect the quality of our perceptions. Recovering, revitalizing, and enhancing our contact functions through practical exercises and activities fine tunes our bodies, opening the channels for sensitive responsiveness which is so necessary for living in harmony with nature.

Listening

"A bird does not sing because it has an answer. It sings because it has a song."
Ancient Proverb

When listening, most people habitually listen for content, for the literal meaning of the words. They gather information. The transmission of information is complex process of encoding and decoding sounds and symbols, and even under good conditions and with skilled listeners, miscommunications are not uncommon. Indeed, when one realizes all that goes into even the simplest communication, it's amazing that we get along as well as we do.

As a counselor in training, I was taught "active listening skills." We were trained to listen for more than just the content of the words, but to listen also to "the music behind the words," the voice tone, pitch, volume, and rhythm. These are the concrete components of sound that make up the sensory awareness of listening.

Sounds can warn us or relax us. Infants everywhere are sung to sleep by the soothing sounds of a lullaby. There is music for grieving, for loving, for dancing, for marching and war making, and most likely for every other purpose under heaven. There is certainly music for spiritual joy and religious ecstasy. The chanting of mantras or the pulsing rhythms of drumming can open doors leading us into a variety of states of consciousness.

Our modern cultures rely more and more on disembodied forms of communication. Sounds come from the speakers of radios, televisions, and computers bringing us messages from impersonal sources great distances away. You may never meet the author of these messages. Before writing, television, and computer networks, all cultures were held together by an oral tradition. Listening was live and in person. Communication was up close and personal. The collective myths and stories, repeated over and over from birth to death, created the collective memory of a people. These face-to-face meetings have now been greatly reduced as the mass media plays a more dominant role. Celebrities on television have replaced elders telling stories by the fire.

Music and song, when they serve as threads that weave together a common tapestry of beliefs, customs, traditions, and rituals, bind the people of a culture together. Sound in the form of myths and legends, music and song still plays a prominent role in seasonal celebrations and religious rites. In many cultures over the centuries, vision questers have ventured out to a sacred place in nature to seek guidance for their mission in life. Receiving their own unique "spirit song" was one gift they might receive. Their spirit song gave them a unique source of inspiration to support them in implementing their vision.

In nature, rhythmic sounds are never reduced to the hum-drum monotony of mere mechanical reproduction. The mechanical precision of the metronome takes the life out of sound. When each pulse of the rhythm is an exact replica of the others, there is no spirit. With living music each pulse has its own uniqueness. This wildness of rhythm is present in the spirited performance of all great music, yet the wildness is contained within a preciseness of the natural laws of rhythm, not straying into disjointed chaos of unrelated sounds, noise which jolts the senses. Nature's sounds and rhythms are inspirational resources from which humans have created much great music.

Paying attention to the physical sensations of sound entering the ear and the body's response provides the raw data for a particular kind of listening. Listening to content without awareness of tone, rhythm, or pitch is to lose contact with often-ignored nonverbal messages. In counselor training, I was encouraged to actively listen for deeper meanings submerged under the surface message. A favorite quote of mine illustrates this point: "What you are doing speaks so loudly that I can't hear what you are saying." Staying open to the emerging meanings of the message without cluttering it up prematurely with your own projections is not easy. This involves learning to separate out your own interpretations and hunches about deeper meanings from the actual message received. While these interpersonal communication skills are the basic tools of my trade, everyone can benefit from learning them.

Active listening skills need not be narrowly restricted to the interpersonal world but can also be meaningfully applied to the natural world as well. Learning to tune into the nonverbal dimensions of nature's communications and learning to make sense out of these sounds is like learning a foreign language for most of us. When the earth speaks, we can learn to listen and to understand.

"Language is the very voice of the trees, the waves, and the forests."
Maurice Merleau-Ponty *The Visible and the Invisible*

Activity Twenty-One ➢ Listening to Nature

Pick a natural area to explore. Close your eyes and listen to nature sounds as you would a musical composition. Listen for rhythms, patterns, feeling tones, percussion, melody, and so on. (There are frogs, crickets, birds, wind, raindrops, ocean waves, rustling leaves, and on and on . . .) Pay attention to the silence. Pay attention to your inner response to these sounds. Imagine that these sounds are a foreign language that has meaning which you haven't learned to understand yet. This language is so foreign that you have to use a different part of your brain to comprehend it. Compare and contrast this experience of nature's sounds with your experience of man-made sounds in the city and the impact they have on you.*

* Also, try the Exploring Attractions Activity in Chapter 7, p. 79, using only listening as your source for attractions and repulsions.

Smelling

Smell is the most primal of our senses, yet the least developed by humans. On the evolutionary timeline, the small lump of olfactory tissue atop the fish's nerve cord evolved into a brain. The cerebral hemispheres were originally buds from the olfactory stalks. Considered our weakest sense, it is most likely to be ignored. Yet, smell is often a trigger for some of our earliest and most profound memories. Odors associated with events and people can trigger intense feelings and vivid memories. While our powers of smell can't compare with those of many of nature's other life forms, including hounds which have 200 million smell-sensing cells, our five million cells are nothing to sneeze at either. The human nose still has greater discriminatory powers than any instrument designed to analyze odors.

The cells in our olfactory centers are specialized to respond to each of more than fifty basic kinds of odors. Despite efforts over many years, scientists have found no easy system for classifying types of smells. Here are some of the more common ones: fragrant (floral), nauseous, aromatic (spicy), repulsive, ethereal, burned, redolent, pungent, fetid, and sweet.

Cultural historians claim that our powers of smell have been in decline since the dawn of the modern era. European explorers and settlers, who had come to rely on dogs for hunting, were amazed at the tracking skills of Native Americans. A keen sense of smell has important survival value for hunters and gatherers, but it is not a critical skill for getting around in supermarkets.

Use and training can improve our sense of smell considerably. Most of us can identify a few thousand of the estimated 400,000 smells on earth today. With training, however, humans have been able to identify up to 10,000 discrete odors. Experienced hunters still report that they frequently smell their prey before they see them.

While our powers of smell may have been on the decline for centuries, our concern with smell borders on the obsessive. Conditioned by advertising, we have become hypersensitive to "bad" odors as a social stigma and source of embarrassment. Deodorizing began in France around the sixteenth century. Now, everything imaginable needs deodorizing whether it's our breath, armpits, toilet, bathroom, cat or car, and then re-odorized with other "pleasant" smells. Contemporary society has become odor-phobic. Never have so-called bad odors been so systematically pursued.

Most cultures have sought to capture the positive powers of smell. Premodern medicine was closely linked to smell. Up until the 19th century, most preventative or curative measure relied on the use of odorous processes and products. Shamans used medicinal plants whose virtues were closely linked to smell. Recently, aromatherapies have resurfaced and are growing in popularity.

Pheromones, odorous substances secreted by the body, have been observed in many animal species to function as chemical signals that trigger, parental, social, and sexual behavior. Odiferous potions have been used to allure people throughout human history. However, during periods of asceticism, both philosophers and Christian moralists condemned the use of smell for sensual purposes. With the decline of Puritanism came the flourishing of the perfume industry. The current perfume industry is huge. In addition to carnal purposes, smell in the form of incense is used in religious practices to create an atmosphere conducive to spiritual experiencing. Exploring nature's smells is not to be overlooked.

For enhanced smelling, consider the following practical tips. Smell is better in moist air because more of the odor can be absorbed. To smell as much as possible, stay low to the ground where scents are more prominent. For determining the direction of a smell, sniff briefly as you turn your head from side to side. Head movements and continual shifting help locate the source of a smell by noticing small differences in intensity.

Activity Twenty-Two ➤ Banquet of Smells

Collect a variety of aromatic natural objects in advance on a nature walk, or go on a smell walk. Tree smells, cones and needles, aromatic shrubs, leaves, twigs, seeds, flowers. Smell with your eyes closed. Draw the fragrances inside you. Pay attention to what happens as you do this. Compare active sniffing verses just letting the scent come to you. Explore at what distant you can first begin to smell an object and how far away it can be moved before you lose the scent. Note your inner response to each smell. This activity can be done in pairs with one partner's eyes closed so that the objects are identified by smell only.

Try the Exploring Attractions Activity in Chapter 7 (p.79) using only your sense of smell as a guide. Follow your nose. Many animals navigate through the woods relying on their sense of smell to find food, avoid danger, and so on. See what happens when you follow your nose.

Seeing

Like all organisms, humans are sensitive to light. Seeing is not a passive process, but an interactive cycle of nature. Every second the retina performs 10 billion computer-like calculations. Seventy percent of all the body's sense receptors are in the eyes. One third of the brain, fifty percent of the cortex, is thought to be involved in processing visual perception. Our eyes bring us information from the greatest distances, unlike touch which requires physical contact.

We live in an eye dominant culture. We say "see you later" not "touch you later." *See* what I mean? We also say "seeing is believing." Yet, many experts on perception believe that sight is the most easily duped sense. Perceptual psychologists have spent much time studying optical illusions. The expression, "your eyes are bigger than your stomach," took an interesting twist of meaning when researchers found overeaters consumed considerably less when blindfolded. Our eyes may play a contributing role in addictive behavior. Our eyes may also be bigger than our pocketbooks, contributing to problems involving over-consumption of material goods.

With seeing, unlike touch, we can keep things at a distance. We can glance at our world, skipping over the surface, taking in almost nothing. We can be detached observers. We can watch without becoming involved with what we see. We can keep a vigilant eye on things while keeping them at a safe distance.

On the other hand we can look into each others eyes with an intimacy that is deep and profound. The eyes have been called the windows to our souls. Both sexes have identified the eyes as the feature of a person's appearance that is the most powerful source of attraction. Looking into the eyes of an animal in the wild and having your gaze returned can be a powerful and exhilarating experience. People can be delighted when seen with love and admiration or shrink with embarrassment or shame when under the scrutiny of a judgmental eye. Not being noticed by others can make us feel ignored, like a no-body. Children, for example, often prefer negative attention to no attention at all. We give the world our attention so that it can be mirrored in our eyes.

Even though we live in an eye dominant culture, how many of us take the time to really see. We often look just long enough for identification and orientation and then move on to the next. Photographers and painters, the visual artists, take the time because the tasks of their art require it. Yet, even then the artist can distance from intimacy by hiding behind the camera lens. An opportunity for intimate dialogue with nature will be lost by the landscape painter who places the dominant focus on the technical details of applying paint to the canvas. On the other hand, these artistic activities can be windows which open our eyes to the appreciation of beauty in the world. Ultimately it is not what you do, but how you do it.

Looking is active seeing. Watching with fascination, with absorbed curiosity. Looking may take the form of rigid staring, gazing at the whole scene, or sharp pinpointing of detail. The focus of watching can be light (brightness), color, movement, shape, patterns, depth, size, or perspective. The brain processes motion first. Color is a luxury. When we don't take our seeing for granted, paying attention to the process can be enlightening.

Oftentimes, our eyes are not seeing clearly because they are tired, stressed, and strained. They need some special care.

Activity Twenty-Three ➢ Eye Relaxation

Close your eyes. Gently place your slightly cupped palms over your eyes to further close off outside light. Allow your eyes and facial muscles to relax with the warm, gentle, comforting touch of your hands.

On the other hand, there may be times when your eyes need the benefits of some active exercise.

Activity Twenty-Four ➢ Looking Warm-Up

Wake up your eyes with some calisthenics. Open eyes wide and then close them tightly 5-10 times. Then look side to side out of the corners of your eyes without moving your head. Next, look up and down. Then move your eyes in circles clockwise, then counterclockwise. For the next few minutes, focus your vision for just one second on one thing at a time, shifting from objects up close to objects at a distance, shifting from objects from the left, center and right of your field of vision, and from high to low.

The eye movements that cause seeing are called saccades, very tiny rotations of the whole eyeball. Flickering at speeds of two to ten hundredths of a second, they create a strobe light effect which stimulates the retinal nerve cells. Dr. William Bates (1860-1931) studied how muscle tension of the eyes can slow down and disrupt these eye movements. When relaxed and harmonized, eyesight becomes especially bright, acute, and colorful. This "centralized" vision comes from the "fovea centralis," the special area of the retina where the cone cells, our color and detail receptors, are packed closely together. Dr. Bates developed eye movement exercises designed to help people with poor vision, publishing them in a book entitled *Better Eyesight Without Glasses.* A variation of his basic exercise designed to enhance vision is included below.

Activity Twenty-Five ➢ Imaginary Outlining

Imagine that you have an imaginary pencil extending from the tip of your nose. Loosely draw the outlines of objects around you with the tip end of your pencil. Move your whole head as you trace. Begin with outlining large objects that you see best. Proceed to smaller shapes. Then sketch shapes that are near and far. Stay relaxed, yet alert. Do not make any special effort to be precise. Stay loose and playful. Take your time. Don't rush. Let your sketching flow from one object to the next. Continue sketching throughout the full range and depth of your field of vision. Note that doing this activity requires a kind of active, conscious marking of what you see.

One problem experienced by many in our intense, highly focused, goal-oriented culture is tunnel vision. There is a tendency to set our sights on one thing to the exclusion of everything else in our field of vision. We get lots of up-close use of the eyes, but less frequently do we step back and take a broader perspective.

When growing up I learned the value of wide-angle vision when my basketball coaches taught me the importance of seeing the whole court. I remember how acquiring this skill took considerable effort and how easy it was to abandon, especially under the pressure of a close game. Until just recently, I had no idea that it had applications off the court. Native Americans use this technique to spot game while hunting. Deer and other animals use it to spot predators. To help counter this tendency for tunnel vision, try the following activity.

Activity Twenty-Six ➤ Wide-Angle Vision

Stretch your arms out wide, away from your sides and slightly behind you, parallel to the ground like a pair of wings. Point your fingers up. Then, gazing straight ahead towards the far horizon, slowly bring your arms forward wiggling your fingers until you can see them moving in your field of vision. For most people the angle is almost 180 degrees. To check your vertical field of vision repeat, but this time with one arm stretched up high above and behind your head and the other low and behind by your side bringing one arm down in an arc and the other up. For most people the angle is about 150 degrees.

Practice the above until you get the feel for unfocused gazing into the distance that enables the largest field of vision. Notice how the periphery of the field picks up movement. Contrast this with narrow focusing on an object. Objects in your direct line of vision can be brought into clear focus while objects in your peripheral vision remain fuzzy. Shift back and forth between narrow focusing and wide-angle vision, separating them by intervals of just a few seconds.

Practice outdoors in a variety of settings. Shift in and out of wide-angle vision. With practice you will likely double your chances of picking up all kinds of nature's movements including spotting birds, insects, deer, and other critters. It's easiest to learn standing or sitting still. Once you get the hang of it, challenge yourself more by trying it while hiking down a trail, kayaking, gardening, or during other activities.*

While seeing has been identified as a sense that enables us to receive input from great distances, we can also explore the world of up-close vision. The following activity, my version of an activity also designed by tracker Tom Brown, invites you to find out more about this perspective on life.

---

* Adapted from Tom Brown

Activity Twenty-Seven ➤ Small World Exploring

Mark off a small section of ground (no more than 1 or 2 square feet) that draws your attention using a length of string or sticks. First, look at it from a standing position. Notice what you see and describe the area. Then kneel down on your knees, and again notice and describe the area. Finally, lie on your belly and explore the area in minute detail. Imagine you are a small bug exploring never-seen-before territory. Stay with your natural attractions, whether a tiny flower or insect. Then, wander on to the next. See if you can stay absorbed for at least ten minutes. Then get up and return to your standing vantage point. Don't analyze or evaluate, simply notice the differences in perception and response from the different vantagepoints.

"Nature will bear the closest inspection.
She invites us to lay our eye level with her smallest leaf,
and take an insect view of its plain."

Henry David Thoreau

Touching

All creatures great or small react to being poked, prodded, pressed, or caressed. Touch is the earliest sense to mature. The skin is both boundary and antenna. Our skin has sense receptors for exploring the textures of our world. Pain is the alarm that warns of tissue damage causing us to withdraw from contact. Pleasure, on the other hand, draws us into intimate contact. On a primal level, our attractions and repulsions are often governed by the sensations of pleasure and pain which serve to ensure our physical survival and health. While vision and hearing are the senses best suited for perceiving from a distance, touch is a local sense for exploring what is within reach.

Our nearest relatives in the animal kingdom, the primates, spend hours each day preening each other. Healthy emotional development depends on receiving adequate touch. Unfortunately, touch is probably our most repressed sense. Lots of touch taboos remain in our culture. Still struggling with our western puritanical heritage, we tend to be hyper-concerned about sexualizing touch. The boundaries between the sensual, erotic, and genital arousal are so blurred as to cause confusion and threat in many touch situations. As a result, people are likely to be touch-deprived in our culture. Sadly, people are all too often sexually and physically abused as well.

Reconnecting with nature reawakens us to our erotic nature. The superficial sexual exhibitionism or titillation that gets so much press in our contemporary culture are symptomatic of our touch dis-ease. Placing our sexual-erotic nature in the broadest context of our existence as sensual beings and learning to be more discriminating about the wide array of our physical engagements with the world holds the most promise for leading us in a healthy direction, one that will help us escape the puritanical-hedonistic conflicts that have plagued us for centuries.

Wearing layers of clothes and shoes on our feet cuts much of our skin off from tactile stimulation. Tactile stimulation of all parts of the body is revitalizing. Touch is not just for the hands. You can rub your back up against a tree or rock for example. Touch can be relaxing or invigorating. There is a great variety of touch to be explored: stroking, rubbing, tapping, patting, scratching, kneading, caressing, squeezing, preening, shaking, tickling, kissing, pinching, punching, twisting, hugging, fondling, stretching, poking, pressing, holding, pushing, pulling, and so on. By connecting with nature in this up-close physical way, you will be touched deeply by many of your experiences. There are countless touch opportunities in nature.

Activity Twenty-Eight ➤ Touching Nature

Collect a variety of natural objects with a wide range of textures in advance on a nature walk, or go on a touch walk. Moss, leaves, twigs, bark, flower petals, smooth and jagged rocks, pine cones, shells. Explore these objects with your eyes closed. Find out as much as you can about each using only your sense of touch. In addition to exploring them with your hands, touch them to various parts of your body to see what it's like to experience their touch on your body. Try holding, rubbing, tapping, rolling and stroking them. Pay attention to your internal response to these objects as you experience their varying textures, sizes, weights, densities, temperatures, pliability, softness, hardness.

Activity Twenty-Nine ➤ Receiving Touch

Get a massage from a friend or professional. This can be a great preparation for receiving nature because it will help relax you, stimulate and invigorate you, as well as open up your sensitivity to touch.

Activity Thirty ➤ Nature's Massage Walk

When you are open to it, nature provides many wonderful massages. Take a walk in nature. Feel the breeze on your skin, the warmth of the sun, refreshing water of a stream, the sand between your toes, . . . Fair weather and minimal clothing, including bare feet if terrain permits, is ideal for this activity.

Tasting

To experience eating is to become familiar with a most fundamental process of nature. Life lives on life. Eating is the passage of life from one form to another.

Taste is the sense most involved with conscious behavior because it requires both attention and coordinated activity for putting things in the mouth. Like the four primary colors of sight, there are four primary tastes: salt, sour, sweet, and bitter. Taste is not discrete but is intertwined with the sensations of temperature, texture, and smell. Life can be filled with a variety of flavors and spices. Taste is involved in selecting what is to be admitted into the body. Breast milk is sweet. Most poisons are bitter. A person may respond to taste with gut-wrenching disgust or with powerful craving. Sweets, like chocolate, are the stuff of addiction. We describe paradise as the "land of milk and honey." We eat food by plucking fresh berries right off the vine or by sitting down to a multi-course meal that has been painstakingly prepared by a great culinary artist.

Many seasonal celebrations involve eating, sometimes fasting, sometimes feasting. Christian Communion is an example of how eating can be infused with special significance when part of a religious ritual. The Lord's Prayer includes, "Give us this day our daily bread." Humans all over the world treat eating as a sacred act preceding it with a mealtime prayer. For many, saying grace before a meal is not to be forgotten.

Activity Thirty-One ➤ Taste Sampler

Prepare in advance a platter of sample tastes, using very small portions. Include a glass of cool water to clear the palate between tastes. Select natural foods with no additives, no cooking. Pick a wide variety of tastes (sweet, sour, salty, and one or two bitter) including if available small slices of *fresh* fruits, berries, vegetables, nuts, honey, herbs and spices. Settle into a comfortable place to eat that will be free of distractions. Take some time to relax and focus your awareness. Then slowly, with full awareness, taste each sample. Pay attention to your internal response to each taste. "Right now I am tasting, . . . and my response is . . . ") Clear your palate with a sip of water between tastes.

In my life, Wednesday morning is Farmer's Market day. I regularly buy a bag of mixed greens for our family salads. The dozen or so different greens change throughout the season, providing me a regular opportunity to enjoy the Taste Sampler Activity. This morning, an apple vendor at the market provided tasty samples of ten different varieties. The melon man was there offering five or six varieties to sample. Yummy.

Activity Thirty-Two ➤ Full Taste of Life

Select a special fruit to explore: orange, tangerine or tangelo, peach or pear. Read through these instructions in advance so you'll remember what to do. When you're settled in and ready to start, hold the fruit in the palms of your hands and close your eyes. Sense its weight, its shape, its temperature. Feel the texture of its skin. Squeeze it to sense its hardness and density. Roll it on parts of your body (legs, tummy, arms, shoulders, then your face. How close must you bring it to your nose to be able to smell it? Open your eyes and explore it visually. See its shape, color, markings on its skin. Then slowly begin to peel the fruit. Listen to the sounds, see the juice, watch the skin break and come off, notice the texture of the inner flesh. After it is peeled, close your eyes. Smell it again. Then slowly break it into sections. What can you feel inside your mouth? Your teeth? Your tongue? Your saliva? Keeping your eyes closed, take your first bite. How does the flavor change from the first bite until you swallow? How long can you continue to taste that first bite? Slowly continue to eat the fruit one small bite at a time. Listen to the sounds of your eating. Savor the taste, feel the juices in your mouth. Experience your teeth sinking into it, chewing, swallowing. Continue to experience every detail of the whole experience until you feel finished. How does this compare with the way you usually eat?

Activity Thirty-Three ➤ Full Taste of Life: Partner Variation

Do this activity with a friend. Select a special fruit for your partner to explore: orange, tangerine, or tangelo. Don't tell them what it is. Have them blindfolded or keep their eyes closed so they cannot identify it by sight. Put the fruit in the palms of their hands. Tell them to find out as much as they can about this object. Let them explore it in their own way. Yet, encourage them to take their time to explore slowly and thoroughly in as many ways they can. You want them to have a rich experience; so if they seem to run out of ideas quickly, suggest some ways to explore. (for additional ideas see those suggested in the previous activity) Keep talking to a minimum. Do they remember to smell it? After awhile, ask them to open their eyes and explore it visually. Encourage them to pay attention to every detail and aspect of this experience. Then have them peel it. After peeling and exploring it peeled, then have them close their eyes again. Then invite them to eat it, slowly and carefully so they taste every bite.

5

Exploring the Impact of Language

"The major problems in the world are the result of the difference between how nature works and the way people think."

Gregory Bateson

Language is both our jailer and our liberator. We can use language in ways that cut us off from our experiencing; and we can also use language in ways that plunge us ever more deeply and intimately into our world. This chapter explores both sides of the language coin with activities designed to help you use language in the service of your liberation.

Language as Jailer:

"Surrounded by our thoughts or imaginary objects, living in our ideas, not one in a million ever sees the objects which are actually around him."

Henry David Thoreau

In Chapter 4's section on sensory awareness, I introduced how our use of language can block and dilute experiencing. Emptying the mind of distracting chatter helps us focus on our sensory experience. Seeking causes and reasons, interpreting, and explaining are mental activities that often take us away from our direct experiencing. Mental activities point the flashlight of our awareness toward the midzone of the mind and away from the direct experiencing of ourselves and our world. By thinking and talking about experiences we've had in the past or expect to have in the future, we can lose touch with our here-and-now experiencing. We need to be wary of using words in ways that disconnect us from our concrete life experience.

Labeling often brings sensory perception to a halt. When we name our experience and immediately move on to the next, the label becomes a conceptual box that signals the end of exploring and discovery. We box ourselves in with words by limiting and selecting out experiences to conform to our preconceptions about how the world is. This tendency is strong in people who, having a low tolerance for the ambiguity of not knowing, grasp for the feeling of security that naming provides.

Caught up in the cognitive dimension of interacting with signs and symbols, we abstract ourselves out of participating in our organic connection with the living earth. Modern technologies, beginning with the revolutionary shift from oral to written cultures brought on by the invention of the printing press, invite us to spend more and more time out of touch with the natural world. Entranced by the electronic cyberspaces and information highways of the mass media, we live more and more in a midzone world of abstract images and symbols. We live indoors, surrounding ourselves with our technology, encased within the human constructed world of cement, windows, mirrors, and screens. We cut ourselves off from our bodies and our sensuous immersion in the earth's body, living encased in our brains which have no sense organs whatsoever.

A little too abstract, a little too wise,
It is time for us to kiss the earth again,
It is time to let the leaves rain from the skies,
Let the rich life run to the roots again.
                    Robinson Jeffers (excerpt from "Return")

Language as Liberator

"Any given word is a bundle, and meaning sticks out of it in various directions, not aspiring toward any single official point. In pronouncing the word "sun," we are, as it were, undertaking an enormous journey to which we are so accustomed that we travel in our sleep. What distinguishes poetry from automatic speech is that it rouses us and shakes us into wakefulness in the middle of a word. Then it turns out that

the word is much longer than we thought, and we remember that to speak means to be forever on the road."
Osip Mandelstam, "Conversations About Dante" (essay)

On the other hand, language can reflect an authentic effort to fully describe our experiencing. Do we conform our experience to our language or do we form our language to reveal our experience? In the words of David Abram, "We regularly talk of howling winds, and of chattering brooks. Yet these are more than mere metaphors. Our own languages are continually nourished by these other voices—by the roar of waterfalls and the thrumming of crickets. It is not by chance that, when hiking in the mountains, the English terms we spontaneously use to describe the surging waters of the nearby river are words like "rush," "splash," "gush," "wash." For the sound that unites all these words is that which the water itself chants as it flows between the banks."

You can learn to recognize when your thinking is disconnected from your senses and when it is being informed by and grounded in your perceptual experience. The zones of awareness activities in Chapter 2, help you learn to pay attention to the relationship between your thinking (internal zone) and your perceiving (external zone) in your ongoing experiencing of your world.

Our cognitive structures guide our perceptions. All perception is enmeshed with our construction of reality as expressed through our language system. We can loosen the knot between language and perception but it cannot be completely untied.

Personal and societal constructs are the templates for sifting through and ordering massive amounts of complex sensory data. New conceptualizations of nature can guide us to perceive our world differently. For example, Eskimos have many more words for snow in their language than we do which reflects their more refined experience and understanding. T. H. Huxley put it this way, "To a person uninstructed in natural history, his country or seaside stroll is a walk through a gallery filled with wonderful works, nine-tenths of which have their faces turned to the wall."

Words are more than just labels. They're packed with meaning. Words carry with them both positive and negative connotations. They are linked with powerful images. They represent our construction of reality, coming together like pieces of a puzzle to form a worldview. The following activity invites you to explore the formative power of words in creating our values, attitudes, and understandings of nature. What roads do these words take you down?

Activity Thirty-Four ➢ Constructing Nature

Below are pairs of words for contemplation. Relax and settle in. With your eyes closed, silently say each word to yourself alternating back and forth between members of each pair. Each time you say a word to yourself, pause and pay attention to your inner response. What feelings, thoughts, and images are triggered by this word? Then, compare your response with the other member of the pair. Slowly repeat each pair several times before moving on to the next pair. Try out other pairs of nature words that come to mind.

Jungle	Rain forest
Weed	Plant
Swamp	Wetland
Beast	Pet

Individual words, like single pieces of a puzzle, do make a difference in the way we experience our world. Sometimes the overall way the pieces come together in relationship to each other undergoes a shift. Paradigm shifts occasionally occur that radically alter our perspective and worldview in ways that create a profound impact. For example, John Briggs states at the end of his book on the patterns in nature called fractals, "Whatever the study of fractals and chaos may bring in terms of practical applications, the deepest gift may be the opportunity these ideas offer for radically changing the way we look at nature." As stated in the introduction, I believe that we are in the midst of a revolutionary shift from a mechanistic to an ecological worldview. This guidebook invites you to actively participate in this transformation.

Here are some other ways our use of language can effect our experiencing. We can use "objective language" to structure our world into a world of unchanging things, to objectify it. "There are three roses in a vase on the table." Or we can use "process language" which is descriptive of our ever-changing, emerging, world of experiencing. "Enthralled, I find myself being drawn in, gazing further into the radiant red folds of color in the center of the rose." We can live in a language world that emphasizes nouns or one that emphasizes verbs.

Language can be personal or impersonal, intimate or distant. For example, I-language verses It-language. "It is a soothing stream." verses "The swishing and trickling sounds of the stream soothe me at my core."

Language can be disembodied and factual or it can be sensual and feelingful. "My father died." verses "As I looked at my favorite picture of my dad, I felt an empty longing sensation in the pit of my stomach."

The following activities help you explore how these different ways of using language effect our experience of nature. By participating in these activities, you will better learn to notice how your "self-talk" during nature experiences, and the words you use to describe your experiences after the fact, create a powerful and formative impact on the quality of your experiencing.

Activity Thirty-Five ➤ Language Impact

Try saying the following sentences to yourself. Pay attention to your inner response to saying them. "That tree." "This tree." "My tree." Repeat several times and notice your feelings with each. Then compare: "It's a hot day." and "I can feel the penetrating warmth of the sun on my face." Repeat several times noticing your feelings. Then try these two pairs: "It's a very good day." and "Today, I feel good all over." "It was a funny movie." and "I smile and chuckle inside as I remember scenes from the movie."

You can experience the formative power of language by paying attention to the words that come to mind as you experience the nature activities, and by noting how you describe your nature experiences to others or write them down in a journal.

Activity Thirty-Six ➤ Language Awareness

Select a nature activity. Describe your experience of the activity in the words that emerge at the time or immediately after by either writing it in a journal or telling a friend. Do you find yourself using objective or process language? Are you using intimate or detached language? concrete and specific or highly abstract language? Do you find yourself using sensual and emotional or factual and sterile language? Repeat the words and feel your inner response. Try changing the way you describe your experience to include more process, personal, concrete, and emotional language. Tell this version of your experience and feel your response.

Poetry is the creative art of putting together words that point beyond themselves in ways that open us more deeply into our experiencing. Words, like the air we breathe, can be life giving or stale. Poetry is inspirational, opening us to new dimensions of life. I have included special quotations and poetry in this book that will hopefully have this energizing effect on you as they have for me.

As with singing, dancing, and so many other creative activities, we don't have to abdicate to the professionals. We can enjoy participating in creative wordplay.

Activity Thirty-Seven ➤ Wordplay

Immediately after completing one of the nature activities write down a few words and phrases that come to mind. Then play with them, arrange them, develop them in ways that better bring your experience in its fullness to life. See if you can find words and create images that point beyond their literal definitions and meanings to the essence of your experience.

We are language-creating beings. The midzone of our thinking will not go away. By paying attention to our use of language, we can uncover how it impacts our experiencing of ourselves and the world. Our use of language reflects both our I-It instrumental approach to the world and our I-Thou relationship with our world. We can discover ways to use language which will validate our ongoing life experiences and creatively reveal to us new perspectives and depths of meaning as we penetrate the mysteries of our existence in the universe. Whether it be through the recitation of poetry, prayer, sacred chanting, or the ritual use of "mantras," the repeated sounding of sacred words of invocation, we can rediscover the transformative power of the word. They are a means of acting upon ourselves to create a greater receptivity to the living earth so that it can flow through us in all its manifestations.

The living "word" is made flesh through the sensuous interplay between the human body and the living landscape. This felt meaning can be represented in words which may then be expressed by the human voice. At this most primordial level, the sounding of the words invoke sensations in the body, the massage of the message.

The intoned words of incantations, by modifying the airwaves, physically transform the atmosphere of a place. The chanting person, whose own body is the instrument of transformation, first creates within himself the desired state, such as harmony and well being. Then the chanter sends outward this inner state of en-chant-ment.

Buddhist monk Thich Nhat Hanh has created simple meditation techniques that combine breath awareness (See Breathing Section of Chapter 3) with mantras in which the practitioner identifies with an aspect of nature (See Identification Section of Chapter 7).

Activity Thirty-Eight ➢ Flower and Mountain Meditations

In sitting meditation, gazing at or imagining a special flower, repeat the following mantra to yourself silently, *"Breathing in, I see myself as a flower . . . Breathing out, I feel fresh."* Synchronize each statement with your breath.

In sitting meditation, gazing at or imagining a special mountain, repeat the following mantra to yourself silently. "Breathing in, I see myself as a mountain . . . Breathing out, I feel solid." Again, synchronize each statement with your breath.

Experiment with creating some of your own. Try tree, stream, star, and . . .

It's Sunday, the week before Easter. I go to my sacred space for my morning meditation. Meditating on the experience of Spring, the words emergence, blossoming forth, fertility, and opening to the sun parade through my mind. "Emergence, blossoming forth, fertility, opening to the sun; emergence, blossoming forth" when my eyes are drawn to the bright red tulip on my altar which, fully closed minutes before, is beginning to open. Instantly entranced, I spontaneously begin repeating the mantra, "Breathing in, I am one with the tulip; breathing out, I am opening." Ah . . . I am drawn into the blossoming. Moment by moment, I experience opening into the light as never before . . . Passionate red. Emerging from within, on the tip of the stamen, are three pairs of tiny bright yellow petals of sunshine bursting forth from a black and yellow hexagonal pattern. Fully open now, ready for the bee. I bring my nose to the blossom and inhale its fragrance. Ahhhh . . . Just as I sense the experience coming to an end, the sun shines through the window, its penetrating light bringing a beautiful glowing translucence to the petals. Praise for the enlightenment of the Earth. Gratitude for this morning's teaching. I know Spring more fully than ever before.

Here is an out-loud invocation activity to try:

Activity Thirty-Nine ➤ Invocations

Select an inspirational poem, prayer, or passage that expresses your own deep feelings for nature. Go to a place in nature that is special to you. If there is a close correspondence between the words selected and the landscape chosen so much the better. Sit in a comfortable place where you can remain still and silent for awhile. Begin with the Calm Breathing or Centering Activity. Then repeat your selection silently to yourself. Say the words with reverence. Allow the words to penetrate yourself and your surroundings so that you can feel their meaning. Repeat your selection several times to create the desired mood. Then sit quietly in silent meditation and drink in your setting. Experiment with the effect of increasing the number of repetitions. RESOURCES: *Earth Prayers* or *The Earth Speaks* (Collections of poems and prayers)

The following poem has become a personal anthem that I have used many times to invoke a powerful connection with nature. I can't resist sharing it with you. If the poem speaks to you, try calling it out to the universe from one of your favorite places in nature.

> *For I have learned*
> *To look on nature, not as in the hour*
> *Of thoughtless youth; but hearing oftentimes*
> *The still, sad music of humanity,*
> *Nor harsh nor grating, though of ample power*
> *To chasten and subdue. And I have felt*
> *A presence that disturbs me with the joy*
> *Of elevated thoughts; a sense sublime*
> *Of something far more deeply interfused,*
> *Whose dwelling is the light of setting suns,*
> *And the round ocean and the living air,*
> *And the blue sky, and in the mind of man:*
> *A motion and a spirit that impels*
> *All thinking things, all objects of all thought,*
> *And rolls through all things. Therefore am I still*
> *A lover of the meadows and the woods,*

And mountains; and of all that we behold
From this green earth; of all the mighty world
Of eye, and ear,—both what they half create,
And what perceive; well pleased to recognize
In nature and the language of the sense
The anchor of my purest thoughts, the nurse,
The guide, the guardian of my heart, and soul
Of all my moral being.

William Wordsworth
"Lines Composed a Few Miles
above Tintern Abbey"

6

Barriers to Being Fully Present in Nature

"I feel a little alarmed when it happens that I have walked a mile into the woods bodily, without getting there in spirit . . . What business have I in the woods, if I am thinking of something out of the woods?"

Henry David Thoreau

Decompressing

Decompressing from our fast-paced, goal-oriented, task-filled lives often takes time. Time to unwind. Time to settle in. Time to let go of digital time and enter into nature's time. Joe, a client of mine, who in his own words, "lived in the fast lane," took a hard-earned weeklong vacation to Hawaii with his wife. Afterwards, he reported in his counseling session, "It took me five days to slow down. I was restless until the last two days, but those two days were the best I've had in a long, long time." Colin Fletcher, author of *The Complete Walker*, describes the adjustment this way, "And, so, by slow degrees, you regain a sense of harmony with everything you move through—rock and soil, plant, and tree and cactus, spider and fly and snake, and coyote, drop of rain and cloud shadow." Sometimes this transition is not so gradual or gentle.

Our feelings as well as our language can be a barrier to opening up to nature. This was especially true for me on one of my first solo backpacking trips. I'd arrived at the trailhead at sunset for a few days of hiking and fishing. Anxious to get a few miles behind me before darkness set in, I hoisted my pack onto my shoulders only moments after turning off the ignition and bounded down the trail. My mind raced with excitement and anticipation. "What a gorgeous place! Isn't this going to be wonderful? Weather's perfect. Not a cloud in the sky. Eden, here I come."

As it began to grow dark, my anxious energy started to dissipate. Less than a mile down the trail, no more whistling or humming tunes, the bounce in my step gone. Walking into a thick cloud of silence, I came to a grinding halt, suddenly feeling utterly lost. My body shuddered, and into my head popped the thought that I could hightail it back to the car before dark. What for? What's going on here? Then it dawned on me. Even though I was telling myself this place was beautiful, I was not really taking in its wonder and beauty. My words unmasked as wishful thinking, I just stood there in the middle of the trail, dumbfounded, the self-deception of my good time exposed. A big tall conifer, standing off by itself on a nearby knoll, caught my eye. In response to its beckoning, I staggered over beneath its branches, dropped off my pack, plopped down and pressed my back against its massive trunk. I pulled my legs up to my chest, grasped them with my arms, and dropped my forehead to my knees.

Well, I went a little crazy right there under that tree as waves of confusion and fear, then pain and sadness surfaced. On the hike in, I was carrying a burden of psychological junk that was blocking my responsiveness to this beautiful setting. I surrendered to my feelings and accompanying thoughts as they surfaced. I sat there under the tree and grieved. I uncovered some hidden layers of myself. I had no person to cheer me up, distract me with talk, or help me rationalize it all away.

By the next day, having done my griefwork, purging myself of the disruptive unfinished business, I was no longer merely telling myself, "This is wonderful." I was cleared out and genuinely experiencing the wonderment of it all.

Beginning a nature trip with a transition experience of this kind isn't unusual for me, or for many others who have told me similar stories. I now know that it often takes time to decompress, to break free of the baggage I'm carrying around. To "get fully present" and "in the flow" so I can more fully enjoy my nature experiences oftentimes involves breaking through a wall of grief or other feelings that need to be emptied out. You may find this to be true for you.

"Only in the stillness and simplicity of presence can we really appreciate our life and reconnect with the ordinary magic of being alive on Earth."

John Welwood

I have come to accept and plan for decompression as part of the transition process. When I work with groups, I sometimes have them try the following decompressing activity.

Activity Forty ➤ Decompressing

Sit quietly for a moment. Pay attention to any obsessive thoughts, worries, problems, concerns, anxieties about the future, unresolved conflicts, . . . any and all psychological baggage that is blocking your being fully present, your here-and-now openness to what nature has to offer you. As these obstacles come up, take at least a few moments to examine each of them. Acknowledge and accept them. Then, one by one toss them in the river and let them float away. In the absence of a river, select another place where you can toss them. For example, you could toss them in your campfire and let them go up in smoke. Wherever you toss them, just let them all go. If there are concerns that are too important to let go of in this way, ones that carry important lessons for you, put them in your pocket or other special place for safe keeping. You can then take them out again after you've returned from your nature experience. When you discover psychological baggage surfacing at other times during your nature experiences, repeat this activity.

In addition to diffusing the barriers of feeling that currently block us, we can choose to dig deeper and struggle with our core issues of loneliness and solitude.

Loneliness and the Human Condition

"No man is free who will not dare to pursue the questions of his own loneliness. It is through them that he lives."

Christopher Fry

Loneliness is part of the human condition, a natural human response to our separate-but-relatedness. There is the loneliness of the city, the loneliness of the country, forest, desert, and sea. Experienced by young and old, at home or thousands of miles from home, alone or in a crowd, it will remain a part of the human experience. Loneliness tends to be experienced with more intensity during periods of transition and crisis. When habits and routines give way, when there is a questioning of the meaning and value of one's life, loneliness is likely to make its presence felt.

As a culture we're caught up in an ongoing crisis of rapid social change, popularized as "future shock" by Alvin Toffler. Culture has a powerful effect on how loneliness is experienced and handled. Modern societies, like our own, are especially conducive to the state of loneliness.

In addition to the rate of cultural change, the way a society is structured can create conditions of isolation and alienation. Sociologists have been writing about alienation and modern man for a long time. Alienation is another term referring to our disconnectedness. Much of the focus has been on our alienation from work and each other, but it can also apply to our relationship to the land.

Erich Fromm, in *Man for Himself* contends that our "marketing orientation" is the source of the problem. When this orientation dominates a society, then everything is treated as a commodity, and worth is determined by its exchange value. All relationships are weighed in terms of how profitable they are. Relationships are treated as means to ends. Instrumental, I-It relationships are the norm. Contact is specialized and organized for task completion and lasts only as long as needed to finish each task. The result is "emptiness." And emptiness, according to Rollo May, is the "chief problem of our day."

The widespread geographical uprooting that takes place in our highly mobile culture greatly increases our contact with the new and unfamiliar. Indigenous cultures that have occupied the same territory for many generations are disappearing at an alarming rate. So are migratory hunters and sheepherders, who by following the same routes season after season and generation after generation, have also maintained a deep connection to the land. Displacements from homelands cause major upheavals that destroy communities and entire cultures by removing the ground upon which they were founded. For most of our evolutionary history, humans have remained geographically rooted for centuries at a time. Until very recently, the experience of being uprooted was the rare exception. Now it is commonplace.

The US Bureau of Census reports mobility rates of 20% of our population moving every year in the 50's and 60's and continuing at rates in excess of 10% into the 90's. Human displacement, primarily to urban areas, is now increasing worldwide. We can be banished or exiled from our homelands for political or economic reasons. Or we may choose to move because of a promotion or because we want to leave a polluted environment to live in a more hospitable setting. Whatever the reason, when we move, we estrange ourselves from our roots in both the human community and the biotic community of our home landscape. Having left the familiar, most people, at least initially, experience the loneliness of being strangers living in a strange land. Some never succeed in putting down roots in their new place.

> *"We **must** get back into relation, vivid and nourishing*
> *relation to the cosmos and the universe . . .*
> *Vitally, the human race is dying.*
> *It is like a great uprooted tree, with its roots in the air.*
> *We must plant ourselves again in the universe."*
>
> **D. H. Lawrence,** *Lady Chatterley's Lover*

The Fear of Loneliness

> *"Loneliness is such an omnipotent and painful threat to many persons that they have little conception of the positive values of solitude. Many suffer from the fear of finding oneself alone and so they don't find themselves at all."*
>
> **Andre Gide**

Our culture tends to view loneliness as a negative emotion that should be avoided. For many, the painful emptiness of loneliness is so fearful that they attempt to escape from it, pushing it away through compulsive socializing and staying occupied with busywork. For these people silence and being alone are threatening since they might expose one's loneliness. Therefore, they engage in constant chatter about anything and everything, devoid of any meaningful or productive content. They may prefer the noisy city where silence is seldom experienced.

People's fear of loneliness can translate into a compulsive drive to be well liked by others. Fear of abandonment dominates their social behavior. Being around others supports the illusion of not being lonely. This person works hard to be well liked, conforming to others' expectations. Psychology itself falls into this trap when it describes human health in terms of adjustment and being normal. People seek to belong by striving to be like others so they can fit in to the group's expectations. Sociologist David Reisman first characterized this "other-directed" person. Psychologists have described these people as having an "external locus of control." That is, these "co-dependents," to use the current popular term, have a radar set tuned in to the needs and wants of others around which they organize their behavior in order to please them. Their own point of view, their own needs, wants, feelings, ideas, and values get lost in the process. Being in positions of high status and prestige can provide them with a sense of self-worth and belonging, but only in the eyes of others, and sometimes not even in their eyes. Ironically this neurotic path taken to escape loneliness is ultimately the most isolating and lonely of all. The person gains acceptance not of oneself but of the image presented for acceptance. Inner conflicts between the person's true inner self and the image presented for acceptance makes alone time inwardly directed and increasingly uncomfortable. In the end, the person one is lonely for is one's self! It becomes impossible to distinguish between one's true feelings and the other-directed roles that he or she plays. This emptiness is the deepest loneliness and most difficult to face. In this situation, to be alone is to face an identity crisis.

Clark Moustakas describes this condition of running from loneliness well, "It is absolutely necessary to keep busy, active, have a full schedule, be with others, escape into fantasies, dramas, and lives of others on television or in the movies. Everything is geared towards filling and killing time to avoid feeling the emptiness of life."

Out of Loneliness into Solitude

The way out of this unhealthy response to loneliness begins with the full acceptance of one's feelings of loneliness. The way out is through surrendering to the feelings of loneliness. Through loneliness, a person enters into a significant intimate experience of communing with oneself. The initial identity crisis leads to self-discovery: new insights about who one is, one's wants, desires, and values. Lost aspects of oneself that have been covered up in the habits and routines of daily living are uncovered. Moustakas puts it this way, "In utter loneliness, one can find answers to living; one can find new values to live by; one can see a new path or direction." The presence of loneliness testifies to the existence of a deeper human self-identity that can be reached. Facing one's loneliness leads to personal growth. According to Moustakas, it "leads to deeper perception, greater awareness and sensitivity, and insight into one's own being."

Breaking through the wall of loneliness allows us to enter into ourselves in contemplation, to discover ourselves, to separate out living one's own life from living a life designed to meet the expectations of others. When successful, this process leads us to the experience of solitude, the glorious experience of being at one with oneself and one's world. When a person has confronted one's illusions and worked through their feelings, has struggled and fought their intra-psychic battles, then one may be restored to one's self in solitude. Silence is experienced as a peaceful fullness, immersed among the subtle energies of the living earth. In solitude one can discover the peace and tranquillity of nature.

Psychologists have tended to focus on the negative aspects of being alone as being egoistic, narcissistic, and an escape from reality. These are legitimate concerns. However, we need to be alone to engage in self-reflection, self-confrontation, and meditation. In this process, we search within ourselves for new feeling, awareness, and direction. Being alone, silent, getting out of the hubbub and routine activity is essential for maintaining a genuine relationship with ourselves. To satisfy this need, especially in mass society, involves a decision to spend time alone in self-reflection to gain a clear sense of how your today is part of your life story.

Being alone in nature is often an invitation to deal with your psychological baggage. Research on solo experiences in the wilderness indicates that these experiences can be distressing as well as rewarding. The personal demons of loneliness must be faced and challenged on the journey to solitude. Sunset of the first night alone is a common low point. An inner sense of peacefulness may take time to develop. Overall, solo outing participants report very positive experiences (Kaplan, *The Experience of Nature*). Robert Greenway, reporting on his studies of 1,380 participants in his wilderness programs, found that 92 percent cited "alone time" as the single most important experience of their trip.

> *"Only by going alone in silence can one truly get into the heart of the wilderness. All other travel is mere dust, hotels and baggage and chatter."*
>
> **John Muir**

Activity Forty-One ➢ Solo Time

Select a time period, anywhere from ten minutes to a day or more, to be entirely alone. Then pick a quiet solitary place in nature where you can be undisturbed by phone calls or other interruptions. Take no work. Plan no activities. This is time to just sit with yourself and nature in silence. Sitting in meditation, see what happens in this state of non-doing. Be especially attentive to yourself and your response to your natural surroundings. Check in with yourself for feelings of loneliness, restlessness, boredom, emptiness, or solitude. Accept each feeling as it arises and learn what you can from it.

> *"The more I see of life the more I perceive that only through solitary communion with nature can one gain an idea of its richness and meaning. I know that in such contemplation lies my true personality."*
>
> **Palinurus**

Only a naive Pollyanna would claim that nature provides us only with joy. Nature can also plunge us deeply into our grief. It can trigger both profound despair as well as joy. Opening up in nature can be painful. Uncovering how disconnected we have become can be a very painful process. When we reconnect, it hurts to face the loss and pain about the times that we have not been connected. The pain of loneliness runs deep. There is also a deep sorrow connected to our longing to experience our original nature, the source of our being which we experience so rarely.

When some people lose a love through separation, divorce, or death, they may try to protect themselves from future pain by cutting themselves off from loving attachments. No longer following the proverb, "Better to have loved and lost, than to have never loved at all," they fall into the trap of "to protect myself from more pain, I'll not risk loving again." As a counselor, I experience this interpersonal dynamic all too often. What initially surprised me was recognizing how it also applies to our love of the land.

Cindy was uprooted from her childhood home at age eleven when her dad was transferred to another job. With tears streaming down her face, she began to uncover the pain of this loss and to recognize how this unhealed damage had effected the rest of her life. "Ever since that move, I have never allowed myself to become emotionally attached to any place, to really make it my home." The places Cindy lived were little more than crash pads. She "went out" to enjoy life. Uncovering this unresolved grief from her past helped Cindy rekindle her desire for a personal connection to place, a place where she felt she belonged. Only then did she begin to transform the house she currently occupied into her new home.

To summarize, in order to connect with nature, old traumas, past psychological damage, and other unfinished business may need to be faced. Breaking with the bonds of habit and changing the way we view our world can be a real struggle. I encourage you to have a group of supportive friends and professional resources available for support whenever you might need it.

Communing with nature can sometimes be as helpful as meeting with a good counselor or therapist. If you feel safe in nature and have learned your own methods of self-help from books or through coaching from a counselor, trips into nature settings can be a valuable adjunct to personal therapy. On the other hand, nature trips are no substitute for a good counselor. The challenges triggered by your nature experiences may precipitate the need for counseling when the intensity of feelings or the confusion that surfaces becomes overwhelming, or when you find yourself stuck and needing some feedback and guidance to sort it all out.

Fear of Nature

> *"Alone in a field or at the seashore . . . we feel closer to the mystery of life and death than when actually at risk crossing the street or riding in a fast car, when death may be literally just around the corner . . . Nature seems to want us to remember death. Is that why it's so hard to get us out of the house, out of the car, off the boat?"*
>
> **James Hillman,** *Talking on the Water*

Nature engenders powerful feelings in us that range from deep desire for connection to terror. We can feel very small and helpless, a little speck, lost and insignificant amongst billions of celestial light-years of space-time. Nature has its own horrors: earthquakes, floods, volcanic eruptions, hurricanes, tornadoes, fires, and diseases caused by harmful bacteria. Severe weather conditions cause massive destruction, suffering, trauma, and death. When engulfed by nature's harshness, nature seems totally indifferent to our welfare. We desire creature comforts to shelter us from these severities. We create heating technologies to protect us from the bitter cold and air conditioning to provide comfort from oppressive heat. Yet this cultural cocooning isolates as well as protects us.

You are not likely to be open to the beauty, power, and majesty of rapidly approaching thunderheads if you have no shelter and will soon be soaked to the bone. Fearful fantasies of impending death from hypothermia are likely to interfere. Blisters, mosquitoes, ticks, sunburn, bee stings, poison oak, snakebites and frostbite are just a few of nature's thorns that come with the roses; not to mention wildfires, cyclones, earthquakes, floods, comet collisions, and exploding supernovas.

Some of our fears of nature are real and warranted. Honoring those fears helps ensure our safety. By not having practical knowledge about nature, we lack survival skills for knowing how to be safe in the wilderness.

On the other hand, many fears of nature are born out of ignorance. Lack of familiarity and knowledge creates ideal conditions for fearful fantasies and phobias. Many people develop unfounded fears of harmless snakes and spiders, for example. Isolation from nature also creates fears of the unknown. Many of us are educated to survive only in our urban jungles. Although we may feel more safe in familiar urban settings, they're often more dangerous than most wilderness settings.

Struggling to face our fears of nature comes with the territory. Initially, I was surprised how, when the subject of wilderness came up, even veteran outdoor enthusiasts would begin to talk about bears, mountain lions, snakes, near drownings, slipping from ledges, windstorms, swarms of savage mosquitoes, and the like.

On a recent rafting excursion, participants shared personal stories which revealed their fears of nature. As darkness set in and thunder clapped in the background, one of the guides told us of her snake fears. When she was a little girl, her dad and older brother killed a dozen large copperheads and hung their skins on a line to dry. This dramatic event, done to make their camping area safe from these dangerous poisonous snakes, made a strong impression. Ever since, she has reacted as if all snakes were lurking copperheads.

The next day, while participating in a nature activity, she was startled by a snake darting out of the brush while exploring the riverbank. This time she was able to recover from her initial fear reaction and watch the snake harmlessly slither about the rocks and brush. As her familiarity grew, her fears diminished.

An important prerequisite for intimate relationships is trust. If we are to be intimate with nature, we must learn to trust her. Becoming familiar with each other, spending time in others' presence, helps build trust. All too often we do not venture beyond the familiar. For urbanites, exploring often stops where the pavement ends. A 1990's study found that 97% of those who visit our national parks never travel more than 100 yards from their cars. (Joe & Carol McVeigh "Mt. Rainier and the Wonderland Trail" video, 1995) No wonder park rangers have coined the term "windshield visitors" for these park tourists. Our illusory notion of wilderness as scenery limits us to experiencing it safely packaged in "views." To explore new territory, we must break out of our habitual patterns and overcome our fears of the unknown. (The Repulsions Activity in the next chapter can help in overcoming fears of nature.)

During the Middle Ages vast stretches of European forest were regarded as places of danger and chaos, where demons and monsters lived. Evil lurked in raw nature, while good was advanced by the development of civilized gardens. Many individuals and whole cultures find nature most beautiful when tamed, arranged, and dressed up in an English, Italian, or Japanese formal garden: flowers in groups and rows, terrain flattened or landscaped in geometrical terraces, trees pruned. "Civilized" people often prefer nature in its domesticated forms: farm animals and family pets rather than mountain lions and snakes, nurseries and arboretums rather than rainforests, cut flowers specially arranged, trees pruned with Euclidean order and symmetry, rather than fields of wildflowers and forests of trees. Orderly, neat, and tidy is preferred over messy and dirty.

People struggle to find the security of order in a complex and dynamic universe where there is not simple left-right symmetry, but jagged, interwoven networks. The natural world is a world of endless variety where nothing is ever the same. Nature does not exist in a simple static and balanced harmony, but rather a wavering, sometimes lurching, animating harmony.

Becoming connected with nature also involves acknowledging the cycle of life. Life thrives on energy. The flow of energy through most ecosystems begins with sunlight, which is converted by plants through the process of photosynthesis into the chemical energy of life—living tissue. A plant or animal uses energy for motion, growth, maintaining health, and reproduction. The web of life is one great food chain. Life lives off life. Nothing is wasted in this system in which everything nourishes something else. The food chain involves the passing of energy from one organism to another, from one life form to another, and these combustion systems are the same throughout nature. Each of our cells contains from one to thousands of tiny power plants called mitochondria, which turn food into cellular energy.

The food chain is made up of predator-prey relationships. A lone white blood cell prowls through tissue stalking and devouring bacteria. When an organism dies, however, bacteria have their way breaking it back down into inorganic compounds, which plants with the aid of sunlight can again transform into proteins. Thus, the recycling of energy goes round and round.

Watching a cat kill a mouse, or a lion bring down a zebra is not for the feint hearted. A client of mine shared the story of his son becoming extremely upset when watching a crocodile attack and devour a wildebeest on a television nature program. Soothing talk and the comfort and safety of a father's arms did not prevent a recurrence of the fear in a nightmare that evening. Imagine your reactions if you were to experience this crocodile attack first hand, up close. Being connected to the realities of nature means being confronted with the daily realities of life and death.

We do not experience the death of cattle when we pick up our prepackaged meat at the supermarket. We are distanced from the hunting and gathering that created an intimate relationship between predator and prey. We seldom experience ourselves as either predator or prey. If we were more intimately involved in all phases that precede our consumption of food, I wonder how our appetites and eating rituals might be effected?

Even pacifists who develop a strong compassion for life ultimately can't avoid killing. Buddhists and Jaines, for example, take vows to "save" all sentient beings. Albert Schweitzer with his reverence for life philosophy and lifestyle wouldn't kill insects, including mosquitoes. However, we can't even breathe without killing microbes in the air. The whole purpose of our immune system is to kill off noxious microorganisms. Killing is an integral part of being alive, but for most of us it is not part of our daily firsthand experience. Paradoxically, we live in a culture which denies death while at the same time exposes us to massive amounts of senseless violence and murder via television and the media. Exposure to a real corpse is rare, while dramatized images of death are common. Our fear and denial of death is one of the most powerful barriers to our developing an intimate relationship with nature. Compassion, reverence for life, come out of our facing the realities of life and death rather than its avoidance and denial.

In Greek mythology, Dionysus is the god of vegetation, of earth, of theater, as well as ecstatic dance. The Dionysian approach involves depths, wilderness, raw death, underworld, souls, ancestors, depths of consciousness, going down, into the womb, into the cave, into the formless origins. It involves entering into wild, untamed spaces where eater and eaten are one, where life consumes life. The Dionysian dance takes place close to nature, in the woods, and is an expression of forces of nature. It is an expression of our love for nature, for the earth, for the web of life, for the source, for nourishment, for union, for the paradise of our origins.

Our civilization has isolated itself from wilderness. If we are to develop an instinctive camaraderie with nature, we need its living presence. By experiencing Mother Nature's many gifts, by facing our fears rather than ignoring them, we will awaken our yearning for her presence just as we do for a loved one. The powerful feelings of ambivalence that accompany intimate loving relationships: the risk, vulnerability, the pain of loss, as well as joyful union, also apply to our love of nature.

> *"To follow nature means being able to accept her support and her cruelty as one state, undivided. Gentle rains or spring floods, the havoc of a landslide or the beauty of mountain mists—all are part of the whole to which the Sage belongs."*
>
> **T. H. Barrett**, *Tao: To Know and Not Be Knowing*

7

Taking in the World

"Drink it all in. Everything, the redwood forests, the sea, the sky, the waves, the birds, the sea-lions. It is in all this that you will find your answers. Here is where everything connects."

Thomas Merton

The Boundary

Each human organism, like all other living organisms, has a permeable boundary through which it both draws on and influences its surroundings. The process underlying all relationship is what gestaltists call "contact." Contact takes place at the boundary between organism and environment, between self and other. Taking in the world happens at this boundary.

Relationships grow out of our ongoing contact with the environment. The new and strange become familiar. Individuals grow and form identities through contact. The process of living one's life may be understood and experienced as a series of contacts, of meetings between self and other, between what is experienced as "me" and "not me."

Gestaltists explore the quality of the contact that takes place at the boundary between the person and the environment. People may contact the environment in ways that establish effective boundaries for meeting their needs, or they may contact the environment in ways that result in boundary disturbances which frustrate or prevent the meeting of their needs. This book is about establishing effective boundaries with nature that will nurture and foster your personal and spiritual growth.

Everything is enhanced in the presence of nature, the fresh air, the vegetation, the rocks, flowers, sea, mountains, and sky. But these gifts to the senses can only be given if we are open to receiving them. When we don't get input from nature, we end up not having much sense of smell, hearing, or vision. When we diminish our exposure to nature, we diminish the quality of our sensory awareness. Skylab astronauts complain of the sensory sterility of their orbiting man-made environment. They miss the colors, textures, and smells of earth. Natural settings, in contrast to sterile indoor man-made environments, are ideal for learning sensory awareness. Nature is a powerful presence that can draw us out of our preoccupations with practical concerns and daydreaming, and bring us into the immediate present. The activities in this chapter guide you in exploring natural settings with enhanced awareness.

Developing our sensory awareness helps us develop a growing sense of our coexistence with nature. We become more aware of shifts in our state of being in response to our surroundings. We bring ourselves, even if only for a moment, into the intimate awareness of the greater world from which we are inseparable. The Buddhists have a term for this experience. "Tathata" refers to the "suchness" of experience, the unmediated reality in which all appearances become lost in the one ultimate being. Meeting the earth with openness gives rise to new thoughts and systems of knowing. Most importantly, we awaken to our love for life in all its countless manifestations.

Oftentimes in our rushing about, we lose our connection to the earth. The following activity helps you learn to maintain your connection to the earth as you walk about.

Activity Forty-Two ➤ Walking Meditation

Begin with the grounding activity on p.30. If the terrain is safe, walk with bare feet. Now, in slow motion, with complete conscious attention, lift one of your feet from the ground, slowly move it forward a short ways, and then carefully again with your full attention place it down on the ground. Pay attention to every nuance of the process of lifting, moving, and setting down your foot as you very slowly walk. Pay attention to your sense of connection to the earth as you walk. See how you maintain your sense of balance and receive support from this grounding activity as you move upon the earth. Pay attention to your relationship with the earth as you continue.

If your mind wanders, gently bring your awareness back to what is right in front of you. If you would like additional support for staying focused repeat silently to yourself the phrases, "Now I am aware of . . . And my response to this is . . . " Then, try letting all self-talk fade out as you focus on direct unmediated sensing. Explore what presents itself to you as you slowly and consciously take one step at a time.

The activities that follow reveal the dynamic dance of reciprocal influence between you and your environment. You will be able to explore how your unfolding inner process influences, mirrors, and is influenced by your interactions with the external environment. The first activity helps you discover how your inner nature is drawn to connect with different aspects of the natural world, and how these connections effect your inner nature.

Activity Forty-Three ➤ Exploring Attractions

Select a natural area that you would like to explore. Be careful not to select a vulnerable meadow or area with small plants and vegetation which would be damaged by moving about off trail. Begin with one of the Tuning Your Organism Activities in Chapter 3. Then simply allow the area to call to you rather than consciously choosing where to go. See if you can let go of thinking and reasoning. Navigate by sensing your environment. Navigate spontaneously, by intuition, by feel. As you explore try not to assign any labels or terms to your experiencing. Stay with the raw data. Allow yourself to go from attraction to attraction like a bee or butterfly. Pay attention to what you are drawn to. What feelings are triggered? pleasure, calmness, excitement, sadness, joy? Let yourself fully explore each attraction in detail until you feel finished and are drawn to the next attraction. Move gently on the earth, leaving it as undisturbed as possible.

Many participants love the childlike spontaneity, playfulness, and freedom that is often elicited by this butterfly way of navigating through nature. The next activity invites you to examine your fears, reluctances, and avoidances of nature.

Activity Forty-Four ➤ Exploring Repulsions

This activity calls for some restraint and caution rather than simply going with the flow of your spontaneous attractions. Pay attention to something that repels you. Rather than avoid and move away from it, be curious about what it is that repels you. If there is no clear and present danger to you, carefully and cautiously move toward it taking care not to force yourself too far out of your comfort zone, overloading yourself with fear or anxiety. Find out as much as you can about it. Be aware of what feelings are triggered in response to it. Check your breathing and see if you can let it be calm. Continue to close the distance as you feel safe and ready to explore. What are all the qualities and characteristics of this object that repels you? Can you discover something that you can appreciate, something that actually attracts you toward it? Continue to discover more about it. When you're ready, move slowly away from it. Be aware of how you feel and move as you do this. Take a moment to process what you learned from exploring your repulsion. If you would like to explore more, scan your environment for the next repulsion and continue on in the same way.

One of my workshop participants recorded her response to this activity in her journal: "I remember my mother trying to get rid of slugs in her garden when I was a small child. I learned that slugs are slow, slimy, gushy, destructive . . . right? They are disgusting and to be avoided . . . Here's a slug in our garden. It has a dividing line between its 'head' and body. At first I see no tentacles on it. Then the top tentacles come out, exploring leaves and grass. Two smaller tentacles come out further down. This isn't just a slimy blob after all . . . A fast moving slug is crossing the deck. It pulls itself up and forward like an inch worm. It's moving in a determined direction—a very straight line . . . I'm like that slug. I usually lollygag around taking my time—but when I have a goal I can really move . . . Two slugs are 'curled up' together on the upper road. They barely touch, but each is curved into a half circle, and the head of each is in the curve of the other. Each slug is a different shade of brown. How beautiful! They've formed a yin-yang symbol."

In the following activity, by eliminating seeing which is our dominant way of sensing the world, your other senses will be awakened to compensate. You will also be able to compare and contrast with your partner's experience, which may also open up new possibilities and discoveries.

Activity Forty-Five ➤ Silent Blind Walk

This is a pairs activity. Take turns being a guide for your partner who will keep their eyes closed during the activity. The guide will provide a wide variety of touching, smelling, hearing, experiences on this nature walk. Keeping your eyes closed will tend to heighten the sensitivity of your other senses. The guide is to provide a safe and pleasant experience. No talking. Guide by holding hands, and direct by gentle touch. Begin slowly at first, allowing time for your partner to become more trusting and get used to the situation. Allow your partner plenty of time to fully experience whatever is being explored. Don't abruptly interrupt or rush them. Be responsive to your partner and allow them to take some initiative if they are so inclined. You can signal your partner to open their eyes for 1-3 seconds by a pre-arranged signal such as gently squeezing their hand. As a guide, you can also position their head for a particular view before signaling them to open their eyes. Lead them to a variety of objects to give them a rich sensory experience. Remember this is a silent activity. No talking.

A woman biologist guiding a man visiting from Australia, related her experience of the blind walk activity: "At first I had a hard time with the no-talking rule. I wanted to share with my partner the names of all the new things he was exploring for the first time since he was from another part of the world. I wanted to explain how they all fit into the great phylogenetic web of life. First, I led my Aussie friend to a large Sitka Spruce. He put his nose amongst the stiff, pungent-smelling leaves. I handed him one of its reddish-brown cones. His fingers traced its shape and felt its texture. Then on to sword fern, trillium, and other species of herbs and shrubs. Deciding to help him explore low to the ground, I eased him down on his hands and knees. First he crumpled the dirt in his hands, letting it slip through his fingers. Then his groping hands brushed a kind of mushroom which I couldn't identify. After intently stroking its smooth surface with the tips of his fingers, he bent down and began stroking it with the tip of his nose. This big guy on all fours rubbing a little mushroom with his nose, in other circumstances might have struck me as funny, but at that moment I felt a unique blend of both passion and reverence, and then an urge to join him. Totally absorbed in discovering that mushroom, he could care less what it was called. Meeting eclipsed naming. From then on, I joined him in my new-found spirit of exploring without labeling. It was wonderful."

> *"Whatever aid is to be derived from the use of a scientific term, we can never begin to see anything as it is so long as we remember the scientific term which always our ignorance has imposed on it. Natural objects and phenomena are in this sense forever wild and unnamed by us."*
>
> **Henry David Thoreau**

Expanding Your I-Boundary

> *I live my life in widening circles*
> *That reach out across the world.*
> **Rainer Maria Rilke**, *The Book of Hours*

Your "I-Boundary" (another gestalt term) is the range of actions, ideas, feelings, values, images, memories, and *settings* which you are willing to engage in fully. Your style of life, including your choice of friends, work, and *geography*, is a manifestation of your I-Boundary.

A healthy person's I-boundary will not be rigid and closed, but open to expansion. In Abraham Maslow's words, "The healthy . . . [human] *spontaneously, from within out, in response to his own inner Being*, reaches out to the environment in wonder and interest . . . can return to these experiences, repeat them, savor them . . . can move on to more complex and richer experiences." Rather than cling to the familiar, healthy people have the confidence for risk-taking and overcoming fears of the unknown. They have the self-support needed to follow their natural sense of curiosity into new experiences. The primary emphasis of this book is on expanding your I-boundary in the area of the natural world and the reverberations within yourself that this engagement awakens.

There is a basic existential trust involved in opening yourself up to the world in ways that will change and transform you. In an I-Thou encounter there is a softening of one's boundaries. Fear of letting your defenses down, of being engulfed and losing your autonomy, can keep you from surrendering to the influence of the emerging encounter. In a genuine I-Thou encounter both beings are open to being touched and moved, to being changed by the experience.

The process of alienating oneself from one's experience and surroundings increases one's isolation. We can say to ourselves, "That's not me, that's something alien, something different, something that I should stay away from. That's something to avoid because it is unfamiliar, risky, or might cause me unpleasantness."

Through the process of identification we can extend our sense of connectedness to the world. We can say to ourselves, "That's like me, I am closely related or a part of that, that's kin." The greater our openness to a broad range of identifications the greater is our capacity for empathic attunement. By learning to loosen and extend our I-boundaries, we can begin to experience our deep belonging, our being at one with our world. The most powerful and all-inclusive of these experiences were named "peak experiences" by Maslow. William James explored these experiences in his classic work, *The Varieties of Religious Experience.* You will find guidelines for cultivating your own peak experiences in Chapter 14.

When we experience a change in this boundary, as when we act out of character, we often feel strange, alien, anxious or threatened. When the experience turns out pleasant and the change is viewed positively, we feel freed up, expanded, excited and grateful. The healthy maintenance and extension of our sense of self is one of the central components of our maturation and growth as humans. Human development through the various passages from one stage of life to another necessarily involves the ongoing process of identity formation and reformation stimulated by the integration of new life experiences. The challenge is to safely pass through a series of changes of identity without losing one's core sense of self.

Identification With The World

Connecting with nature through "identification" increases your sense of belonging in the world. Taking in nature in this way extends your sense of self. Your ego boundaries loosen and expand to include a greater range of self as you identify more and more with what you share in common with the rest of nature. Identification also goes hand-in-hand with the development of empathy, which Carl Rogers identified as a core condition for growth-enhancing relating (See next chapter). Practicing the following identification activity will help you further develop this capacity.

Activity Forty-Six ➤ Identification with Nature

Pick a spot in a natural setting. Begin with the Flow of Awareness Activity. Let your awareness freely drift until you notice a natural object that stands out strongly or that you return to repeatedly, something to which your awareness is especially drawn. Continue to explore this natural object, becoming more fully aware of its many aspects. What is it like? . . . What are its characteristics? . . . What does it do? . . . Take time to experience it in all its particular details. What is its color? texture? smell? motion? sound? density? size? How does it fit in with its surroundings? How is it unique?

Now identify with this natural object. In your imagination, climb into it, merge, become one with it. What are you like? What are your qualities? Describe yourself as this natural object, "I am . . . I have . . . I move . . . I . . . "? What is your experience like as this object? Explore all that you can about your experience of being this natural object. Try assuming the postures, gestures, movements of this object. If it produces sound, try mimicking the sounds it makes.

When you reach a point of completion, climb out of the object, returning to your own sense of self. Again, view it from where you are. How do you experience it now? Take some time to reflect on this experience. How involved did you become in the activity and what did you discover about yourself? To what extent was it revealing accurate statements about some aspects of yourself and your existence? Did the activity elicit strong physical and emotional responses or did you feel untouched and remote? Did your experience of yourself as this object shift your idea of what you are like? Did it reveal any untapped potential that you might develop in yourself?

The following variation of the Silent Blind Walk will also help extend I-boundaries by experiencing how nature can serve as a mirror to enlarge your sense of self.

Activity Forty-Seven ➤ Identification with Nature Silent Blind Walk Variation

This variation of the Blind Walk Activity (p.81) invites you to identify with what you see as a reflection of your larger self. In this version everything is the same except as the guide you say, "look into the mirror" when you signal your partner to open their eyes. This is the only exception to the no talking rule.

The following identification activity combines the Exploring Attractions Activity with the meditative approach of Thich Nach Hahn (previously presented on p.61). By participating in this activity, you can experience the transformative effects of identifying with your natural attractions.

Activity Forty-Eight ➤ Identification Walk

Try the "Exploring Attractions Activity" (see p.79) only with this added twist. When you come to a natural attraction that has a special quality or staying power, add the following variation of Hahn's meditation mantra. For example, when you come to a special flower, you would repeat to yourself, "Breathing in, I experience myself as this flower (or other natural attraction) . . . Breathing out, I feel . . . (fill in the internal response of the moment stimulated by projecting yourself into this natural attraction)." Repeat a few times so you can settle in and explore your response before you move on to your next attraction.

Ideally, these activities and other variations of empathic identification exercises are meant to be repeated over and over as part of a regular practice. Mastering this method of identification provides a way to experience the Buddhist idea that full concentration and meditation on anything can lead to full knowing of our inner nature.

8

Dialoging with Nature

"If you love it enough, anything will talk with you."

George Washington Carver

As a helping professional, I have spent much of my life studying the therapeutic relationship. What kinds of relationships help people grow? What conditions promote personal growth in contrast to those that are damaging? I've now discovered that what I've learned over the years about human relationships also applies to the human-nature relationship. The distinguishing characteristics and dynamics of healing and damaging relationships are operating whether the other we are relating to is another human being, an animal, an insect, a tree, a rock, a mountain, or a sunrise. My work is based on the proposition that the dynamics of healthy interpersonal relations also apply to human-nature relationships.

The Facilitative Conditions

Carl Rogers, who has had a profound influence throughout the helping professions, was one of the first strong influences in my approach to helping others. His "facilitative conditions" for developing relationships that promote personal growth, I believe, are as relevant for relating to nature as they are in the world of interpersonal growth.

Genuineness

To be genuine is to be honest and open, both with yourself and with others. The more you are able to be in touch with what is going on within yourself, the more you can be fully yourself. You are able to be more *congruent*, communicating to the outside world what is going on inside yourself. The superficial "putting on a smile" for the world will not work. The outward presentation needs to be a manifestation of an authentic inward state. You can live more transparently rather than hiding behind roles or facades. The awareness activities in this book are designed to help you develop this sensitivity to yourself and your experience.

Empathy

Empathy involves entering into the world of the other. Sensing the other's point of view is only possible to the extent that we have contacted our own sense of self, yet without the self-absorption that blocks tuning in to the other. We can learn empathic attunement, the ability to sensitively understand the world of the other rather than simply understanding it in our own terms. In Carl Rogers' words, we can learn "to resonate more freely within oneself to the significance of those expressions" of the other. You can employ empathy, not just with humans, but with all of nature's expressions. (See Identification Activity on p.84) You can challenge yourself to enhance your listening skills to higher and higher levels, to receive more of the subtle meanings expressed nonverbally in gesture, posture, movement, and sound. When you are truly open to the world of the other and take it into yours, you are changed in the process. Allowing the life of other beings to enter yours in this way is an important and valuable catalyst for personal growth.

Positive Regard

This is Rogers' term for approaching relationships with a warm, positive, accepting attitude, neither paternalistic nor sentimental, but a genuine respect for the worth of the other. Positive regard requires real caring, a prizing of the other. We can steep ourselves in nature as a source of guidance. We can approach nature with the same respect as one would approach a great wise teacher.

> *Believe one who has tried,*
> *you shall find a fuller satisfaction in the woods than in books.*
> *The trees and the rocks will teach you*
> *that which you cannot hear from masters.*

St. Bernard of Clairvaux

Preparation for Dialogue

The way you approach an opportunity for relating can have a powerful effect. The attitudes and feelings that you bring to an encounter are formative ingredients that will make a difference in how you are received. Approaching a situation with trust or suspicion, arrogance or humility, disparagement or respect, hostility or affection, will illicit very different responses. As outlined above, the facilitative conditions are important ingredients in growth enhancing relationships. You can consciously learn to develop these conditions. Try the following meditation as a preparatory activity, a way of "getting psyched up" for dialogue.

Activity Forty-Nine ➤ Maitri Immersion

"Maitri" is Sanskrit for friendliness or loving kindness. Close your eyes. Go inside yourself and find your heart center, the place from which your loving kindness emerges. See if you can access these genuine feelings. (Caution: If you find yourself in the grips of an angry, upset, or otherwise contrary mood, you may need to give yourself a rain check for this activity.) Next, by immersing yourself in this loving kindness as a mother holds her beloved child, see if you can further develop these feelings into a more solid and enduring mood. Then, visualize warmth and kindness radiating out from your heart center. Exude this mood. Now, gently open your eyes. Continue to sustain and extend this warmth and kindness outward as you reach out to explore your natural surroundings. See if you can approach each new encounter with this predisposition. (Adapted from Jon Kabat-Zinn. Joanna Macy & Sam Keen also have their versions)

Dialogue

Dialogue is the cornerstone of the gestalt approach. Relationships grow out of ongoing contact with the others in our environment. Entering into authentic intimate dialogue is central to the gestalt vision of the healthiest way to be in the world.

I-It vs. I-Thou Relationships

To clarify the nature of human dialogue, the gestalt approach incorporates Martin Buber's theory of I-Thou and I-It modes of relating. The I-Thou mode of relating has the qualities of directness, openness, presence, and mutuality. I-Thou relating is integrative and affirmative of one's wholeness, whereas I-It relating is more narrowly task-oriented, relating to the other in terms of its functionality or usefulness. Thus, the I-It mode has more of a conditional quality, in contrast with the unconditional acceptance that is more characteristic of I-Thou. When in I-Thou mode, we recognize the subjective presence of the other and willingly enter into relationship with the other.

The I-It mode recognizes the other as an object to be manipulated to one's advantage and thus is experienced as more distant rather than intimate. "I-It" ways of relating are overwhelmingly predominant in modern technocratic society. The natural world has been largely reduced to "natural resources" to be utilized for human production and consumption. Entranced by the powers of the industrial revolution to provide material marvels beyond our ancestors' wildest dreams, the overzealous and misdirected leadership of this global industrial complex has precipitated an unprecedented assault upon the planet. The "Midas touch" has spun out of control and, as the story goes, threatens the human touch that feeds the essence of our humanity.

However, the "I-It" mode itself is not bad. It is necessary. We couldn't get rid of it even if we wanted to. Both modes of being have an important place in our world. We could not live in an ordered practical world accomplishing tasks and making progress towards goals without the I-It mode. Both dimensions co-exist in dynamic relationship. One or the other may become the dominant focus of attention. Ideally the "I-Thou" remains active as the underlying container of the I-It. Or in Maurice Friedman's words, "The I-It is in the service of the I-Thou." Healthy living involves creatively balancing these two modes of existence. What is unhealthy is when the I-It mode dominates to the exclusion of the I-Thou. As Buber in the text of his most famous work *I and Thou* stated, "Without *It* a human being cannot live. But whoever lives with only that is not human."

The I-Thou mode of relating can be extended to include not just the interpersonal domain, but the whole of nature. Early in the text of *I and Thou*, Buber, himself, expressed this belief in an often overlooked statement, "But it can also happen, if will and grace are joined, that as I contemplate the tree I am drawn into a relation, and the tree ceases to be an It." The creatures of the natural world, nature's phenomena can all be addressed and experienced as "thou." Native Americans relate to "mother earth," "father sky," and the earth's winged, four-leggeds and creepy crawlers as "kin." Adopting this point of view helps us extend our bonds of empathy and compassion to include all of creation. The activities in this book invite you to explore I-Thou relating with nature.

To be is to be related, for relationship is an essential aspect of existence. The universe, rather than existing in an inert objective way, is a *"mutually evocative reality."* We can see the value the natural world places on relatedness in the intricate mating rituals that have evolved. So much plumage, coloration, dance, and song of the world comes from this desire to enter into relationship. To be cut off from intimacy with other beings, to be incapable of entering into the joy of mutual presence, to be alienated from life, is a great loss indeed!

Your beliefs can work as a self-fulfilling prophecy. If you believe, for example, that all people are selfish and untrustworthy, you are not likely to act in ways that encourage the development of trusting relationships. If you believe the universe exists only in an inert objective way, that it has no compassion for your well-being, no morality, that it is basically a harsh and cruel reality which dishes out suffering and death, then what are the chances that you will be reaching out to commune with it? On the other hand, what if you view nature as a wise teacher and yearn for its lessons? What if you have already experienced nature as a living presence or are at least curious and open to the possibility? Approaching nature hoping for an I-Thou encounter greatly enhances the likelihood of experiencing these special moments.

Scientific paradigms and methods can also be examined in terms of whether they promote or assume I-Thou or I-It relationships with nature. John Briggs in his book *Fractals* expresses it this way, "The question is, shall we inhabit a world shaped (as we have long believed) by lifeless mechanically interacting fragments driven by mechanical laws and awaiting our reassembly and control? Or shall we inhabit a world . . . that is alive, creative, and diversified because its parts are unified, inseparable, and born of an unpredictability ultimately beyond our control?" This emerging paradigm shift within science involves changes in perspective and values that are essential for our continued survival on the planet.

In Dialogue with Nature

"All over the world learning the language of animals is equivalent to knowing the secrets of nature."
Mircea Eliade, Anthropologist

Trees, atoms, animals, all have their own modes of communication, their own languages, different from human language, yet intelligible. We have an innate capacity for earth literacy, an ability to understand the languages of the natural world, but we don't develop it. By entering into dialogue with nature, we can become more conversant in her ways of communicating.

Except for humans, nature cannot be taught to speak English. To what extent animals can learn language is a matter of current debate. The boundaries between ourselves and our close relatives, the chimpanzees and gorillas, regarding the development of language skills have become increasingly blurred since researchers began using sign language as the mode of communication. (See book *Next of Kin*) In any case, we need not limit the dialogue by operating from the anthropocentric position of teaching animals our modes of communication. Even among humans, linguists estimate that as much as 75% of the meaning in face-to-face conversation is communicated nonverbally through body language and intonation.

We can learn to understand the nonverbal languages of nature. We can learn to understand the gestures and movements of her dance and the sounds of her music. Our bodies, experiencing the sensations of nature, can learn to understand the meanings of her *massage*. So while nature does not communicate with words to be heard by our ears or read on the printed page, it speaks to us nevertheless. Communing with nature is a form of meditation which involves paying careful attention to the nonverbal sensations, images and impressions flowing into us and our responses in body, heart, and mind. Author James Elkins identifies the transformative power of this kind of intimate connection, "an image has the potential to tunnel into me, to melt part of what I am and re-form it in another shape."

As we use human awareness to explore not just our intrapsychic and interpersonal worlds, but the natural world as well, our views of nature are transformed, sometimes gradually, sometimes dramatically. For example, the development of intimacy and trust can no longer be confined to human relationships but must be extended to include our relationships in the natural world.

Exploring the Subjective Frontiers of Nature

A radical shift in our understanding of the world takes place when we entertain the possibility that all of nature has a subjective consciousness, an inner dimension of its own. Gestalt founder Frederick Perls, as early as 1959, ventured into this worldview:

"I propose the idea of universal awareness as a useful hypothesis that runs counter to this tending to treat ourselves as things . . . From our aware experiencing we can look on the rest of existence and suppose

that there are varying degrees of awareness in all things. The flower that turns to the sun is aware of sunlight . . . By the hypothesis of universal awareness we open up to considering ourselves as intrinsically like the rest of existence. Starting from isness, this awareness here now, we consider ourselves as we are, living, varied and similar to others and the rest of existence. It puts us in a position to contact, to move over boundaries, to range across differences . . . Whether our awareness is greater than or more intense than that of animals, bacteria, cells, plants, or stars I do not know. We need to suspect the vanity of saying we are the most conscious."

Frederick Perls

Psychologist, Laura Sewall, in an article on "ecological perception" examines how our participation in the world shifts with the adoption of this worldview.

"Giving full credence to subjective reality means valuing our participation with the world. Participation implies inserting one's consciousness into the space between ourselves and the Other. The insertion of consciousness makes meaning and metaphor, it allows frogs to become princes, ravens to become messengers, and gnarly old oaks to be grandfathers. As we attribute meaning and dynamism to water and rock, and as we allow animism and vitalism to exist in the field of our consciousness, we might also perceive ourselves as part of an exchange, the human dimension of which is observation, story, and 'reading the signs.' 'Reading the signs' is the attentive observation of the landscape, and refers to both the meaning we attribute to the landscape and to believing the message. Although this process may challenge our culturally constructed reality, it represents a highly prized ability among the Yoruba people of Nigeria; it guides the tracker and the shaman, and may be the essence of creating a mutually respectful relationship between ourselves and the nonhuman world."

Laura Sewall

To what extent is discourse possible in human-nature relations? My own personal worldview has been changing as a result of my experiences of communing with nature. Here is a personal in-dialogue-with-nature experience adapted from my 1994 vision quest journal. I hope that sharing this special experience of my own will entice you to try this approach to nature for yourself. At the time of this particular experience, the book was in progress. Just prior to the quest, I had been focusing on this chapter and the section in Chapter 9 on communicating with the animal world.

Each morning of my vision quest I greet the sun while standing out on some floating logs on a lake. Facing the eastern horizon, I spontaneously create a ceremony of meditation, prayer, and chanting that is responsive to both my natural surroundings and my inner experiencing. Some are short and simple. Others develop into longer, more elaborate "sunrise services." Here is my sunrise experience excerpted from my journal.

Wednesday morning. As I hop out to my place on the logs, the sunlight is already showing on the treetops behind me. I begin as I often do with a combination of praying, gently "ohming," and singing "thank you for this day." The energy level is not high, yet very pleasant. For whatever reason I expect a short ceremony. As the sun begins to break the horizon, I settle more deeply into the serenity of gentle ohming. The soothing sounds of my chanting reverberate within and without. When the sun is half way up, I look to my left and sitting on the same log, about twelve feet to my left, is an otter! I fall silent, being careful not to make any sudden gestures. I sit very still, containing my excitement about what will happen next. "He?" stays there only briefly before slithering off the log. Breaking my own guidelines which call for silence, I resume my gentle ohming chant. A few moments later, his head pops up in front of me and slightly to the right; close enough so that if I bent over and leaned out I could have touched him. Eyeball to eyeball, we look into each other's eyes for one long second. Then, the otter opens its mouth, and in a raspy low moan out comes the sound, "ohm." As soon as he finishes this startlingly good otter version, he drops out of sight again. In the silence that follows, I feel astonished, exhilarated and blessed.

I resume ohming, which now resonates with special feeling for my surprise visitor. This time when I sing "Thank you for this day," I include "Thank you for this otter." A short while later, I notice a nose sticking out from between two logs just 2-3 feet to my left and slightly behind me. My otter friend has joined the ceremony. I continue to ohm and once again he responds with his own ohm sound. I am sharing my sunrise ceremony with an otter! After awhile he disappears beneath the water.

Soon after his departure, I express my gratitude for this wonderful event and start to leave. Two steps into leaving, a loud moan startles me as I step onto a log. Recoiling with dread that I might have squished him under the log, I bend over, scanning the surface of the water for some sign of him, saying, "I'm sorry. Are you OK?" Immediately, the otter appears and swims around and right up to my right foot which he would be touching if it weren't higher up on the log. Looking right into my eyes, he "ohms again." I "ohm" back. Again, we are eyeball to eyeball. I find myself talking to him, "Isn't this a wonderful home" and "I am writing a book that I hope will help save this place and others like it for us all." After this brief encounter, he once again submerges. I pause a moment to see if he will re-emerge, and when he doesn't, I return to my campsite.

When I try to tell my friend what happened, I can't get started. I just laugh and laugh for several minutes before I can contain myself enough to tell him the story. When I settle down, I tell the story with much specific detail, "He was right there, 2-3 feet away and slightly to the right." When I finish, my friend says, "you're telling me this as if you're trying to convince yourself that it really happened." Instantly, I recognize that he's right.

The Practice of Dialogue

In the classic gestalt therapy "empty chair" technique, the client creates a dialogue with someone, something, or a part of oneself by imagining the other to be in an empty chair. The person then switches chairs and responds from the empty chair as if they were the other person, moving back and forth between chairs to create a dialogue. The empty chair represents the part the person projected onto the other. The dialogue continues until the unresolved issues are worked through. The projection, may have varying degrees of accuracy in depicting a real other. This "imaginary" dialogue often has a great deal of real impact, carrying within it much substantive meaning for the person. Growth is achieved through owning and integrating these projections of the self.

What if we approach nature in this way? Rather than relating to an imaginary person in an empty chair, the dialogue is with a particular manifestation in nature. In this case, not a guided visualization into a nature setting, but actually focusing awareness on a particular bird, animal, insect, or any other of nature's subjects in their natural setting. This natural "subject" becomes the trigger for your developing awareness. Approaching nature as subject rather than object is a core ingredient for transforming your worldview. No longer is nature merely an object to be acted upon, a natural resource, a gymnasium for outdoor recreation, a place in which relating occurs. Rather than remain in the background, nature as subject becomes the point of focus for your awareness in a way that opens you to the possibility for dialogue.

Activity Fifty ➤ Opening to Nature's Messages

Select a natural setting to explore whether it be your backyard, ocean, woods, city park, or . . . Begin with the Centering (p.28) or Grounding (p.30) activity as a warm up. Then, spend some time fully taking in your surroundings. Pay attention to what you see, to what you hear, to what you smell, to temperature and other tactile sensations. Really take in your surroundings becoming more and more aware of what is there. Continue until your attention gets drawn towards something in particular: a tree, an insect, a bird, an animal, a flower, or some other of natural creation. Open yourself to it and see what feelings and thoughts are triggered inside you. Drink it in. Pay attention to the changes that occur as you quiet your thoughts and let yourself be led into the world of the "subject" of contemplation. If you pay attention, it is as if it speaks to you and your situation. Most often what happens is a wordless exchange, like the kind of communication that happens when you dance with someone. Yet, sometimes words pop into your head. A tall tree might trigger words like, "Look how gracefully my branches sway in the breeze. You would really find pleasure by swaying smoothly and gently like this. Join me in this motion." Listen carefully to messages that come to you as you respond to connecting with your environment.

The next activity invites you to add your response to the messages being received from nature. Speaking is added to listening creating a back-and-forth dialogue.

Activity Fifty-One ➤ Nature Dialogue

Begin with the previous Opening to Nature's Messages Activity. Select the part of nature you are drawn to as your "nature partner" for the activity. When you connect with something in your environment that triggers a message in you, simply respond and answer spontaneously. In the example above, you might respond, "Thanks for the suggestion. I'll try swaying." Continue to pay attention to nature's other as you do this. See if you notice through the nonverbal behavior a response that triggers the next response in you. In this way you begin to create a dialogue between you and nature.

As you focus your awareness on a tree or some other particular manifestation of nature, to what extent are these thoughts and words that pop into your head perceptions and to what extent are these imaginings? On the one hand, these activities encourage us to anthropomorphize nature, to project human qualities onto it. On the other hand, from a totemic perspective common among many indigenous peoples, these activities allow us to take into ourselves the incredible range of nature's energies as manifested in animals, plants, and other natural subjects with whom we commune. These activities, unlike guided visualizations and dreams, encourage us to engage nature more deeply in concrete specific sensory ways.

To what extent is communication actually taking place? To what extent are we picking up meaning from nature and to what extent are we creating myth through projective imagination stimulated by contact with nature? Wordsworth, in his poem, *Tintern Abbey,* addresses this mystery of the fascinating interplay of sensation, creative thought and imagination, "Of eye, and ear,—both what they half create, And what perceive; well pleased to recognize in nature and the language of the sense; The anchor of my purest thoughts . . . " I doubt you or I will find simple answers to these questions, but we can live the questions and learn from our experiences. With these activities in particular and with your other encounters with nature, you can explore for yourself, penetrating this mystery of dialoguing with nature.

Part II

Exploring the What, Where, and When of Nature

Each kind of landscape, each season of the year,
and each hour of the day has its special lessons, gifts,
and enchantments that come from the animal, vegetable,
and mineral dimensions of nature.

9

Connecting with the Animal, Vegetable, and Mineral Worlds

"But ask the animals, and they will teach you, or the birds of the air, and they will tell you; or speak to the earth, and it will teach you, or let the fish of the sea inform you."

Job 12:7-8

"We must rediscover our kin, the other animals and plants with whom we share this planet. We are related to them through our DNA and evolution. To know our kin is to come to love and cherish them."

E. O. Wilson

The natural world offers an abundance of inspirational teachers. We need not limit ourselves to human role models. We have much to gain by enhancing our sensitivity to the non-human inhabitants of our world. In general, it is easiest for us to identify with our closest kin. We identify most easily with other primates, like chimpanzees with whom we share 98% of our DNA, than with other mammals, like horses with whom we share about 30% in common, and so on. If we stretch ourselves, we can learn valuable lessons from insects, trees, even from the properties of rocks, fire, water, and the other "nonliving" manifestations of nature. For psychological or more mysterious reasons unrelated to shared DNA, we may find ourselves especially drawn to or repulsed by various creatures.

If we are to benefit from these teachers, we must first overcome the barriers that keep us isolated from them. By respectfully spending time with other species in their home territories and learning their languages, we break out of our anthropocentric biases and limitations.

We can expand our range of understanding to include a much wider range of earth literacy. We can learn a little mountain language, river language, tree language, as well as the languages of the insects, birds, and animals. These "languages" are nonverbal communications that directly penetrate our senses rather than our abstract symbol systems.

David Abram, in his book *The Spell of the Sensuous*, shares a personal experience that provides a powerful description of the nonverbal communication that can take place between human and animal. "While at Pangandaran, a nature preserve on a peninsula jutting out from the south coast of Java, I stepped out from a clutch of trees and found myself looking into the face of one of the rare and beautiful bison that exist only on that island. Our eyes locked. When it snorted, I snorted back; when it shifted its shoulders, I shifted my stance; when I tossed my head, it tossed its head in reply. I found myself caught in a nonverbal conversation with this Other, a gestural duet with which my conscious awareness had very little to do. It was as if my body in its actions was suddenly being motivated by a wisdom older than my thinking mind, as though it was held and moved by a logos, deeper than words, spoken by the Other's body, the trees, and the stony ground on which we stood."

The meanings we attribute to these nonverbal communications are commonly understood to involve the projection of human understandings onto any given situation. How accurate are our projections? Is the eagle joyfully soaring overhead or hungrily in search of prey? Was the bison angry when it snorted in the Abram's encounter? We need to be wary of making the mistake of "anthropomorphizing," distorting reality by projecting human qualities onto objects that don't possess them. Like naturalists, we must pay close attention to our teachers to learn their lessons with minimal distortion. Otherwise we may end up with an overly romanticized Disney view of nature that has more in common with our own psyches than the realities of the natural world. Do grizzly cubs befriend little boys and save them from harm? As a local colleague of mine once said, we need to shed the Bambi and Thumper sentimentality, which is the delusion that all Nature wants is for everyone to be nice to everyone else. On the other hand, we can also err in the other direction by projecting overly negative qualities. Many of us react to bee stings and mosquito bites as enemy attacks warranting a lethal response. Mosquitoes were not put on this earth to be our tormentors. Biologically, female mosquitoes instinctively collect the blood they need to develop viable eggs for producing their offspring.

Anthropomorphizing is not all bad. When we knowingly let the natural world fuel our imaginations, the resulting stories and myths greatly enrich our lives. For example, for the Kwakiutle of British Columbia, biting creatures, including bee, wasp, gnat, and our friend the mosquito, play a role in their creation myths. The Kwakiutle carve masks that they wear to invoke the insects' spirits in their religious ceremonies. For the Kwatkiutle, to be bitten or stung by these ancestral kin was interpreted, not as a hostile attack, but as a transmission of power or a call to action.

To what extent we can communicate with the natural world is a matter of ongoing exploration and debate. A number of psychologists are now suggesting that projection may be a two-way street. Human-nature encounters are understood to take place in an intersubjective field. Not only do humans project their subjectivity onto the natural world, but objects, plants, and animals also project their particular subjectivity onto us. Or in Charlene Spretnak's words, "the human mind, does not merely project its mental processes onto the universe, but also participates in the processes of the larger 'mind'." For example, do you believe that music is created solely within the confines of the head of its composer? Many great composers, like Schubert, were inspired by nature. Creative inspiration, like breathing, involves taking in something from without, participating in an intersubjective field. Artists' muses can be viewed as messengers that connect them to this larger mind.

A review of our current knowledge of perception and the creation of meaning is beyond the scope of this book, but the personal experience of the mystery of communication with all dimensions of nature is not. The three sections that follow are designed to help you explore the animal, vegetable, and mineral dimensions of nature.

> *"We awaken to ourselves at the same moment as we awaken to things."*
>
> **Jacques Maritain**

Encountering Animals

> *"Human connectedness to our animal kinfolk helps us gain a sense of belonging in this world as our home."*
>
> **Nadya Aisenenberg**

Most of us are fascinated by wildlife. Consider that more Americans visit zoos during an average year than attend all professional baseball, basketball, and football games combined. While in zoos, however, our fascination is often short-lived: visitors average less than one minute at most of the exhibits. Looking at strange and alien lifeforms from far away lands barricaded behind fence, cages, or glass invites a detached voyeuristic experience. The zoo setting invites us to be spectators of wildlife, not cohabiting kin. Natural settings, on the other hand, are more conducive to intimate encounters with wildlife. By reminding ourselves that we are present to them as well, we open ourselves for interspecies dialogue.

Animals in the wild offer us important lessons about living in harmony with nature. In zoos, we view animals on our terms in confined spaces of our own making. In museums of natural history, we see them as lifeless specimens in inanimate dioramas. Nothing can replace meeting these creatures in their natural habitat, for this connects us with the earth, the animal, and the mysteries of life. Knowing animals in this way takes a special astuteness, humility, and an intuitive sense for nonverbal communication not required of us in zoos or museums.

By adopting a different approach than the detached spectator perspective common in zoos, we can turn an encounter with an animal into an opportunity for self-understanding. When we behold an animal, it is possible to empathically attune ourselves to its special qualities whether it be strength, agility, or endurance. Think about the times when you were struck by the gentleness of the deer, the grace of the swan, the playfulness of the otter, or the strength of an ox. Through empathic identification, we can sense the potential grace or strength within ourselves and learn to incorporate that quality into our way of being in the world. As I write this, I see outside my study window a squirrel leaping from branch to branch gathering nuts from our walnut tree. Active, energetic, one-at-a-time, the squirrel makes progress in preparing for the future. I wonder how I might incorporate these qualities as I gather words for this book.

Over the course of human history, the dialogue between the animal kingdom and the human psyche has created many fantastic offspring including sirens, centaurs, unicorns, demons, and dragons. Yet even the most bizarre of them are built upon some elements of zoological truth. Animal myths emerge out of our close relationships with real life animals, but different cultures with their own different beliefs and customs may seize on different attributes and behaviors as the basis for their myths. That is why we find that the same animal may carry very different meanings and significance in different cultures. For example, the snake has a very different status and meaning in the Hindu tradition than in the Christian tradition. While revered by Hindus as a symbol of fertility and wisdom, the snake is associated with Satan in the Christian tradition. Depending on the cultural context, the snake, which has inspired more cults and mysteries than any other animal, can symbolize life, death, rebirth, sexual energy, fertility, sacred knowledge and the afterlife. This multiplicity of meanings makes the interpretation of messages from animal encounters a less than straightforward process.

Activity Fifty-Two ➢ Understanding Your Animal Messengers

Both sightings of animals in real life and animals that appear in our dreams carry personal, cultural, and archetypal levels of meaning. If a particular creature comes across your path in a dramatic way or makes multiple appearances, you might look for some symbolic significance or message in these meetings.

Begin with your own unique personal associations and identifications with this animal. Consider first and foremost the specifics of your encounter with this particular animal, giving them the strongest credence: What was going on with you at the time of the encounter? What feelings were evoked by the encounter? How did the animal relate to you and what was your response? What was the landscape like? What was the weather?

Consider the specific details of what happened in the context of your own unique personal associations with the animal. These associations come from your past experiences with the animal, family stories, books you've read, and so on. Next, you might consider the broader cultural and archetypal associations as possible carriers of additional meaning. Start with your own culture, then consider others. Remember that animals do not convey a single true meaning, but simultaneously express many different levels of experience and understanding. The symbolic meanings associated with animal species are embedded within the symbol systems of an entire culture. When exploring cultural or archetypal levels of meaning, be careful about oversimplifying. Taking them out their personal and cultural context may reduce or distort the meaningfulness of the animal as messenger or teacher. Keeping these cautions in mind, for assistance in identifying possible cultural and archetypal meanings, you might consult books such as *Animal Spirits, Medicine Cards* or *Dancing with the Wheel*.

Tilden Edwards, author and Episcopal priest, in the introduction to his book *Living Simply through the Day* shares a modern day example of how animals can bring special meaning into our lives. "I once received the gift of a ceramic sea otter. The otter is floating on its back, energetically eating an abalone from a cracked shell: an alluring scene I have witnessed many times along the California coast. To the casual eye that was a casual present. But it was far more. That otter is a reminder of much that I have come to appreciate about life. I am held up when I trustingly relax into the waters of life, yet I need a certain attentiveness that keeps me aware of just how to ride the waves. Such an orientation reduces the energy put into self-worry and increases the energy available for attending the callings of work, caring, appreciation and play in my life . . . The otter sits on my desk as a reminder of the spacious, bright, confident, upholding, simple Presence that always is there, however obscured by passing clouds." Edwards keeps the otter figurine on his desk side by side with a cross as his "revealers of truth."

Anthropologists tell us that humans have regarded animals as sources of strength and guidance since prehistoric times. Indigenous peoples throughout the world have cultivated deep personal connections with animals. They play an integral part in their day-to-day lives. The peoples of some indigenous cultures even name their members after their personal power animals. Native Americans and most other indigenous cultures have traditionally incorporated personal power animals into their beliefs and customs, linking them not just to individuals but to their culture as a whole.

For example, the traditional culture of the Plains Indians was built upon their relationship with the Buffalo. Dependent on the buffalo as a food source, the tribe honored them with buffalo dances so they would offer themselves up for the hunt. The Sioux bands would wear headdresses made out of buffalo fur and highly polished horns. In their dances, they would sway from side to side, tossing their horned heads, and charging each other as buffalo bulls do. By ritually imitating its movements, they greatly increased their identification with the animal.

Through ritual, animals can also come to us in trance states. Through ceremonial rituals like the Buffalo Dance, humans are able enter into a trance state relationship with a spirit animal. These rituals sometimes involve wearing special animal masks and ceremonial dress to help deepen the connection with the animal. Shamans, the healers in these cultures, are able to enter into a trance state in which they turn themselves into the form of the spirit animal. This practice of shape-shifting is widespread among indigenous peoples. For example, Lapp shamans in Northern Europe turn themselves into wolves, bear, reindeer or fish, the Eskimo of North America into wolves, the Semung of Asia into tigers.

The Plains Indians and most other indigenous peoples throughout the world consider certain special animal species to be their ancestors and/or protector spirits of their clan or tribe. Anthropologists coined the term totemism to refer to this close association and identification between humans and animal species. Kinship groups were often given totem animal names like the "salmon people" or "bear clan." Anthropologist Claude Levi-Strauss reported that hunting peoples held totemic animals in high regard not merely because they were an important part of their diet, but also because they were good food for the imagination.

When I studied anthropology as a young college student, I adopted the popular biases of the times. I believed that the ancient ways of relating to animals had been exposed as primitive anachronisms based on superstition by the so-called advanced cultures of the world. Since that time, my personal experiences have caused me to reconsider. I now find much value and wisdom in the ways of our ancient ancestors as do a growing number of contemporary anthropologists and cultural historians.

In modern society, animals have lost their central role in cultural organization. When animals are no longer viewed as guiding spirits nor connected to us by sacred rituals that guide our behavior, animals lose their significance retaining only their function as secular emblems. Vestiges of these connections between animals and societal groupings remain in the naming of our sports teams and lodges: the Miami Dolphins, Detroit Tigers, and Chicago Bulls; in the Lions Club and Elks Lodge, and in the stuffed animals we buy for our children. Revered spirit animals are reduced to team mascots.

Our modern day knowledge of animals is oftentimes shaped more by the media than by first hand day-to-day experience. The portrayal of animals in the mass media has helped create in us an unrealistic view of the their world. Teams of experts using the latest in high-tech photographic equipment spend months shooting film and then select out only a few minutes of the most dramatic moments in the lives of exotic wildlife for our television viewing. We're not aware of the great patience that's required in seeking out encounters with wildlife. In reality, dramatic moments are few and far between, and often hard earned. On the other hand, we can experience the everyday miracles that are going on all the time if we let go of our expectations for the dramatic. We can begin to reclaim the value of animals as our teachers by reconnecting with them in our day to day lives.

Each lake, marsh, woods, and field offers many opportunities for encounters with wildlife. The opportunities change according to the season of the year, animal cycles of nature, the time of day, and weather. Even in the heart of the big city, nature is present. We need not travel thousands of miles to exotic places nor disturb wilderness areas in order to meet with animals. An abundance of squirrels, birds, frogs and other critters inhabit our own backyards and local parks. We can also learn from pets and farm animals.

There are so many opportunities. Animal life includes not just the larger mammals, but an incredible diversity of lifeforms including birds, fish, amphibians, insects, and all of the other lesser-known classes. These lifeforms are huge and microscopic, warm-blooded and cold-blooded, diurnal and nocturnal. They are vertebrates and invertebrates, herbivores and carnivores. They fly, swim, crawl, walk, run, hop, perch, and burrow in most every imaginable nook and cranny of this planet. All of these lifeforms are potential messengers and teachers. Over the years, I have had special encounters with deer, elk, otter, crow, osprey, hawk, eagle, trout, shark, ant, and butterfly. Here is an example of an encounter that I originally recorded in my personal journal.

Journal Entry for Wednesday — 10/5/94 — 2pm

I'm at home relaxing on the back deck reading Sam Keen's *Hymns to an Unknown God,* the chapter entitled, "Death: The Final Question." He's telling how his father's death affected him and his beliefs about death.

I read, "My linear mind rejects the idea of post-mortem survival, but my father has continued to live in my dreamtime." I tilt my head back and look up into the blue sky. And what to my wondering eyes should appear? A small white butterfly, flutterdances by, hovers inches above my face, then spirals upward and over the grape arbor.

Just a butterfly or a carrier of symbolic meaning? A sign of the spirit! Or, am I just grasping for reassurance? Has nature, at this moment, spoken to me about the mystery of death? I lean toward this latter sense even though my logical mind wants to keep me lodged in my old belief system. With the words, "It's just a coincidence," I'm tugged back toward the familiar scientific view that has no room for divine messengers or synchronistic events.

My wonderment persists. If this is a message from nature, how am I to translate this nonverbal visitation? There is no written message to rely on. While my logical mind tries to claim them as projections, these are the words that come to my mind:

"The spirit lives. Metamorphosis is real. The butterfly is real. I am not dreaming. My father has lived in my dreamtime now for a little over a year since his death. Like the butterfly, he has been transformed."

In the house on my altar is a photograph of a butterfly. Wedged between the photograph and the frame is a piece of paper on which I have written some notes on the symbolism of butterflies: "Very often butterflies are used to symbolize the things of the spirit. Greeks called them 'psychae.' Aristotle used the word to be both soul and butterfly. For the Greeks, the soul could come and go in the form of a butterfly; the soul released from the body; life after death; resurrection of the soul."

The mystery remains. I will continue to wonder in my quest for death's meaning, Yet, I feel like I've just received a vote from nature sent by a butterfly. "Death, John, is not obliteration, but a kind of transformation."

Special moments like the one above may occur as a single incident or as a series of serendipitous encounters with a particular individual or species. For example, my extraordinary experiences with deer began at age five in Yosemite Valley when I ran out into a meadow to romp with some fawns. After accepting my presence for some time, the fun with my playmates ended abruptly when one of the mothers surprised me with a gentle kick in the butt that sent me running back to the family car. During my college years, I was charged by a great stag in the Ventana Wilderness Area and on another occasion followed around by a doe at a retreat center near Monterey. Visits like these, in both waking life and dreams, can occur close together, during a particular stage of development or transition in your life, or be spread out over a lifetime.

Some animals will have unique personal associations and meanings for you. Based on your own history and experiences with them, you might feel kinship, indifference, fear or even repulsion. You may discover that certain animals speak to you in ways that are more powerful than others. Study them closely and a particular species may become your teacher. You may discover that you have a special connection and rapport with a particular kind of animal that seems to keep showing up at important times in your life. In this way you may come to know that you have been blessed with a personal power animal. Whether identified as a power animal or not, developing ongoing relationships with animals can add new meaning to your life.

I am not suggesting that you seek out bears to feed and pet, or swim on the backs of dolphins. There are real dangers for the ignorant city slicker. I consider myself one, having been raised in suburbia and spending the vast majority of my life in cities. Unless we are well informed and very respectful, our encounters with wildlife are likely to do more harm than good. We must learn their language so we can be sensitive and responsive to them on their terms as well as ours. Wildlife need space and shouldn't be intruded upon by us. We must learn how to be unintrusive, respectful, and well-educated about these encounters.

Mary Ann Simonds, wildlife biologist, describes one of her special experiences, which illustrates this reverent sensitive way of encountering wildlife. "I remember watching a young badger and fox play together, while I sat just a few yards away hoping that they wouldn't notice me and leave. Instead, they approached me, sniffing and making funny little noises. My heart beat rapidly with joy as they came closer, bravely poking their noses around me. The feeling is 'borderline euphoric.' . . . I am trying to build a case to justify the communication that takes place when I am in a completely open state of mind. As a scientist, it has been hard for me to accept some of the things I've experienced between wild animals and myself . . . It is this quality of 'being' without judgment, but with feeling and compassion that we will grow closer to understanding other species, all of life."

My favorite way of meeting wildlife is a chance encounter, an unplanned crossing of paths. I find that when I'm most calm, centered, and respectful, animals do not flee but are quite tolerant of my presence, sometimes even approaching me with interest. To meet wildlife, you don't have to be sneaking around as long as you're not driving them away by noisily tromping through the woods.

Staying put, not approaching or making any sudden movements reduces the chances that you will spook them, especially if the wildlife is prey like elk or rabbit. With predators, like mountain lion and brown bear, acting like prey by turning and running away could trigger an unwanted chase. Instead, by staying calm, standing tall, making noise so they are not surprised by your presence, not smelling of food, and keeping a safe distance, you greatly reduce the risk of an unsafe encounter.

If you are not content to wait for chance encounters, you may also intentionally seek out animals by "stalking," following the tracks of an animal, or by "posting," sitting still in an inconspicuous spot with a good view of an area frequented by animals and letting them come to you. Stalking requires more skill and is more intrusive, so I recommend you start with posting.

Guidelines for Encountering Wildlife:

1. Wear clothes that will camouflage your visibility. If there might be hunters around, wear something bright when traveling about. Mask your scent by rubbing strong smelling plants on your clothes.
2. To aid in up-close viewing consider bringing along binoculars and/or magnifying glass. A good telephoto lens for your camera will also reduce the temptation of getting too close.
3. Find areas that offer plenty of food, water, and cover. Try the fringes of forested areas and meadows, along edges of waterways, places where grass, berries, succulent vegetation grow. Return to an area where you have seen tracks, scatch, or other signs of wildlife at a time of day and in weather when they are most likely to be active.
4. Avoid putting yourself in a position in which either the animal or you would feel trapped or cornered. Look for plenty of safe exits.
5. Take high ground, 10' or more above animals. Animals are less likely to look for danger above them as often as to the side or rear.
6. Approach an area quietly and slowly, avoiding sudden movements or alarming noises.
7. Approach an area with the wind in your face. Also, look upwind from your location. Both sound and smells carry downwind.

8. Look into the vegetation, brush and cover; not above, beyond, or around it.
9. Use wide-angle vision to pick up movements. (See Activity p.49)
10. Do not feed or bait the animals with food. Let them do their own foraging and hunting for their own natural sources of sustenance.

"One does not meet oneself until one catches the reflection from an eye other than human."

Loren Eiseley

Activity Fifty-Three ➢ Animal Encounter

Pick a spot where there are signs of wildlife, such as animal trails, tracks, droppings, edge of an open meadow, watering hole, or bird's nest. Pick a time of day when wildlife is more likely to be out and about. (Consult guidebooks on bird watching, tracking, etc.) Wear clothes that will camouflage your visibility. Pick a spot where you blend into the landscape. Approach the area very quietly and slowly, avoiding noises or rapid movements that would startle wildlife. Take your place, sitting as still as is comfortably possible, waiting for the world of nature to return to its normal undisturbed routine. Relaxation helps staying quiet and still. You might settle in by doing the calm breathing, centering activity, or a form of sitting meditation that works for you. This activity can be a lesson in patience. You need to let go of expectations for that dramatic encounter with a cougar or bear. Instead of looking for what is not there, simply pay attention to what is present. When you do this, there is no waiting. If you find your mind drifting away, thinking about worldly or other concerns, gently bring yourself back to the present moment. When new wildlife appears, resist any impulse to chase or close the distance on your part. I find stalking, which may be a latent instinct from our hunting days, especially hard to resist. Your challenge is to remain still, open and receptive to whatever nature presents to you with an attitude of acceptance and appreciation. Observe any wildlife that comes your way with your full focused attention. Follow its movements. Observe how it relates to its environment. See how nature has uniquely expressed itself through this creature. Does this animal have a message for you?

Encountering Vegetation

> *I wandered lonely as a cloud*
> *That floats on high o'er vales and hills,*
> *When all at once I saw a crowd,*
> *A host of golden daffodils . . .*
> *Ten thousand saw I at a glance,*
> *Tossing their heads in spritely dance*
> *For oft, when on my couch I lie,*
> *In vacant or in pensive mood,*
> *They flash upon that inward eye,*
> *Which is the bliss of solitude;*
> *And then my heart with pleasure fills,*
> *And dances with the daffodils.*
>
> **William Wordsworth**

We can learn to commune with such a great variety of plant life, much more than can be covered in this book. Of the many possible choices of flowers, shrubs, herbs, grasses, ferns, and other plant life, I have selected trees. Since humans have such powerful practical and spiritual connections with trees, they make an excellent starting point. Let trees be the beginning of a much longer and diverse adventure. Rather than exploring the other types of vegetation systematically, I recommend simply following your natural attractions. Let your own unique experience, curiosity, and interests take you on an odyssey of exploring the many types of plant life.

Trees

> *I think that I shall never see*
> *A poem lovely as a tree*
> *A tree whose hungry mouth is pressed*
> *Against the earth's sweet flowing breast;*
> *A tree that looks at God all day,*
> *And lifts her leafy arms to pray;*
> *A tree that may in summer wear*
> *A nest of robins in her hair;*
> *Upon whose bosom snow has lain;*
> *Who intimately lives with rain.*
> *Poems are made by fools like me,*
> *But only God can make a tree.*
>
> **Joyce Kilmer**

Trees have played a central role throughout the ages in providing humans with food and shelter. They provide fuel for the fire to protect us from the cold, shade from the heat, homes and furniture, tools, fruits and nuts, and sources of medicine. They fertilize the soil and prevent its erosion. Forests play a critical role in the regulation of our atmosphere. By recognizing the many gifts received from trees, we can experience the gratitude and respect that opens us to feeling our deep connection with them.

Perhaps another reason that we can connect so strongly with trees is that they were home for our prehuman ancestors. Children everywhere love to climb and play in trees. Tree houses are highly prized dwellings for most youngsters.

Trees are astounding. Here are a few of their extraordinary accomplishments. The oldest known trees, the Great Basin Bristlecone Pines, have lived for more than 4,000 years on dry, cold, windy sites in Nevada. The tallest trees are the Coastal Redwoods. With lifespans of 800-1500 years, some grow over 350 feet tall. Touted as "the world's largest living thing," The General Sherman Tree, a Giant Sequoia 2600-3500 old, has amassed 50,000 cubic feet of trunk volume and weighs 4 1/2 million pounds.

Trees provide aesthetic and spiritual sustenance as well. They have carried important symbolic and mythic value in many cultures and religions throughout the world. Trees are symbols of life, abundance, creativity, generosity, stability, uprightness, and strength. Nathanial Altman in his book *Sacred Trees* describes three types of mythical trees: World trees (symbolizing the universe), Trees of Life (symbolizing fertility and generativity), and Trees of Knowledge (symbolizing wisdom and distinguishing between good and evil). The Christian Scriptures refer to trees symbolically in these ways: "the tree of life" (Gen. 2:9, 3:22,24; Prov. 3:18, 11:30, 13:12, 15:4; Rev. 22:2,14) and "the tree of knowledge" (Gen. 2:9, 3:3).

The "tree of life" marks the center of the world. In Christianity, the tree of life is found at the center of the Garden of Eden. For early Egyptians, it stood in the middle of paradise, providing immortality. For the Mayans, a ceiba tree grew at the sacred center of their communities. Black Elk's vision had a flowering tree at the center of a sacred hoop.

Jesus frequently used trees in his parables and teachings. Biblical prophecies of restoration also refer to trees. For example, Isaiah's vision of the wilderness blossoming includes the growth of cedar, acacia, myrtle, olive, pine, fir, and cypress trees (41:19).

Trees also serve as sacred sites for personal inspiration and religious ceremonies. They are connected to legends and historical events. In Buddhism for example, it was under the sacred bohdi tree that Buddha received enlightenment. According to Celtic tradition, oak groves were especially venerated. The word druid, from *dru-wid*, means both "known of oak trees" and "steadfastness." In Japan, pines stand for loyalty and longevity. The Buriat people in eastern Siberia consider groves of trees sacred and always ride through them in silence. Commemorative trees are planted throughout the world for remembering births, deaths, and special events of all kinds. A grove of trees creates a special spirit of community. People want to meet, have picnics, and get married amongst the trees.

My wife and I made love for the first time under a beautiful old oak tree. We were married and celebrated many of our wedding anniversaries under a big locust tree. Our children swung from its branches and climbed it for fun. To benefit from its cool shade on hot summer days, I hung my hammock from its branches. It was our favorite place to rest and rejuvenate.

> *"Trees in particular were mysterious and seemed to me direct embodiments of the incomprehensible meaning of life. For that reason the woods were the place where I felt closest to its deepest meaning and to its awe-inspiring workings."*
>
> **C.G. Jung**, *Memories, Dreams, Reflections*

Activity Fifty-Four ➤ Your Favorite Tree

Do you have a favorite tree? Do you have a favorite kind of tree that you are drawn to? What is it about this tree that attracts you? Does this tree have qualities in common with you or one's that you admire or desire for yourself? Find out as much as you can about your favorite tree including its natural history and the roles that it plays in myths and legends. Visit your favorite tree. Sit beneath it and meditate. Try also incorporating Opening to Nature's Messages (p.96) and Dialogue Activities (p.96) with your tree.

The following activity provides you with another way of identifying your own unique connections to trees. It is also a way of finding out more about yourself by examining through mental imagery your identifications with trees.

Activity Fifty-Five ➤ Imaginary Tree Identification

Begin with the Calm Breathing Activity on page 23. After you have established your calm breathing pattern, continue to relax with your eyes closed. Spend a few moments inside observing your inner feelings and bodily sensations . . . Now see if you can imagine yourself as a tree. Just let it come to you. What kind of tree do you feel like inside? Are you old or young? What size are you? Where are you growing? What are your roots like? Can you sense the kind of ground are they rooted in? What are your branches like? Leaves? Needles? Fruit? Seeds? What season is it? What is the weather like? What are your surroundings like? What is the view, the smells, the sounds? How do you feel as this tree? Continue to discover even more details about your existence as this tree. What is your history? What has your life been like? Let your imagination develop this vision of yourself as a tree for awhile. When you feel finished, gently open your eyes and return to your present time and place. In what ways was your experience as a tree, an indicator of the kind of person you are? the kind of person you would like to be? If you were to meet a tree like this in real life, would it feel more like kin than other trees?

"Trees have individuality. A tree, therefore, is often a symbol of personality . . . It is the prototype of the self, a symbol of the source and the goal of the individuation process."

C. G. Jung

Encountering Minerals

Life spirit is not restricted to animals and plants. It permeates all of nature, including inorganic matter whether it be air, water, ice, metal, or stone. While foreign to our modern way of thinking, this idea that all of nature has a living force within it has been the common belief dating back to our origins as humans. The Polynesians call this life force "mana." The Sioux call it "wakanda." In Japan, from the Shinto tradition, the term "kami" refers to entities with an unusually powerful spiritual function that impart a feeling of awe. These entities can be stones, mountains, rivers, and trees. When nature is known as living spirit, then all relationships with her are personal.

Science confirms how the mineral world is everywhere involved in dynamic interchange with the living systems of the earth. The minerals of the earth, whether solid, liquid or gas, play their part in the three great recycling systems of the earth that are essential for life: the lithosphere, hydrosphere, and atmosphere. Here are some examples of how the earth's lithosphere (literally rock sphere) is inextricably involved with living species. Marble gets its beautiful patterns from the activity of bacterial colonies. All limestone is made up of tiny sea creatures. Other microscopic creatures form continental shelves and reefs. Still others make land soils by eating into rock. A single gram of earth can contain an astounding number of tiny organisms: among other things 30,0000 protozoa, 50,000 algae, 400,000 fungi and 2.5 billion bacteria. Fossilized bacterial communities, some of our most ancient life forms, have been locked in rocks dating back over two billion years.

We can learn important lessons about life by delving into the world of minerals. Rather than examining them from a detached scientific point of view, I invite you to explore how our personal encounters with the mineral world effect us psychologically and spiritually. For example, at a talk I attended recently, an explorer shared with us that glaciers remind him of how slowly time passes and the power of persistence. Such insights can prompt us to examine the role of persistence in our personal lives. Let's explore rocks to discover the lessons we can learn from communing with the world of minerals.

Rocks

"When the hand has once touched the rock, the heart cannot be satisfied until the whole frame has been drawn up out of the waves and stands firm on its two feet on the solid stone."

Phillips Brooks *Light of the World*

Rocks are characterized by their durability, solidity, and cohesion. Unlike water, rocks resist impression. They contain additional symbolic meanings as well as natural scientific understandings. Thus, the rock as a symbol of Spirit is understood as a firm foundation for all life.

For example, the Judeo-Christian testaments refer to rocks in the following ways. In the Old Testament and churches everywhere, the Lord is portrayed as "the rock of salvation." In the book of Psalms (31:3 & 71:3), God is referred to as "my rock and my fortress." Jacob's vision came when he slept on stones for a pillow, which he then raised up as a pillar, anointed it with oil, and called it Bethel, the house of God (Genesis 28:11-22). And in the New Testament, Jesus states in Matthew (16:18), "Upon this rock, I will build my church."

Stones as sacred objects date back to our ancient ancestors. Large stones called megaliths take us back to prehistoric times. The world's largest is Uluru, a gigantic natural red mound, standing 1,260 feet above the Australian plain. For thousands of years it has been the most sacred site of the Australian Aborigines. Renamed Ayers Rock by European explorers, it has become a world famous tourist attraction. Until we regain our understanding of the power of rocks as sacred objects, the secular values of tourism rather than the religious values of pilgrimage will continue to dominate visits to this and other magnificent sites. Like our visits to the zoo, we will parade by to take pictures of the world's largest rock, missing the opportunity for communing with this magnificent presence that has infused people with its powers for thousands of years.

The best-known sacred stone of ancient Greece is the conical stone of Apollo called the *omphalos,* which means "navel." This stone in the sanctuary at Delphi marks the navel of the earth, the sacred center of the Greek world.

Cultures, great and small, all over the world have expended great amounts of time and energy constructing stone temples, stepped stone pyramids, burial chambers, tombstones, monuments, and shrines. Some of humankind's first structures were made out of stone. Menhirs are single upright standing stones, some natural and some sculptured. Erected throughout the world since prehistoric times, they create sacred places by connecting heaven and earth. Sacred ceremonial sites were created by placing groups of these large standing stones in rows or rings like the ones at world-renowned Stonehenge. Many of these formations can also be found in Southeast Asia and Oceania as well as Europe. Piles of stones, called cairns, mark sacred places throughout the world. Set at crossroads, they point the way for travelers and messengers. For example, in Tibet travelers will place a stone on the cairns along the way to gain the favor of the gods for a safe passage through the mountains. Anthropologists have verified over 50,000 of these kinds of standing stone and cairn sites in Western Europe alone.

Stones have also served as the canvas for ancient cave paintings, drawings and carvings on rocks called "petroglyphs." Truths and commandments have been carved in stone since the beginning of history.

Cultures throughout the world incorporate stones into their religious beliefs and practices. When used as sacred objects, they connect people to the divine. Stones used to mark burial sites link the living to the immortal spirits of their ancestors. Small stones are often carried as amulets or talismans for good fortune. Ancient stone carvings of women's bodies, the earliest-known sculptures, were probably fertility fetishes. Native Americans carried small animal shaped stones for powerful medicine. When a Sioux hunter came across a small stone with the natural rough shape of a tiny buffalo, this "buffalo stone" would then be used in special rituals for bringing the buffalo back to their hunting grounds.

In modern times, people carry around "pet rocks" to rub when stressed or worried and wear jewelry made out of their birthstones. The first ever birthday present from my son was a rock he picked out for me from our driveway. I'll bet most of you have collected a special rock or two along the way.

I have two most-special rocks in my collection. The first goes back to when I was a college student. I found it in the surf when walking at twilight on a beach where I spent several solitary days camping over Spring break. The stone, with a perfectly round hole in the middle, dangles on a necklace of shells I collected on the same outing. Of the many who comment on the stone, more than just a few are surprised to learn that Mother Nature was the sole artist.

I found my second most special stone during my second vision quest. Just before I found it, I was in such despair that I was considering calling off the vision quest and returning home. At my moment of greatest doubt, restlessly pacing back and forth at my campsite, I happened to look down and pick up what appeared to be an arrowhead of some sort. Amazed to find a rare artifact at such a critical moment, I received it as a powerful sign that my vision quest path was the right one. A local anthropologist later identified it as a 3-4,000 year old lancelot point that went on the tip of a spear launched from a hunting device called an atl atl. These two rocks, both delivered up to me at special moments in my life, are much more valuable to me than anything that I could ever purchase.

Activity Fifty-Six ➤ Rock-In-The-Hand

Find a special rock that can be held in your hand. It may be a special treasure you have kept over the years or a recent gift newly presented to you in today's nature explorations. Sit alone in a quiet place. Hold the rock in your hand. Close your eyes. Take your time and pay careful attention to your response to each of your explorations throughout the activity. You may support this way of responding by incorporating the Awareness Shuttling Activity. Silently say to yourself, "Now I'm aware of . . . and my response to this rock is . . . " Sense its temperature. Feel its weight. Turn it in your hands and explore its sides from many angles. Feel the surface texture of the rock. Sense its hardness. Rub it. Touch the rock to parts of your body. Bring it to your face. Smell it. Touch it to your face. Gently place it over each closed eye. Place it on the very center top of your head. Place it on your forehead for awhile. Open your eyes and explore its shape, colors, ridges, and indentations. Look at it from different angles and perspectives both distant and up close. Try to find out as much as you can about it. Imagine that this rock can talk. Give it you full attention and listen in your mind to what it has to say to you. When you are done actively exploring your rock in whatever other ways spontaneously occur to you, put the rock in your hands and hold it gently as you again sense its presence and assimilate the overall effect this experience has had on you. Did this rock teach you anything? What feelings emerged for you?

Author Margot Lasher describes her experience with rocks this way, "There are certain places that you come to—the top of a hill, the bottom of a valley, a cover of the ocean—that say, 'Rest.' You stay and you feel a special energy that is alive and vibrant and at the same time peaceful and centered. These are places of power. For me, these places are usually circled with rocks. When I come to these places I want to lie down. I want to lie down with a rock. I want to feel the energy through my whole body. There is something about lying down that opens the body to natural power. Perhaps it is because we are not using any energy to balance, to stay standing. We relax completely into the earth's power." I have a special big flat rock that I go to for rest, another I go to for Yoga, one for meditation, one for sunning, and another for journal writing. My journal writing rock rests up against a big old Ponderosa whose trunk provides back support and whose canopy provides an umbrella of comfort. You might want to follow the putting-a-rock-in-your-hand activity with the next one in which you put yourself in the hands of a rock.

Activity Fifty-Seven ➤ Resting-on-a-Rock

Find a big flat rock that you are drawn to. Lie down on this rock. Feel its energy throughout your whole body. Relax and let the rock completely support you. Pay attention to the way this rock "speaks" to you through the sensations of physical contact. Some participants drift into a reverie. Others fall asleep and wake with a dream. What is your experience?

This type of activity can be extended to include not only rocks, but to any and all of Mother Nature's creations. Another variation is to compare and contrast a man-made object, hand-crafted or manufactured, with a natural object. Below, I have included just one variation. You can create many variations of your own that fit your own unique curiosities and situations.

Activity Fifty-Eight ➤ Natural Object Exploration (Rocks, pinecones, seeds, moss, shells, leaves, wood, bark, coral, bone, and other natural objects)

Select two or three really different rocks that attract you. Or select three different kinds of objects to explore. Repeat the process outlined in the Rock-in-the-Hand Activity with each object. When you've completed exploring all of them, notice the similarities and differences in your responses to each of the objects.

"When you walk across the fields with your mind pure and holy, then from all the stones, and all growing things, and all animals, the sparks of their soul come out and cling to you, and then they are purified and become a holy fire in you."

Hasidic Proverb

RESOURCES:

Duensing, Edward and A. B. Millmoss *Backyard and Beyond: A Guide for Discovering the Outdoors* (Fulcrum Publishing 1992)

Mohrardt, David and Richard Schinkel *Suburban Nature Guide: How to Discover and Identify the Wildlife in Your Backyard* (Stackpole Books 1991)

Saunders, Nicholas J. *Animal Spirits* (Little, Brown and Company 1995)

Sams, Jamie and David Carson *Medicine Cards: The Discovery of Power Through the Ways of Animals* (Bear & Company 1988)

Sun Bear et. al. *Dancing with the Wheel* (Simon & Schuster 1991)

10

Landscapes as Mirrors for Self-Understanding

"It has taken me half a lifetime of searching to realize that the likeliest path to the ultimate ground leads through my local ground. I mean the land itself, with its creeks and rivers, its weather, seasons, stone outcroppings, and all the plants and animals that share it. I cannot have a spiritual center without having a geographical one; I cannot live a grounded life without being grounded in a place. In belonging to a landscape, one feels a rightness, at-homeness, a knitting of self and world. This condition of clarity and focus, this being fully present, is akin to what the Buddhists call mindfulness, what Christian contemplatives refer to as recollection, what Quakers call centering down."

Scott Russell Sanders

The Problem of Uprootedness

As a nation, we are primarily a population of immigrants or descendants of immigrants. Only the Native Americans have a historic connection to the land going back more than a few hundred years. And sadly the European newcomers displaced them onto reservations. A major theme in the stories of the settling of America is one of escaping persecution by seeking a "New World." This message continued to operate as people moved West to find the good life. Our stories, religious, mythological, historical, and ancestral, often carry with them the theme of seeking a Promised Land.

When local conditions get tough, we are prone to seek happiness through what psychologists call the "geographical cure." We believe that our problems will be resolved by moving on to greener pastures. Unfortunately, the geographical cure is most often only a temporary fix that doesn't, so to speak, get to the root of our problem. We tend to bring our psychological baggage along with us and as a consequence create our problems anew. Sooner or later, our past catches up with us. If we are truly to reconnect with the land, we need to emphasize changing our perceptions and way of life rather than changing our location.

Many of us feel compelled to uproot for financial reasons, to go where the jobs are so we can continue to provide for our families. Others, like those at Chernobyl or Three Mile Island, lose their homeland to environmental degradation. Rapid urbanization makes many of our childhood neighborhoods unrecognizable, bulldozed away for new office buildings and freeways.

Most of us have been uprooted at least once in our lifetime. One of my clients, raised in a military family, moved seven times in nine years. Another, the son of missionary parents, grew up moving back and forth between places in Africa and the United States, each with dramatically different climates and landscapes. It's no wonder that we feel like we've lost our roots, that we're in exile from our homelands. Sometimes this loss goes back for generations. The widespread popularity of genealogy, of the TV series "Roots," and of the movie "E.T." whose alien hero longed to return home, all point to the underlying problem of our rootlessness and yearnings for home that arise out of our displacement from the land. When people are living where they know they belong, intimately connected to the land, then they can truly flourish.

The Formative Impact of the Land

> *Consider one born in the desert,*
> *How he must see his sorrow rise*
> *In the semblance of the yucca spreading*
> *Its thorn-covered leaves in every direction,*
> *Pricking clear to the ends*
> *Of his fingers. He recognizes it*
> *And deals with it thus. He learns to ponder*
> *Like the reptile, in a posed quiet*
> *Of the mind, to move on the barest*
> *Essentials, to solve problems*

Like the twisted mesquite sustaining itself.
He puts edges to the nouns of his statements,
Copying the distinct lines of the canyon in shadow
And established cool niches out of the sun
In every part of his dogma. He understands
His ecstasy in terms of fluidity, high spring water
In motion through the arroyo.

That one born in the forest, growing up
With canopies, must seek to secure coverings
For all of his theories. He blesses trees
And boulders, the solid and barely altered.
He is biased in terms of stable growth vertically.
And doesn't he picture his thoughts springing
From moss and decay, from the white sponge
Of fungus and porous toadstools blending?
He is shaped by the fecund and the damp,
His fertile identifications with humus
And the aroma of rain on the deepening
Forest floor. Seeing the sky only in pieces
Of light, his widest definition must be modeled
After the clearing hemmed in by trees.

And consider the child raised near the sea, impinged
Upon constantly by the surf rising in swells,
Breaking itself to permanent particles of mist
Over the cliffs. Did you really think
The constant commotion of all that fury
Would mean nothing in the formation of the vocabulary
Which he chooses to assign to God?
The surge, the explosion must constitute
The underlying dominion unacknowledged
In his approach to the cosmos.

And we mustn't forget to inquire:
Against what kinds of threats must the psyche
Of the Arctic child protect itself in sleep?

Pattiann Rogers, "The Determinations
of the Scene" in *Fire-Keeper*

Since the environments in which we were raised shaped our characters, we can gain greater self-understanding by exploring our geographical roots. Our roots may not be limited to a single place or ecosystem. A member of the Saami people, migratory herders who follow the reindeer from the mountain pastures in the summer to the coastal forests in winter, put it this way, "Home is not a dwelling, but a sense of the land that I recognize as a part of me."

You can discover how the land is an inextricable ingredient of who you are. Scott Russell Sanders, in describing himself, captures this weaving together of sense of self with the land. "I am a toddler digging in the spring dirt of a Tennessee cotton field, and I am a boy staggering behind a plow in Ohio on the lookout for arrowheads, and I am a teenager stalking muskrats along a river that has not yet been dammed, and I am a lone young man lured to the melancholy roar of the ocean on the coast of Rhode Island, and I am a husband and father here in Indiana transplanting ferns and fire pinks into my garden." The landscape is the staging ground upon which our stories unfold. The following Geographical Roots Activity helps you discover how the land has played a formative role in the creation of your identity.

Activity Fifty-Nine ➤ Geographical Roots

(1) **Your original home:** To explore your geographical roots, select one or more of these questions to answer. Where are you from? Where were your ancestors born? Where were you born? Where is your childhood home? How many places have you lived in your life? How did moving away from these places effect you? Recall a story of a special place that you frequented in your formative years that made a strong impression on you. What was it that drew you to that place?

(2) **Your present home:** Do you feel rooted in place, today? Do you have a home, a place where you belong? A place where you feel the land is a part of you and you are a part of it? Tell a story about your present home.

"I am bound to the earth by a web of stories . . . By keeping them fresh, I keep the places themselves alive in my imagination. Living in me, borne in mind, these places make up the landscape on which I stand with familiarity and pleasure, the landscape over which I walk even when my feet are still . . . I have been thinking about stories of place in an effort to understand how the geography of mind adheres to the geography of earth."

Scott Russell Sanders

Self-Discovery Through a Variety of Landscapes

> *"Deep within each one of us lies a garden. An intensely personal place, this landscape grows from a rich blend of ingredients— imagination, memory, character, and dreams—that combine in wonderful ways in our innermost selves."*

Julie Messervy

Wherever we are, the landscape is a teacher. We can learn from nature's teachings as expressed through each unique place. Our particular situation has many lessons for us if only we'll be attentive students. We can discover much about ourselves by exploring how we respond to a variety of different ecosystems. As creations of the universe, nature acts as a mirror that reflects back to us truths about ourselves. Just as different people bring out different parts of your personality, different landscapes will elicit different aspects of yourself. You will feel at home in some settings and alien in others. You will be irresistibly drawn to some and repelled by others.

The experience of place is shaped not only by the place itself and its history, but also by a person's experiences in that place or similar places. Places imbued with a history of creative inspiration contrast with those with a history of destruction. The ambiance of a battlefield may contrast sharply with the site of a monastery. Knowing the history of a place may make your response to it more understandable. However, the effects of personal memories are usually more predominant and immediate than those of social history. Someone who was molested at a monastery would probably feel more comfortable visiting a battlefield.

Each place has a spirit, its own unique atmosphere or personality that generates a particular kind of feeling. The personality or spirit of a place cannot be reduced to a psychological projection. We experience the spirit of a place by relating to the tangible reality of that unique landscape.

Each type of landscape may be viewed as having a certain kind of character structure. This idea is reflected in classical mythology which associates each type of landscape with a different kind of nature spirit: water spirits were called naiads; the spirits of trees and woodlands were dryads, mountain spirits were oreads; and sea spirits were nereids. Similar categories are found amongst indigenous cultures all over the globe. In any case, different kinds of environments "rub us" in different kinds of ways.

Landscapes have a life span. Not only insects, humans, and trees, but also mountains, rivers, planets and even stars are born, move through youth to old age, and die. Just as we respond differently to infants, adults, and seniors, we are also influenced differently by the age of the landscapes we encounter. For example, consider how you would respond moving through these two contrasting landscapes: following along the newly-created bed of a high mountain stream to find its source compared with descending down into an ancient canyon exposing layer upon layer of its million year geological history.

Landscapes can be intimate, up close and personal, or they can be vast, making you feel small in relationship to the immense distances involved. What is the feeling of entering a cavern deep in the earth occupied by our earliest ancestors? What is the feeling of arriving at the top of a youthful jagged peak with a panoramic view as far as the eye can see in every direction? Contrasting landscapes, such as cave and mountaintop, impact us in different ways. We read a landscape by journeying through it with our minds as well as our feet.

Julie Messervy in her book, *The Inward Garden: Creating A Place of Beauty and Meaning* has identified seven archetypal vantage points from which we explore our world.

Landscape Vantage Points

(1)   **The Sea: Withinness.** Immersion, womblike, liquid world.

(2)   **The Cave: Inside to outside.** Close fitting, snugly places from which to look out on the world.

(3)   **The Harbor: Enclosure with a view.** An anchorage, cloister, an enclosed refuge where an area protects one part of the world from the rest.

(4)   **The Promontory: At the very edge.** Daring vantage point, cliffs, bluffs, capes, from which to scan the world.

(5)   **The Island: Awayness.** Safe secret havens from the world; isolated, being at the center surrounded by an endless horizon.

(6)   **The Mountain: Upness.** High, remote, grand panoramic view. Sacred above looking down on profane world below.

(7)   **The Sky: Beyondness.** Flight, soaring, transcendent, celestial, boundless.

Activity Sixty ➤ Vantage Points

As you read over and contemplate the seven types of vantage points outlined above, let memories and images come to you. With which types do you resonate most strongly? Try the nature activities (such as: Exploring Attractions or Opening to Nature's Messages Activities) from each of these vantage points, noting similarities and differences.

There are a great variety of settings to explore: estuaries, marshland, moors, seashore, open sea, coral reefs and other underwater ecosystems, caves, sand dunes, lava beds, glacial moraines, valleys and mountain tops, streams and waterfalls, rainforests and open plains, high and low deserts, farmland, pasture, city parks, gardens, rangeland, tundra, nature creeping through the cracks in downtown megalopolis, and more. The next sections invite you to explore the landscapes of mountain, desert, ocean, cave, and sky. You need not limit yourself to these. You can extend your learning by reading about, visiting, and adapting the activities for each additional landscape you wish to explore. For example, you can do the Exploring Attractions and Repulsions, Identification, Opening to Nature's Messages, and Dialogue Activities in any and all of these settings.

Mountain

"Mountains have been a major influence on the human mind since our ancestors first looked up to them and gloried ·in their splendor, placed their gods and goddesses among them, and accepted their challenges. They continue to inspire."

Jack D. Ives

Summits of mountains provide dramatic sites of vision. They possess the power to awaken in us an overwhelming sense of the sacred. For this reason, peoples from every part of our globe view the ascent of the sacred mountain as a symbol of the individual's ultimate spiritual quest. Whether it be Moses on Mt. Sinai, Mohammed on Mt. Hira, or Black Elk on Harney Peak, their stories share a common theme. The seeker, through the arduous effort of climbing becomes oriented, gains steadfastness, becomes conscious. By learning to confront dangers, to have nerve, the protagonist gains strength. When we meet the challenges of the mountains in our lives, we develop our strength and courage.

The Navajo know this connection. Their word for mountain is also the root of their word for strength.

The accounts of mountain climbers provide insights about this kind of upward journey. Mountain climber Rene Daumal in his book, *Mt. Analogue*, describes entering into dialogue with a mountain, "Often at difficult moments you'll catch yourself talking to the mountain, flattering it, cursing it, making promises or threats . . . Just keep in mind that your dialogue with nature was the outward image of an inner dialogue with yourself."

Mountains are revered by peoples throughout the world. The Greeks built their shrines on mountainsides. For the Greeks, mountains were the homes of the Gods. Their chief god Zeus was portrayed seated on the peak of Mt. Olympus. In every part of Japan, there is a local mountain deity. Each summer over 100,000 people climb Mt Fuji, Japan's most famous sacred mountain. Mt. Kailas in Tibetan Himalayas is considered the center of the world for both Hindus and Buddhists.

According to Native American tradition, powerful spirits live on the tops of the highest peaks. Mountains play prominent roles in many of their legends. For some tribes, the powers of their most sacred mountains were so great that they felt it was a desecration for mere humans to dare to climb on these sacred heights. One kneels before the altar, never stands on it. For example, millions of tourists from all over the world visit Crater Lake National Park to view the famous scenery. However, for the Native Americans who lived nearby for thousands of years, it was taboo. Having great respect for the powers of this sacred place, they sanctioned only special visits for religious purposes by shamans carrying powerful medicine.

For Buddhists, mountains are holy places for retreat, places for prayer and contemplation, even enlightenment. The mountain represents aspiration towards ideals, rising of the soul to higher planes of consciousness, the place where the infinite is revealed. Tibetan Abbott Thuben Norbu, brother of the Dali Lama, proclaims, "Through meditation, we build a spiritual mountain inside." We build this internal mountain by developing virtue, knowledge, and wisdom. Pueblo Indian writer Alfonso Ortiz also expressed this connection between ideals and mountains, "Whatever life's challenges you may face, remember always look to the mountain top, for in so doing you look to greatness."

Great visionaries and prophetic wanderers like Moses and Mohammed came down from their mountaintops proclaiming the need to create a new community on earth. These liberators of humanity, with their heavenly perspective, inspire movements for social change by decrying the gulf between the world as it is and the world as they envision it. Thus, mountains provide support for both individual and cultural enlightenment.

We need not be mountain climbers or religious visionaries to benefit from the upon-high perspective of mountains. After completing my doctorate at the University of Florida, I was considering whether or not to take a teaching position at Oregon State University. I asked the department chair where I might go to see the area. Of the several places he suggested, I chose Mary's Peak, the highest mountain in the Oregon Coast Range. There, from the top, I looked down over the Willamette Valley below. The beauty of this place welcomed me. From this panoramic perspective I contemplated my life path and chose this valley as my new home. Ever since, Mary's Peak has been a special place for me to go to gain some perspective on my life path—a place to clarify my vision.

A hill near my home overlooks Corvallis and the surrounding area, including a nice view of Mary's Peak. Occasionally I take the short trek to the top to enjoy the hawks and vultures soaring in the updrafts while I contemplate my life from a distance.

Activity Sixty-One ➤ Nature From A Distance

Pick a special high point, whether a near-by hilltop, mountaintop, promontory, or other viewpoint. If you can see your home from this spot, that's an added benefit. The geography of such a place supports the process of contemplating your lifepath from a distance, away from the demands and complexities of all the particulars. Select a block of time when you can hike to your spot and spend some time doing just that.

"A large granite mountain cannot be denied—it speaks in silence to the very core of your being. There are some that care not to listen but the disciples are drawn to the high altar with magnetic certainty, knowing that a great Presence hovers over the ranges."

Ansel Adams

Desert

"It's strange how deserts turn us into believers. I believe in walking in a landscape of mirages, because you learn humility. I believe in living in a land of little water because life is drawn together. And I believe in the gathering of bones as a testament to spirits that have moved on. If the desert is holy, it is because it is a forgotten place that allows us to

remember the sacred. Perhaps that is why every pilgrimage to the desert is a pilgrimage to the self. There is no place to hide, and so we are found."

Terry Tempest Williams, *Refuge*

In the desert, you are challenged to accept the empty silence, to endure the heat of the penetrating sun, and to get by with only the bare necessities for survival. The desert landscape is threatening for most of us—poisonous snakes, waiting vultures, heatstroke, dehydration. Death, suffering, and the devil seem nearby. You feel vulnerable. You can easily become disoriented and lost. Misplace something, a watch or compass, and it can be difficult if not impossible to find.

The desolate harshness of the desert is not the setting of choice for affluent hedonists. In the words of writer Belden C. Lane, "The desert, as metaphor, is that uncharted terrain beyond the edges of the seemingly secure and structured world in which we take such confidence—a world of affluence and order that we cannot imagine ending. Yet it does. And at the point where the world begins to crack, where brokenness and disorientation suddenly overtake us, there we step into the wide, silent plains of a desert we had never known to exist. We cross its sands—unwelcomed, stripped of influence and reputation."

In the desert, ascetic discipline is invited and greed confronted. The lean and arid landscape invites you to move slowly and deliberately attending to one thing at a time. Survival demands paying attention. Life seems reduced to the simplicity of bare necessities, both physically and spiritually. Perhaps this is why many monasteries are located in the desert.

The desert contains extreme beauty as well as desolation. Stars are more brilliant in its dry, night air. When the desert plants are blooming, the desert can be incredibly colorful. Unfamiliar with the desert, even though I had heard about the beauty of desert flowers, I was nevertheless amazed at the great quantity and variety of flowers that can blanket this landscape. Getting up close and low to the ground (as in the Small World Exploring Activity on p.50), I have counted hundreds of tiny blossoms within a small patch of only a few square feet. I have gazed on cactus flowers with a magnificence that rivals the blossoms of the most exotic of tropical plants. Terry Tempest Williams proclaims, "In the severity of the desert, I am brought down to my knees by its beauty. My imagination is fired. My heart opens and my skin burns in the passion of these moments."

By voluntarily going into the desert, we invite feelings of vulnerability and loneliness. We learn lessons of self-emptying and self-denial. Laurens vander Post suggests another dimension for self-learning elicited by the desert, "The desert . . . above all is a symbol of what has been most deeply denied in men's own spirit: it's a kind of bright mirror wherein they see the arid reflection of their own rejected and uncared for selves."

When venturing into the desert even for short periods of time, we must meet the challenges of caring for ourselves physically as well as emotionally. Panicking when disoriented can turn a difficult situation into a disaster. If you are not familiar with the desert, you can easily become disoriented and underestimate distances. Going with an experienced guide and learning desert survival skills ensures your safety. You also need to make wise decisions to prevent the dangers of dehydration, heat prostration, severe sunburn, and getting lost. Careful planning also includes: adequate sun protection (hat, lotion, chapstick), water, map and compass, consulting the most recent weather report, and notifying people of your location and time of return.

Activity Sixty-Two ➤ Desert Walk and Meditation

Taking all the necessary safety precautions mentioned above, pick a circumscribed area where you can safely lose yourself in the desert for a short spell, away from roads and other people. After following your own attractions for awhile, pick out a particular spot that calls to you. Sit there in one place for at least fifteen minutes, contemplating a theme in your life that you feel ready to explore, one that fits this landscape, such as: (1) the losses in your life: relatives, loved ones, jobs, interests, missed opportunities, things you've had to give up for health or other reasons. Sit with any loneliness, grief, longings, or other feelings that emerge. Then, listen into the silence of the desert for any messages regarding these losses that might come to you. What would best heal these losses? (2) Without influence or reputation, without job or material possessions, who are you? What are the bare bones essentials of your existence? Finish your meditation by giving thanks for what you've learned.

"What good is the desert? It's good because it's so starkly, stubbornly beautiful, a respite to the eye, a surcease for the mind, a beginning on a beginning. A desert is good because it holds the mountains apart."

Ann Zwinger

Ocean

"The beach is the simplest possible landscape. Sand, sea, sky, and no more. There is a lovely, perfect reductionism in a beach. It was a beach that God was contemplating, I would bet, when He called the dry land Earth and saw that it was good. The beach is a beginning. Walking the good simplicity of the sand, in the sea wind, lets us begin ourselves from scratch."

Kenneth Brower, *Islands*

The beach, like the desert, is typically a simple, uncluttered, spacious landscape: sand, sea, sky, and no more. The differences between the two, however, are even more striking.

The desert is characterized by the scarcity of water, while vast expanses of water dominate the seascape. The ocean, especially in tide pools and coral reefs, is teaming with life, whereas the desert has a sparsity of life. The ocean contains over 95% of our earth's biosphere. As water covers over 70% of its surface, most of life on earth is aquatic, both in terms of biomass and biodiversity.

The desert is a place of silence, while the seaside brings us the constant rhythmic sounds of the surf. Ocean waves create continuous, yet subtly varying rhythms. Unlike the mechanistically precise beats reproduced by a metronome or electronic music, each ocean wave is unique, ever changing, complex, different. This elemental sound of wildness is ever present at the seashore. You can't turn off the sound of the surf.

Called the last great frontier on earth, only a fraction of the ocean has been explored. Many of its wild forces are anything but subtle. Imagine being swallowed up in the belly of the whale or drowning in its unfathomable depths. Being lost at sea and being lost in the desert both present powerful images of disorientation in a vast landscape. The power of the ocean surf crashing into cliffs, your boat being cast about in a violent storm, bring you into the presence of nature's awesome power and fury.

Our evolutionary origins run deep and long in the ocean. Life on earth emerged three billion years ago and the ocean was its first habitat. It took another two-and-one-half billion years before life moved onto the land. The amniotic fluids of the womb and the salty waters that flow in our bodies speak to us of these origins. It's no accident that the salt content of our blood is similar to the salt content of the ocean. The ocean also speaks to us about the nature of death. The river runs down to the sea and joins the vast waters of nature. We return to our origins.

There is a great diversity of landscapes to be explored at the border between land and sea. While living in Florida, I enjoyed visiting the calm ocean beaches where the water is warm and clear; and the sand is white, fine, and soft to touch. The beaches slope gradually so you can walk out thirty or more yards, stand waist-deep in the water, look down and see your toes. Tropical waters boast a special beauty, a turquoise brilliance not seen on the Pacific Coast where I was raised. They radiate tranquillity. Yet, I am personally drawn to the furies of the coastal waters of the Pacific with its cold waters, rocky shores, cliffs and capes, rugged storm blown trees, and the crashing waves of pounding surf. To what kind of ocean seascapes are you drawn? What does this say about your roots and who you are?

"The voice of the sea is seductive; never ceasing, whispering, clamoring, murmuring, inviting the soul to wander for a spell in abysses of solitude; to lose itself in mazes of inward contemplation . . . The voice of the sea speaks to the soul. The touch of the sea is sensuous, enfolding the body in its soft, close embrace."

Kate Chopin, *The Awakening*

Activity Sixty-Three ➢ Ocean Breathing Visualization

See if your calm breathing pattern can become as smooth and regular as rhythmic ocean waves gently rolling onto a sandy beach and slowly receding back to the sea. Find a comfortable place to lie down. Begin with the calm breathing activity on p.23. Imagine yourself resting on a sandy beach. Try visualizing the ocean waves as you continue to experience the flow of your breathing. Allow your breathing to harmonize with the rhythm of these gentle ocean waves moving in and receding out. Try imagining that the incoming waves are bringing in the fresh oxygen with each inhalation and the outgoing waves are washing away any remaining tensions with each exhalation.

Activity Sixty-Four ➢ Ocean Breathing

Instead of visualizing the ocean, explore harmonizing your breathing with your actual experience of the rhythms of the ocean waves. Begin with the Calm Breathing Activity on p.23. Now, sitting or lying down comfortably near the surf, pay attention to the ocean's rhythm and its effect on your breathing? "Right now I experience the rhythm of the ocean . . . and my response to it is . . . " Do not try to force your breathing to fit the ocean's rhythm. Rather, see if you can allow your breathing to become synchronized in its own way with the ocean's rhythms so that they flow together. If this doesn't occur, just experience the contrast between rhythms as information about the present state of your organism. Pay attention to the interaction, if any, between the ocean's rhythms and your breathing rhythms.

"If I ever have to get away from it all, and in the words of a Chinese poet 'wash all the wrongs of life from my pores' there is simply nothing better than to climb out onto a rock, and sit for hours with nothing in sight but sea and sky. Although the rhythm of the waves beats a kind of time, it is not clock or calendar time. It has no urgency. It happens to be timeless time. I know that I am listening to a rhythm which has been just the same for millions of years, and it takes me out of a world of relentlessly ticking clocks."

Alan Watts, *Clouds*

Cave

"Upon first entering a cave, one experiences a feeling of shelter, but on going deeper this is sometimes followed by anxiety. My personal experience in caves is that just ahead, waiting to be formed, is some incredible secret which seems to lure me ever deeper."

Dolores LaChapelle

When I was a graduate student at the University of Florida, I contacted the spelunkers club and arranged to go on my first caving adventure. Here's what happened: Upon arriving at the site, I find myself standing there transfixed staring down into the entrance of my first cave. Suddenly it dawns on me that I'm going to have to get down on my belly and squirm my way into this very small opening, a hole fit more for gophers than humans. I hear myself laughing, but this is not my normal laugh. What I'm hearing is hysterical laughter emerging out of a deep primal fear within me. To enter that cave is to give up my best defense. I won't be able to stand up and run.

Later, when we turn out our headlamps deep in the cave, I experience a darkness so black that it seems to penetrate my entire being. My thoughts return to our discovery of an albino crayfish with no eyes, at home in an environment in which sight and color are completely irrelevant. I'll never forget the delight I felt when emerging from this dark and alien underworld into the warm sunlight and wide-open spaces.

To venture into a cave is to explore dark uncharted territory. Being lost in absolute darkness, trapped in a maze with no way out, arouses deep fear in us. We must keep our wits and mark the journey so as not to get lost in these underground labyrinths. One may be challenged to face fears of the dark and feelings of claustrophobia. The darkness of caves contrasts with the life-giving light of the sun.

The extreme darkness and silence in caves is awe-inspiring. We often experience a sense of entering into the dark past of our most ancient origins. Also, this environment may confront us with dark unexamined parts of the self.

Myths and stories do nothing to allay our fears. In Western mythology, we identify caves with the underworld—the frightening place where heroes test their courage. Caves are places where dragons guard treasure and where maidens need rescuing. Myths and legends throughout the world depict caves as special sites for the enactment of dramatic events of great significance. For example, in the oldest known legend with an identified author, the Mesopotamian hero-king Gilgamesh has to travel through a dark and terrifying passage into the depths of Mount Mashu. The myths and legends of ancient China also carry this common theme: the principles of life are hidden within the bowels of the earth, and in order to find them the protagonist must undergo trials, cross difficult passages, and discover the entrances and exits to these holy places.

Popular stories portray the first humans as large hairy ape-like cavemen armed with big clubs. While these stories contain as much mythological imagination as fact, excavations reveal that our beginnings are linked with caves. The mouths of caves were dwelling sites providing shelter for our Stone Age ancestors for hundreds of thousands of years. Our earliest known paintings, which date back between 35,000 and 12,000 years ago, were discovered on the walls of caverns like those found in the Lascaux Caves in France. The majority of these paintings are remarkable representations of large mammals such as deer, bison, horses, and extinct species such as woolly rhinoceros, mammoth and cave lion. Anthropologists speculate that caverns were sites for some of our earliest initiatory rites and religious ceremonies.

As sites of birth and death, caves symbolize both the tomb and womb of mother earth. Anthropologists believe that cave burial sites have developed into man-made catacombs, vaults, crypts, and sepulchers. Caves have also served well as sites of transformation. For example, in ancient rites of passage ceremonies a child was required to crawl deep into a dark cavern. After gestating in there for a prescribed amount of time, the individual emerged re-born as an adult. In this transformation ritual, the cavern serves as both tomb for the child and womb for the emerging adult.

In most all cultures and in most epochs, caves have been viewed as places for creative emergence. Caves have been used for rites of passage by Australian Aborigines, the Inuit of North America, the Dogon in Africa, Salish in British Columbia, to name only a few. Throughout the Orient, whether it be the man-made Buddhist caves at Ajanta in India, the 2,100 Lung-men Grottoes at Loyang in China, or the Chiang Dao Caves of Thailand, going into caves for spiritual transformation has been a practice of Buddhist, Hindu, and Jain for thousands of years. In America, the *kiva*, a cave structure made by the Pueblo Indians, serves as the ceremonial center of their villages. Archeologists have discovered that the Mayans of Central America located their settlements on top of and around sacred caves where they have conducted religious rites and ceremonies for thousands of years.

A contemporary story of death-rebirth happened to country singer Johnny Cash in 1967. He told the following story which was printed *Parade Magazine*.

"I was in really bad shape. I went down to this friend who lived out in the country, near Chattanooga, to hide out. Nearby is the Nickajack Cave. It goes for miles. I drove my jeep there one night. Had my flashlight. The place was flooded with moonlight at the entrance.

"With my flashlight, I went walking in this cave. I knew I was going as far into this cave as I could until the flashlight burned out. When it finally went out, I lay down and gave up. I thought, 'Surely my heart must have worn out by now, so I'll just lay here and die.' I had no strength. I had no idea how long I'd been walking and crawling to get where I was.

"Then I felt something—that love, the warm presence of God that I knew as a boy. I understood that I wasn't going to die, there were still things I had to do. 'But how can I? I don't know how to get out of here? I got no light.' Then the voice seemed to answer back, 'Get up and go.'

"I was sweating. I got up in the pitch darkness and felt the air moving against me, and I knew the way the air was going had to be the way out. Everything was beautiful and good. I drove all the way back to Nashville. June and my mother were waiting for me."

Even today, caves greatly fascinate humankind. Nature's caverns attract tourists, explorers, pilgrims, and religious seekers. In India, religious mystics spend months meditating in sacred caves seeking enlightenment. If you choose to explore caves, go with proper clothing and equipment, and in the company of an expert guide.

Activity Sixty-Five ➤ Cave Darkness

Select a cave that is deep enough to provide an experience of total darkness. For safety, inform others of your specific plans. Prepare adequate clothing, hardhat with lamp, extra light and spare batteries, climbing rope and equipment if needed, maps and/or guide. Being careful to keep track of your location, begin to explore the cave by following your intuition. One option is to let exploring this cave symbolize exploring dark rooms of your inner self. Select a place in one of the chambers that suites you best. Sit or lie down. Turn out all lights so you are in total darkness. Make no sounds. Immersed in this creative void of sensory deprivation, pay attention to your experience. It's like being a cake put in the oven; or should I say, Jello put in the refrigerator? Allow your experience to unfold on its own. As time passes, you might find that old ways of being fall away and a new sense of yourself may begin to emerge. You may need to combat fears, such as feeling lost and disoriented, that often accompany the transformation process. Being careful to tailor this experience to your own level of challenge, see if you can stay put until you feel done whether it be for 60 seconds or 60 minutes.

Sky

> *"The Sky is the daily bread of the eyes."*
> **Ralph Waldo Emerson**

Most of us live in cities where the view of the heavens is blocked by ceilings, city lights by night and smog by day. However, these practical barriers do not provide sufficient explanation as to why so many people spend little or no time contemplating the vast reaches of the sky. Stargazing may not be a popular activity for many because it can be profoundly disturbing as well as profoundly inspiring. Blasé Pascal experienced it this way, "The eternal silence of these spaces strikes me with terror . . . When I consider the short extent of my life swallowed up in the eternity before and after, the small space that I fill or even see, engulfed in the infinite immensity of spaces unknown to me and which know me not, I am terrified and astounded to find myself here and not there." In moments like this, illusions that have provided us with a comforting sense of self-importance can be shattered in ways that make us feel as insignificant as a speck of dust.

The story of Galileo provides us with an excellent example of how we resist having our self-importance shattered. For centuries, Western Civilization lived securely within a worldview that placed the earth at the center of the universe with all the heavenly bodies moving about it in perfect circular orbits. When Galileo pointed his telescope towards the night sky, he found evidence to support the Copernican theory that the sun, not the earth, was at the center. However, this theory was unacceptable to church doctrine which required humans to be at the center of God's creation. When Galileo persisted and published his ideas, in 1633 the Catholic Church sentenced the almost 70-year-old Galileo to prison for life. The Church also required that he sign a document disclaiming any belief in the Copernican point of view. If he had refused, he probably would have been burned at the stake as was Giordona Bruno in 1600.

While our beliefs about our place in the universe generate much discussion and controversy, few, if any, would dispute the claim that the sky is a source of awe and wonder. We've been fascinated with the heavens from the beginning. Our oldest written records, including petroglyphs, cave drawings and clay tablet inscriptions contain references to lunar cycles, constellations, comets, and eclipses. Our earliest civilizations, whether the Babylonians in Mesopotamia or the Maya and Aztec in the Americas, developed surprisingly accurate calendars based on their sophisticated knowledge of the seasonal movements of the sun, moon, stars, and planets. This knowledge was linked to the earth for practical applications in agriculture and navigation.

Some of our first great architectural structures were linked to the heavens. In the 1960's, astronomer Gerald Hawkins found evidence to suggest that Stonehenge was a complex observatory that could be used to predict solar and lunar eclipses. Another megalithic circle at Callanish on the Isle of Lewis in Scotland was situated in the surrounding landscape so that it served as a vast lunar calendar. The Incas in South America laid out their civilization with its Sun Temple at the center. There were 328 straight lines, called "ceques," which radiated out from this center. Many of the alignments of these ceques, which matched the number of days in their calendar, were discovered to have astrological significance.

Peoples everywhere on our planet, whether Eskimo, Bushmen, Navaho, or Greek, have believed throughout their history in a multitude of sky spirits and deities. The tremendous number and variety of myths and folklore generated by our encounters with what nature presents to us from above seem as boundless as the heavens themselves.

Stargazing provides us with an opportunity to experience nature on its grandest scale. Let's look at what is so unique and special about directing our gaze towards the sky. The immensity of the view provides the awe-inspiring and humbling impact that can send powerful currents of religious feelings coursing through our veins.

Stargazing offers us a visual experience of light traveling vast distances. We see but do not hear, smell, taste, or touch the stars. Our unaided senses cannot discriminate whether what we see is hot or cold, or calculate the distances, or count them. As the technological tools of telescopes and other scientific instruments continue to improve, the mystery grows to more and more unimaginable proportions. In just a few hundred years, our Western view of the world as a fixed flat surface with sun, moon, and stars above created thousands of years ago has been revealed to us as an ever-changing universe containing billions of stars within billions of galaxies which exploded into existence billions of years ago.

Gazing into the heavens we look back in time into the origins of the universe. The light reaching our eyes from the most distant stars originated billions of light-years ago.

One way to explore your deepest spiritual, religious, psychological problems is to go out and look at the sky. You can get to know where you are on the grandest scale. Heaven is here for all to see. Its vastness gives us the sense of the infinite.

"In this silent, starry night around me I stand in all my naked simplicity face to face with nature. I sit down devoutly at the feet of eternity and listen, and I know God, the center of the universe."

Fridjof Nansen

Activity Sixty-Six ➢ Night Sky Watching

Go to an area, away from city or other lights, where you can see a large canopy of open sky. Pick a time when there will be little or no moonlight. Open desert or mountaintops are wonderful places. If travel is inconvenient or a problem, you can make do with your backyard or some less-than-ideal place. To prevent neck strain, arrange a comfortable place to lie down on your back. Begin with one of the breathing or relaxation activities. Then, try the shuttling activity, "Right now I sense the sky (star, moon, . . .) . . . and my response to it is . . . " If you find yourself distracted, gently bring yourself back to your experiencing of the sky. What does this experience say about who you are and where you live?

The next activity invites you to make a radical shift out of the heaven-above earth-below perspective that has dominated human understanding from the beginning. See what happens when you turn your worldview upside down.

Activity Sixty-Seven ➤ Looking Down at the Milky Way

As you lie on your back beholding the Milky Way, imagine the earth floating in space. Put yourself on the bottom of this visualized earth peering down into the chasm of the night sky. With this shift may come the startling realization that you're not falling into this star-filled abyss. Engaging the modern understandings of the nature of gravity, you know that it's not simply your weight that keeps you from flying up into the sky, but the earth's hold on you that keeps you from falling. Spend time gazing at the Milky Way knowing that mother earth is holding you to her. Next, know that you're not looking out at the Milky Way, but you're in the Milky Way. Our sun, being one of its 300 billion stars, is situated two-thirds out from its center, inside one of the two long thin wings of this gigantic manta ray shaped galaxy. Spend some time gazing at our cosmic neighborhood from this grand perspective. (adapted from activity in Brianne Swimm's *The Hidden Heart of the Cosmos*)

By participating in the All Night Vigil Activity below, you will have the opportunity to experience the rotation of the earth. Since humans aren't nocturnal, you will likely be exploring nature from an unusual perspective, the one most familiar to our nocturnal kin.

Activity Sixty-Eight ➤ All Night Vigil

This variation of stargazing involves extending the time frame to include dusk, viewing the first stars of the evening, and continuing until the dawn when the last stars fade away. Face West at sunset to experience the earth rotating you away from the sun. Then experience the rotation of the earth through the night as your view of the heavens changes. This activity is a challenge because of the difficulty of staying alert, feeling tired yet not falling asleep. Stay up to view the Milky Way when it's most bright and beautiful. Note how you can incorporate the previous Looking Down at the Milky Way Activity and other activities into this extended time activity. Drifting in and out of the dream-state between waking and sleep consciousness adds a special quality to this experience. Face East at sunrise to experience the earth rotating you toward the sun. The length of the activity adds to the power of the experience as you move through the full sweep of nighttime from sunset to sunrise. Another option for making your experience even more elaborate is to include the Sunrise and Sunset activities presented in the next Chapter.

"One way to spiritual peace is still, as Plato said, to contemplate the 'revolutions of the universe,'"

Eleanor Munro, *On Glory Roads*

11

Experiencing the Passage of Time in Nature

"One of the best things for me when I went to the hermitage was being attentive to the times of the day: when the birds began to sing, and the deer came out of the morning fog, and the sun came up . . . The reason why we don't take time is a feeling that we have to keep moving. This is a real sickness. Today time is a commodity, and for each one of us time is mortgaged . . . we are threatened by a chain reaction: overwork-overstimulation-overcompensation-overkill."

Thomas Merton, *A Seven Day Journey with Thomas Merton*

Out of Sync with Nature's Time

Like all life on earth, we evolved in the warm glow of the sun. Sunlight, with its stable daily and yearly patterns, supplies the ideal ongoing stimulus for the synchronization of our biological rhythms. Our inner biological clock, eons in the making, adjusts our inner states to the earth's daily rhythms of day and night. To live in harmony with nature, we need to recognize and be responsive to our body's natural rhythms.

To disrupt these natural systems, called circadian rhythms, throws us out of balance. Unstable work hours that rotate from day, swing, and graveyard shifts create organismic stress. Jet lag is a common malaise unique to modern civilization. The restful darkness of nighttime can be brought abruptly to an end with the flip of a switch. Nature's transitions of sunrise and sunset are much more gradual. Organizing our lives around the culturally created pressures of digital time, regardless of our organismic rhythms, throws our lives out of balance with nature. As a result, we respond by taking drugs, stimulants to keep awake and sedatives to get to sleep. In attempting to fulfill the demands of our culture, we disregard and override our organismic needs, throwing our systems even further out of whack.

Entranced by the rapid material and technological progress attained by contemporary industrial societies, we have created a stressful relationship with time. Like most everyone else, psychologists joined in with this worship and devotion to the materialistic gods of increased productivity and technological wizardry. Industrial psychology originated with the now classic time-motion studies which were designed to find ways to make workers more efficient so they could keep pace with the technological advances of production. Assembly line workers displaced local craftsman and artisans who could not compete with the speed and efficiency of producing manufactured goods. Like the Sorcerer's Apprentice, seduced by the powers of mass production, we've become frantic trying to keep pace. And when our work-saving technologies fail, we become anxious and frustrated trying to mop up the massive environmental spills that can rage out of control.

A company's success depends on its ability to produce more, faster, cheaper. And people must work harder and longer to achieve a successful standard of living as measured in materialistic terms. As a result, people driven by these economic incentives feel rushed. Many of us constantly check our digital watches to see if we are on time. We manage our time. We run our lives on tight schedules. We become obsessed with wasting time, losing time, running out of time.

We treat time as a commodity. We spend time and buy time. In a materialistic society, time is money. To waste time is to lose money and to lose money is to lose out to your competitors in the market economy. We believe that we must work longer hours to compete, that we have to stay productive if we are to get ahead in life. Even though we bemoan our fate, and try to resist, few of us escape getting caught up in this production-consumption rat race.

Workaholics cycle between compulsive over expenditures of energy into the doings of their unbounded work schedule and a burned out state of exhaustion. Because they're caught up in this vicious cycle between frenetic activity and exhaustion, no energy remains for balancing their lifestyles with other ways of being in the world. Workaholics make little or no time for contemplation, relaxation, recreation, hobbies that would add variety to their unidimensional lifestyles. Many of these hard charging people buy the latest recreation gear, but use it rarely or not at all.

Too exhausted for active participation when not working, many become passive spectators of life. Retreating to our most common pastime, they reduce themselves to couch potatoes. Zoning out in front of the TV, they watch fantastic action-packed images flash by that require nothing of them. They escape from work by losing themselves in the world of entertainment and the lives of media celebrities. Distracted from their own life stories, many simply pass the time rather than live in it.

In another variation, the compulsive doers schedule and approach their exercise, recreation, and vacations in the same way that they work. When these folks finally do make time to use their latest recreation gear, they cram the activity into their busy schedules, recreating at the same frenetic pace as they work. They work hard and play hard. Time urgency becomes a way of life, no matter what they're doing. Here's an experience of mine that makes the point.

I'm up at 6am writing in the quiet solitude of the early morning at the Sunrise Visitors Center at Mt. Rainier National Park. I look up to see a black Honda Accord pull into the empty parking lot and a couple bolt out. By far, the earliest tourists yet. The man leading the way, they jog to the viewpoint just outside my window. They each peek in the telescope. The massive snowcapped mountain is aglow with the colors of sunrise. Next, the man pans the scene with his camcorder, and in less than a minute they're jogging back, scrambling into the car. The car starts up, lurches forward a few feet and stops. The man pops back out of the car with his camcorder and in one sweeping motion pans the visitor center, restrooms, and lodge. He slides deftly back into the driver's seat, and they speed away. Wow! Mt. Rainier in record time. All is silent again. We're alone once more, just me and this magnificent mountain at sunrise, which goes on and on and on, most beautifully.

The Problem of Time Urgency

The existential psychotherapist Ludwig Binswanger (1881-1966) studied the relationship between mental illness and the experience of time. He described the temporal mode of "urgency." His patients felt "caught up in a whirlpool" or "being driven." They were "continuously on the alert for danger," filled with fear, anxiety, and dread.

Contemporary industrial societies are concerned about combating stress. Millions of books, including numerous bestsellers, address the issue. We know "Type A" people live with greater health risks. Heart specialists have identified "time urgency" as a major cause of premature heart disease. Psychologists and other health professionals study the negative side effects of our lifestyles, yet treatment oftentimes takes the form of helping people adjust and cope with these unhealthy conditions, rather than change to healthier, less frenetic lifestyles.

We rushed headlong into the industrial age with high hopes. In the fifties we were told that the new technology of labor-saving devices would bring us more leisure time. Sociologists and futurists were wrong. Leisure time has gone down. People are working longer, harder, and faster. Half of Americans don't get enough sleep.

So, what is by far the most common leisure time activity? Overworked and stressed, exhausted people park in front of their television sets, too tired to do something more active, creative, or rewarding with their leisure time. Europeans work less and watch less television than Americans; Japanese work more and watch more television. (*Ecopsychology*)

As a result of people spending long hours away from home at work and then camping out in front of the TV at home, family time suffers. Couples take, on the average, less than 15 minutes a day to talk to each other. With two-career families, parents spend less time with their children. Adolescents form gangs attempting to create a sense of belonging which is not readily available because our social structures fail to provide adequate opportunities for healthy participation in family and community life.

"Running Out of Time," a PBS television program (1994) presented an excellent overview of the problem. The program did, however, fall into the cultural trap, as most of us do, of treating time as a commodity, a commodity we are "running out of." Yet, the world is not rotating faster on its axis, nor is it traveling around the sun at a faster rate. Objectively, the pace of nature is remarkably constant. We all have the same amount of time each day and we've had that amount for our entire existence as a species. The problem is not the amount of time, but rather the conditions under which we live. When the pace of our lives is fast, the way we experience the passage of time changes. The problem has to do with the rhythms of our lives.

Seeking to Reconnect with the Natural Rhythms of Our Lives

"Free the mind from the domination of time and everything takes on a curious beauty. Experience then seems to exist for its own sake with a flavor and a color and a fragrance it had not before. The scene is no longer blurred and streaming away from us, broken by an anxious heart."

James Fitzgerald

If you change the conditions under which you live, you will experience the passage of time in dramatically different ways. For example, and by way of contrast, consider the vision quest ritual of finding a special place in nature, creating a circle of stones 8-12 feet in diameter, and remaining there within the circle, experiencing the passage of time from sunrise to sunrise. (See Circle of Stones Activity on p. 206) A single rotation of the earth will be experienced in a dramatically different way than the same amount of time spent in our busy, complex, and demanding day-to-day lives. This change in structure drastically slows down the pace and invites us to reconnect with the earth's natural rhythms.

The patterns and rituals of a culture dramatically effect the pace of our lives. All cultures have their ways of marking the passage of time. Before the wrist watch, most people marked time by hearing the bells ringing from the top of the church steeple, the tallest building. The pace of community life emerged from a sacred center. When I was growing up, our culture still observed the Sabbath, one day for rest and religious observance every week. Traditionally, societies imposed strict sanctions for breaking the Sabbath. This holy day when business as usual comes to a halt has slowly eroded away.

Many cultures observe daily rituals for rest and reflection, such as tea time or afternoon siesta. The Muslim practice of prayer at six specified times of day is another example. Our modern work-related time outs are called coffee breaks or smoke breaks. These secular rituals involve the taking of drugs with stimulating effects, caffeine and nicotine.

Time is related to space. There is a pace to each place, whether inner city or desert. Cultural conditions dramatically influence the rhythms of our lives and the way we experience the passage of time. They may encourage lifestyles that are in harmony with our biorhythms, or they may put stress our biological systems to the point that our immune systems are weakened and poor physical and mental health become the norm. For example, sleep researchers are currently trying to find out how the disruption of healthy sleep is associated with depression, our most prevalent mental disorder.

Chronological time is measured by clocks and calendars. It is linear, orderly, quantifiable. Striving for ever-increasing efficiency and productivity, we submit ourselves to the demands of scheduled clock time. We even measure how fast the race is run within hundredths of a second. On the other hand, we can also choose to pace ourselves by tuning into the natural rhythms operating within ourselves in our situation of the moment. This enables us to respond out of a personal sense of timeliness.

Earth time is organic, rhythmic, bodily. Linked to the earth's cycles of day and night and the passing of the seasons, it has its own cadence. Our lives are meant to be synchronized with those of the earth. We can attune to these earth rhythms which will reawaken within ourselves our own natural biological rhythms.

All life is inter-linked in a rhythmic web, composites of rhythms within rhythms that intermesh—electrical brain wave rhythms, heartbeat rhythms, breathing rhythms, hormone release rhythms, fertility rhythms, as well as the sleep-wake rhythms. These rhythms range in frequency from milliseconds, as in the electrical activity of the brain, to much longer cycles, such as the blooming of a Chinese bamboo called Sleeping Beauty which occurs every 125 years. All life is synchronized with the earth, its daily rotation, the monthly moon cycles, the annual cycles of the seasons. The field of chronobiology, which studies these relationships, has studied human biorhythms and their relationship with the earth's rhythms since the 1960's.

The natural process by which one rhythmic system falls into sync with another is called "entrainment." For example, the menstrual periods of women who live together tend to come at the same time. Give a group of children a variety of rhythm instruments to play, and without any conductor they will come together in a common rhythm. When functioning well, our internal rhythms synchronize with their natural patterns. The beepers, sirens, and alarms of modern times produce a cacophony of sounds very different from those heard by our ancestors. A stressful environment, discordant and overriding nature's interplay of rhythms, threatens to throw us out of our natural rhythmic patterns. By attuning ourselves to the sounds of birds, the wind in the trees, waves on the shore, and other natural rhythms, we can entrain ourselves back into a healthier rhythmic internal state. (For example, see the Ocean Breathing Activity on p. 23)

Earth time also moves in a linear, evolutionary direction. Unlike the more obvious and frequent cycles of day, month, and year, the scale of geological time is measured in millions of years. The earth was born; the biosphere was born. Cells, plants, fish, birds, animals, and humans evolve over time. New species are created, evolve, and become extinct. Geological as well as cultural history, in this sense, does not repeat itself. As individuals and as a species, the earth will not give us a second chance to back up and do it over. Life is once and for all. There is no rewind button.

Since the 1960's cosmologists have extended our understanding of history. We now know that the whole universe has been evolving since the "big bang" approximately fifteen billion years ago. The cosmos and everything in it continues to evolve. The mystery of our existence becomes more and more fantastic. Today's understanding of realty dwarfs the unbelievable science fiction of our grandparents. While geological time opens us to our ancient past, cosmological time evokes a sense of the infinite horizon of eternity.

Here's a brief entry from my journal: I'm cruising down the road on my way to my next vision quest when I spot a revival tent up ahead. As I drive by I read on the marquee, "Eternity Ahead." I smile a knowing smile.

In religious and peak experiences the passage of time is transcended or opens up in ways that we break through to the sense of the eternal. Our experience seems timeless, the urgency of getting someplace dissolves completely. We taste what some have called, "the eternal now." Ludwig Wittgenstein put it this way, "If we take eternity to mean not infinite temporal duration but timelessness, then eternal life belongs to those who live in the present." Some of the activities in the next part of the book are especially designed to invite this kind of experience.

There is an Islamic proverb that advises us to live every day as if it were our last and as if we were to live forever. The ultimate challenge of integrating these two polarities into your way of living in time involves learning to embrace the unique preciousness of each moment, while simultaneously knowing the patience and serenity of living in the eternity which contains each moment. Can we learn this well enough together to re-create our cultures in ways that support living our lives according the wisdom of this proverb?

The following activities provide opportunities for you to explore your relationship to earth time.

Activity Sixty-Nine ➤ Entering Nature's Time

Plan a period of time when you can take off your watch. Explore what its like to let go of organizing your day into the hours and minutes of digital time. See if you can withstand the urge to check your watch to find out what time it is. Find out what it's like to let the sun be your guide for the passage of time. Follow nature's time for the duration of your time in nature. If you can arrange it, an excellent time period is from sunset one night to sunset the next.*

"The Western mind has trouble stopping its clock. It conceives its inmost life as a biological clock and its heart as a ticker. The electronic gadget on the wrist encloses in a concrete symbol the Western time-bound mind ... We even seem to see time itself."

James Hillman, *The Soul's Code*

---

* See also Mountain Circumambulation Activity, p. 204, Medicine Walk Activity, p. 200 and Circle of Stones Activity, p. 206.

When on my vision quests, I leave my watch in the car. One time, my wristwatch was held on by only a single thread of its badly worn leather band when I arrived at the trailhead. As I was putting on my pack, the last thread broke and it fell to the ground. Great timing. On the next quest, I left my watch at home.

When I leave my watch behind, I learn lessons about myself and time. Time is something I "watch." I discover how dependent I've become on organizing my life according to chronos. When hungry, I catch myself checking to see if it's lunchtime. When I get restless, when I'm unclear about how to involve myself, when I'm in transition from one experience to the next, or when time for whatever reason seems to be dragging (which really means I'm dragging), it is at those times that I want to know what time it is. Over the years, I've made progress, going for longer and longer periods without even wondering what time it is. I know late afternoon is the hardest time of day for me because that's when I'm most likely to want to know the time.

I've found that taking the time to greet the sun in the morning and watch it set in the evening is a great way to attune myself to the natural rhythms of earth time. Incorporating some special ritual activity into these transition times also provides support for orienting myself to each daylong page in the story of my life.

Activity Seventy ➤ Greeting Sunrise

Select a place in nature where you will have a good view to the East for watching the rising sun. Plan ahead so you can arrive there an hour or two before sunrise and remain there awhile after. Pay attention to the changes in light and how this effects the colors. Notice the changes in temperature. Look all around you at the changing sky, changing clouds, the horizon, the moving shadows, landscape, nearby trees & shrubs, the ground at your feet. Taking it all in, pay attention to how this gradual transition from darkness to daylight effects you.

Caution: Do not stare directly at the sun. Short glances only or you may damage your eyes.

"The seeds of the day are best planted in the first hour."
Dutch Proverb

Starting the day well is important. The way you begin your day can set the tone for the rest. "Did you get out of bed on the wrong side this morning?" is an old saying that contains more than a grain of truth. Robert Greenway found that 73 percent of his wilderness program participants identified getting up before dawn and climbing a ridge or peak in order to greet the sun as their second most important experience of their trip. (*Ecopsychology*, p.129) Consider how you might start the day in a healthier way. Begin your day with meditation, prayer, or a special poem.

Here's a morning invocation that I often use:

> *Listen to the exhortation of the dawn*
> *Look to this day, for it is life, the very life of life.*
> *In its brief course lie all the verities and realities of your existence,*
> *the glory of action—the bliss of growth—-the splendor of beauty.*
> *For yesterday is but a dream,*
> *and tomorrow is only a vision,*
> *but today, well lived,*
> *makes every yesterday a dream of happiness,*
> *and every tomorrow a vision of hope.*
> *Look well therefore to this day.*
> *Such is the salutation of the dawn.*
>
> **The Koran**

Ending the day well is also important. We need rituals to help us slow down at the end of a busy day. Settling the affairs of the day, reviewing gifts given and gifts received, lessons learned, and anticipating the new day ahead are healthy parts of bringing the day to a close. These end-of-the-day rituals pave the way for surrendering to the darkness, the creative dreamscape of inactive sleep. We have ritual ways of putting our affairs in order prior to each night's sleep, just as we put our affairs in order for the "big sleep" at the end of our life. A good night's sleep will rejuvenate us, charging our batteries for the next day's activities.

Activity Seventy-One ➤ Greeting the Sunset

The same as the sunrise activity, except for the planning of time and place. Select the place with the view to the West for watching the sunset. Plan to arrive awhile before sunset and to remain an hour or two after.

Bring a jacket or be otherwise prepared for a drop in temperature. Again, take it all in. How is this sunset transition similar and different to your experience of sunrise?

Part III

Experiencing the Sacred in Nature

The Creator gave to us all the living things so that we would know how to act. The natural world is our Bible; by watching the chipmunk and the meadowlark and even the tiniest flower we learn the lessons that the Creator has put before us. Everything is sacred. This very land is our church.

Chief Fools Crow of the Oglala Lakota

12

Religion, Spirituality, and Nature

"I feel that I draw nearest to understanding the great secret of my life in my closest intercourse with nature. There is a reality and health in present nature which cannot be contemplated in antiquity. I suppose that what in other men is religion is in me love of nature."

Henry David Thoreau

Examining Your Relationship to Nature from a Religious Perspective

How we view ourselves in relation to nature is expressed through our religious beliefs and practices. The scriptures and traditions of the world's religions contain numerous references to nature and our relationship to it. For many of us, religious beliefs and practices form some of the underpinnings of our personal worldviews. For others, they've been supplanted by our scientific understandings of the world.

As stated before, language both guides and describes our experience. Our religious concepts and beliefs, for example, have a formative effect on the way we experience nature and our human nature. By re-examining these cognitive filters, some of which may be unquestioned assumptions adopted from childhood catechisms, we can re-open the doors of perception.

Until just a few years ago, if you were to ask me how my childhood exposure to religion affected my relationship to nature, I would have struggled to come up with anything positive. The services and church activities that I attended at my suburban Presbyterian church (1950-63) were all held indoors. I don't remember our relationship with nature ever being discussed as a concern. God was presented as a transcendent otherworldly being, apart from nature. There was heaven and earth. And the earth was definitely below heaven.

Recently, however, I made a surprise discovery when visiting my childhood church. My mother and I attended the eleven o'clock Sunday Service as was our family custom. The sanctuary was exactly as I remembered it. We sat where we usually sat. Losing interest in the sermon, my gaze was drawn upward above the altar to meet the light coming in through the stained glass window. A sense of the deeply familiar flooded me with feeling. The intensity of my response puzzled me at first. As a child, my gaze would often go there, to this most intimate and private place of personal refuge. Then came the moment of understanding. There revealed above me by the light shining through from the outside was Christ kneeling, arms outstretched upon a large flat rock, praying in the Garden of Gethsemane. I realized that the scene portrayed in this most familiar stained glass window powerfully confirmed my current beliefs about nature being a catalyst to spiritual seeking. In that stained glass window I found that there was an important link between my childhood experience and my present religious affections after all!

The activity below raises questions to help you identify formative experiences from your childhood.

Activity Seventy-Two ➤ Religious Roots

Do you remember any special childhood experiences that influenced your beliefs about nature? Identify one or two major beliefs about nature and human nature that you were taught in childhood? At Sunday school? At home? How do they compare with your current beliefs?

The next activity invites you to review your perspectives on nature, cleaning the dust off old lenses and trying on new ones for experiencing nature afresh.

Seventy-Three ➤ Refreshing Your Religious Views on Nature

Re-examine the scriptures of your current religious orientation for references to nature and our relationship to it. See if you can let go of preconceptions and view them afresh. Does your current reading and interpretation of these scriptures differ from your prior understandings? How do these religious beliefs match up with your personal experience? Is your behavior consistent with these beliefs and values? Explore a variety of views about nature from other religious traditions and compare them with your own.* Now, as in the previous activity, identify two or three of your core beliefs about nature. Any changes?

Examining the Influence of Science on Your Worldview

Like most of you, I was raised with a natural scientific view of nature. I looked into the classroom microscope and telescope, and I replicated objective experimental methods which revealed the laws of nature. Natural events, especially the observable and measurable, did not need spirits, demons, angels, or divine intervention to explain them. In studying history and anthropology, I learned that primitive religious views of nature were the superstitious beliefs of less advanced peoples who were deprived of the knowledge of modern science. The exploration of nature, I found, was a scientific rather than a religious activity. How did your exposure to the natural sciences effect your beliefs about nature and human nature?

---

* See, for example, Lewis G. Regenstein's *Replenish the Earth*, (1991) or Peter Marshall's *Nature's Web: Rethinking our Place on Earth* (1994). They provide overviews of the Christian, Jewish, Buddhist, Hindu, and Islamic beliefs about nature.

Activity Seventy-Four ➤ Comparing Religious and Scientific Worldviews

Is your religious worldview consistent with your natural-scientific knowledge about nature? Compare what you were taught in school with what you were taught in church and at home. Are these views compatible?

As a young adult, my traditional religious faith could not withstand the assault of questions raised by my rational scientific mind. In the monkey trials of my mind, evolution won out over Genesis as the viable explanation of our origins. This questioning of my religious beliefs sent me into deeper seeking. I took a course in the philosophy of religions. I began a meditation practice.

Creation myths crumble, as they did for me, under the scrutiny of those who expect religious scriptures to be recounting literal historical facts. However, when I gained an understanding of the nature of metaphor, I was able to reclaim religious myths and stories. I learned to experience them as powerful conveyers of truths without having to be literally correct, historically accurate, rationally free of inconsistencies, or subject to the laws of science.

Our problem, some argue, is not that God is dead, but that our scriptures no longer sing to us. Our scientifically trained ear isn't tuned in to their music, so they no longer connect us with the divine. Others argue that we, not god, are dead, spiritually that is. We have become disconnected with the divine. As we intimately reconnect with nature, to the divine energies of God's creation, then our religious paths will come alive for us in powerful ways.

Some believe that our precious religious traditions are salvageable. Others believe that our age needs a new updated creation story that better reconciles our modern scientific and religious worldviews. From this viewpoint, the transition to the new ecological age involves a new spiritual transformation which will inspire the creation of new religious beliefs, traditions, and practices.

To summarize, our cultural-environmental crisis is also a spiritual-religious crisis. We struggle to find viable myths for our times to bind people together with a common meaning and purpose in life. Some believe our traditional myths can be salvaged. Others believe we need a new religious myth, one that is consistent with our current scientific understandings and more responsive to the realities of modern global environmental issues. Still others believe that our transition into an ecological era will lead us back full circle to the ancient truths of our hunter-gatherer ancestors who lived in harmony with nature. What do you believe?

While the path hasn't been easy, I've made much progress in reconciling my religious and scientific perspectives with my experiences in nature. I now find that many of the findings of modern science support my religious yearnings by revealing a divine design governed by universal laws. For me, the revelations of science have greatly enhanced the glory of creation by including billions of stars in billions of galaxies, lasting billions of years, and microscopic worlds filled with micro-organismic life, and black holes, black matter, millions of species, and other magnificent phenomena. Consider the biblical reference "for dust thou art, and unto dust shalt thou return." (*Genesis* 3:19) In the light of modern cosmology, I rewrite this scripture in my mind as "for star dust we are, and to star dust we shall return." I now understand that the assumption of a universe, in the first place, is an outgrowth of our monotheistic heritage which posits a single unity of which all the great diversity is a part. In the words of philosopher Alfred North Whitehead, "God is the unification of all things." In many respects, thanks to science, I now experience the mysteries of creation and the grandeur of nature with more awe and wonder than ever before possible.

Common Ground

"In Nature, there is a fundamental unity running through all the diversity we see about us. Religions are no exception to the natural law."

Ghandi

Fortunately, regardless of where you stand on these great philosophical and theological issues, there is growing hope for positive change based on recent developments worldwide. Throughout the 1980's, there has come a burgeoning of activity in the pulpits, pews, seminaries, and headquarters of many religious denominations throughout the world. Ecological, environmental, and "earth and spirit" issues gain attention like never before. Religious institutions, including my childhood church, sponsor programs that advocate for an ecological worldview. Religious leaders everywhere call upon us to be better stewards of God's Creation. The view that only one true religion can show us the way is, I believe, both undesirable and dangerous. Religious diversity plays as important a role in maintaining the creative viability of the spirit as biodiversity does for the ecosystem.

When we emphasize uniqueness and individual differences, we can say that there are as many religions as there are people. On the other hand, there is the common ground of the earth that we all share, from which a diverse number of creative healthy responses to these ecological problems can sprout. And the burgeoning activity mentioned above is an indication that this movement has already begun.

The time is ripe for change. We must come to understand that the body of nature and the human body are inseparable, that any violation of nature is equally a violation of the human mind and spirit. Joseph Campbell (in *The Power of Myth*) describes mythology as "the song of the imagination, inspired by the energies of the body." Rituals are the dances that go with these songs. The lyrics of the songs are the poetic storylines of the myths. The experience of nature and the human body in daily life are going to be quite different for bands of hunters and gatherers, agricultural groups, and modern city dwellers. Campbell studied "the transformation of myths through time" as cultures changed throughout human history. Our images of the divine change over time to reflect our common experience as determined by the patterns of the culture within which we live.

In modern times, we have lost touch with our natural organismic selves and our relationship with nature. We have lost touch with the earth religions that were at the core of indigenous cultures. Instead of the ritual sacrificial hunting of revered totem animals which have spirits that must be appeased and that serve as sources of the wisdom as well as food, we go the supermarket for bloodless processed food in cans or wrapped in plastic. The energies of the body are going to be very different gathering berries in the woods compared to picking up a package of frozen berries at the local supermarket. In indigenous cultures an individual's daily survival depended upon ecological awareness. Successful hunting, fishing, gathering, and cultivation of the land require intimate knowledge of the natural environment. Most of us are far removed from directly experiencing the ecological impact of our actions. While we may hear about it in the mass media, most of us "know not what we do" in this more immediate visceral way.

Reestablishing a harmonious connection with the laws of nature is the challenge confronting us. We must understand what it means to be natives of this earth, to reconnect with our roots in the earth. In a highly mobile technological society, the task becomes much greater!

Our cultural-environmental crisis is a spiritual-religious crisis. One of the reasons we destroy our planet is that it has lost its sacred dimension for many of us. We desperately need cultural practices that resacralize the world, that re-infuse the land with sufficient symbolic and social significance to govern behavior. We must come to know in the deepest way that diminishing the grandeur of the earth robs us of the powers of divine presence.

If we learn how to reconnect with the land, then we will treat our world again as a sacred place with reverence and respect. The reintegration of earth mythologies and rituals with our societal mythologies and rituals will help us bring our cultures back into harmony with nature and our own human nature as we better understand how we are inextricably entwined in the web of life. Looking to the wisdom of the ages, we can rediscover nature mystics throughout human history representing a wide variety of traditions from around the globe. I cite a few of them in the remaining sections of this chapter to help us find our way.

> *"You know, I think if people stay somewhere long enough—even white people—the spirits will begin to speak to them. It's the power of the spirits coming from the land."*
>
> **Crow Elder**, *Deep Ecology for the 21st Century*

Communing with the Divine through Nature

> *"Every natural fact is a symbol of some spiritual fact. Every appearance in nature corresponds to some state of the mind."*
>
> **Ralph Waldo Emerson**, *On Nature*

Nature has a spiritual dimension. It is infused with divinity. The universe is the ultimate context for all religions whose creation myths attempt to tell the great story of it all. If God moves in and through all creation, then to be closer to nature is to be closer to God. The universe itself can be sensed as a divine revelation. In Dante's words, "Nature is the art of God." Nature is an expression of God, the creative force and intelligence of the universe. When we explore the sacramental qualities of the natural realm, we tap into a great resource for our spiritual-religious growth. Anthropologists maintain that our religious origins emerged from feelings engendered by the awesome powers of nature. Nature can be viewed as an ongoing primal source or wellspring for religious feeling.

I-Thou Dialogue with the Divine

Throughout this book, I advocate viewing nature not as an *it*, but as a *thou*. For the moment, I'd like you to consider viewing nature-as-a-whole as *Thou*, a manifestation of the divine. In this context, reflect on the following quote by Martin Buber, "Spirit in its human manifestation is a response of man to his *Thou*."

If God is the verb energizing the universe, then turning toward God is attuning oneself to be in rhythm and harmony with this universal energy. In defining the religious life, William James asserted that "harmonious relatedness is the supreme good."

The compassionate lover, the person with reverence for life, feels the incarnation of the spirit in the things of this world. Again in the words of Martin Buber, "The world is an irradiation of God . . . A divine spark lives in everything and being, but each spark is enclosed by an isolating shell . . . (Humans) can liberate it and rejoin it with the Origin; by holding holy converse with the thing."

Nature as Fertile Ground for Holy Dialogue

*"Nature gave the word **glory** a meaning for me. I still do not know where else I could have found one . . . And if nature had never awakened certain longings in me, huge areas of what I can now mean by the 'love' of God would never, so far as I can see, have existed."*

C. S. Lewis, *The Four Loves*

Developing an intimate connection with nature can plunge us into realms not typically explored. Truths can be revealed in nature that are not mere projections of one's wishful fancy. There is a mysterious process by which perception turns into vision, in Wordsworth's words, "planting, for immortality, images of sound and sight in the celestial soil of the imagination." Nature is a valid source from which we may collect divine inspiration.

Our religion, defined in its broadest sense as reconnecting with our Source or the Ground of our Being, comes most intimately alive for us through being deeply immersed in the experiencing of ourselves and the world in which we live. By avoiding intimate experiencing, we often end up seeking god solely in the confines of the mental gymnastics of analyzing and debating of dogma and creed. Theology has its place, but religion lacks substance if it is all menu and no meal.

Nature and wildlife have served as sources of inspiration and revelation for religious mystics and prophets throughout the ages. For example, the most powerful revelations of Moses, Jesus, and Mohammed all occurred during vigils in the desert. Throughout human history, people on solitary ventures into the wilderness report experiencing communion with a force much greater than the self. Philosopher Alfred North Whitehead defined religion as "what man does with his solitariness." Some religious seekers return from their solitary journeys with visions for their people that challenge the conventional wisdom of their times. Transcendent sensations of elation, oneness with the universe, and an appreciation for natural grandeur are common components of these experiences. You do not have to be a religious mystic or prophet to explore nature as an inspirational resource. The beauty and solitude of nature invite us to awaken to the spiritual dimensions of our existence.

"My heart is tuned to the quietness that the stillness of nature inspires."
Hazrat Inayat Khan

Silence as a Gateway to Solitude and Communion with the Divine

"How can you expect God to speak in that gentle and inward voice which melts the soul, when you are making so much noise with your rapid reflections? Be silent and God will speak again."
Francois Fenelon, *Spiritual Letters, XXII*

Simple exposure to the grandeurs of nature does not guarantee religious inspiration. Environmental educator, Joseph Cornell once observed approximately 150 tourists visiting a popular viewpoint on rim of the Grand Canyon. Only three appeared to be intently gazing at this natural wonder for over thirty seconds. Most of the brief visits were dominated by fiddling with cameras and talking with fellow sightseers.

Our problems, worries, concerns about love and work, daily chores, and other mental baggage sometimes bug us like a swarm of hungry mosquitoes. Being so preoccupied keeps us from feeling our relationship with the natural world. Leaving our everyday concerns behind poses a great challenge. Our continuously broadcasting minds fill us with the noisy chatter of self-talk that blocks our sensitivities to the gifts of the moment. The meditation and awareness activities presented in this book are tools for learning to switch off the self-talk so we are better able to tune in to receive.

Silence is the gateway to solitude. Communion with the world grows out of this silence. And this silence has a voice, a spiritual voice. A Serbian Proverb tells us that, "Solitude is full of God."

Activity Seventy-Five ➤ Listening for Silence

Select a quiet, peaceful place in nature for this meditation exercise. Sit quietly in an erect and comfortable position. Begin by simply listening to your own breathing. Pay attention to the quality of each inhalation and exhalation. Then notice that after each inhalation and exhalation, there is a silent pause. Enter into these silent moments between each inhalation and exhalation. Then begin to listen outside yourself to the sounds of nature. Notice how there is silence between each sound, whether it be the chirp of a bird, the splash of a frog jumping in the water, the rustling of leaves. Observe the ever-present silence behind each of nature's sounds. Notice how all sounds fade into silence. Silences may be experienced as thick, solid, powerful, spacious, even never-ending. How do you experience this silence? Discover how you quiet down inside when you experience the silence as soothing, or become anxious when the silence feels spooky. Silence is often the palate upon which we mix our feelings. And their reverberations also, in time, fade into silence. Continue to explore the silence.

"There is in all things an inexhaustible sweetness and purity, a silence that is a fountain of action and joy. It rises up in wordless gentleness and flows out to me from unseen roots of all created being."
Thomas Merton

The experience of solitude is both aesthetic and mystical. Mystical seekers, both east and west, have sought out places of silence to find solitude. They maintain vows of silence, choose a monastic life, live alone in a hermitage, even go off alone to meditate in caves for months at a time. Thomas Merton, who himself lived in a hermitage, wrote "I have only one desire and that is the desire for solitude—to disappear into God." Psychologist Clark Moustakas found through his studies of loneliness that, "In absolute solitary moments man experiences truth, beauty, nature, reverence, humanity."

The practice of meditation offers a systematic method for entering into a state of solitude. Meditators become centered by sitting still in a meditative posture, the opposite of busywork. They often struggle with restlessness, boredom, and emptiness in their efforts to reach that place of inner calm. T.R. Kelly in *A Testament of Devotion* describes the inner place sought by meditators and religious seekers throughout the ages: "Deep within us all there is an amazing inner sanctuary of the soul, a holy place, a Divine Center . . . Life from the Center is a life of unhurried peace and power. It is simple. It is serene. It is amazing. It is radiant." Some meditators seek to gain the ultimate insight into their deepest inner nature—enlightenment.

As with most religious experiences, moments of solitude are rare and fleeting. Inevitably loneliness returns in the face of boredom, emptiness, rejection, separation, and death. Each moment of solitude must be earned anew. Out of solitude, we may receive a new vision for our lives. It may set the stage, but it doesn't start the new drama. We must return, hopefully renewed, inspired, and with a deeper understanding of ourselves and the world, to re-engage ourselves in the business of our daily lives in ways that include communing with nature.

> *"Master of the Universe, grant me the ability to be alone; may it be my custom to go outdoors each day among the trees and grass—among all growing things—and there may I be alone and enter into prayer, to talk to the One to whom I belong. May I express there everything in my heart, and may all the foliage of the field—-all grasses, trees, and plants—awake at my coming, to send the powers of their life into the words of my prayer so that my prayer and speech are made whole through the life and spirit of all growing things, which are made as one by their Source."*
>
> **Rabbi Nachman**

In the chapters that follow, I present ways for you to make it your custom to seek out your connection with the spiritual dimension of nature. Explore for yourself whether or not cultivating your own intimate experiences with nature will provide fertile ground for religious experiences that serve as sources of inspiration and revelation.

13

Entering Sacred Time and Space: Ritual Activities in Nature

"There is an impulse still within the human breast to unify and sanctify the total natural world—of which we are."

Gregory Bateson, in *Dharma Gaia*

Bedazzled by our own technological wizardry, we may be operating under the illusion that our rational scientific society has progressed beyond primitive ritualism to a less superstitious, more realistic and pragmatic approach to life. Being caught up in daily humdrum distracts us from seeing the mythmaking and ritual power of our modern technologies. Clock, car, TV set, computer, credit ratings, tax returns, diet charts, all pattern our activities. Our lives can be ordered by the rising and setting of the sun, the ringing of a bell calling us to prayer five times a day, or by the beeping of our digital watches and the ringing of our phones. All beckon us to activity and all have their own rhythm.

Could it be that our secular society, blindly and frenetically struggling for materialistic progress, is caught up in a compulsive shallow ritualism of its own? Could it be that as a culture we are not anchored in a spiritual and religious worldview that provides both depth of meaning and experience? Ritual, broadly defined as formalized patterns of behavior, is not an option, but a given. Will these patterns be expressed in our outer world and experienced in our inner world with a sense of richness or poverty? Creating and maintaining rituals that are meaningful and alive is very important. Will our rituals be expressions of our deepest yearnings or compulsions driven by neurotic anxieties?

Rituals become powerfully ingrained in a people. When conquering nations impose their religions, the original practices of the conquered find their way into the practices introduced by the conquerors. If the old practices are forbidden, they often continue to be performed in secret and at great risk by at least some of the local population. Bloody battles are fought over religious ritual. Disagreements about ritual cause congregations to split and new denominations to form. Why the strong attachment? Effective rituals serve as catalysts. They energize the very lifeblood of entire communities. To be robbed of your sacred rituals is to have the practices that support your spiritual life taken from you. On the other hand, when a culture is in decay, rituals may degenerate into empty repetitions that are lifeless, habits that carry no spark or fulfillment. To continue to participate in rituals that no longer inspire or are contrary to your beliefs, whether through force or obligation, is to damage your spiritual life. How well do your rituals serve you?

Rituals transport us into the realm of the ineffable, a consecrated place where we experience changes we cannot articulate. Wordiness can ruin them. Our most powerful rituals maintain plenty of room for the eloquence of silence. These silent spaces, these pauses, the between-the-notes-and-words places, are essential in great music, in great art, and in living a great life. Great ritual, like great theater, is not limited to mere oration. The transformative power of a ritual depends upon its ability to inspire active participation with symbolic gestures and actions as well as listening to sermons. Effective rituals take place in powerful settings and frequently include music that stirs the soul and lifts the spirit.

Rituals provide demarcation and support for change, for transforming one season into another, boys and girls into men and women, ill persons into healthy ones, lay persons into priests, men and women into husbands and wives. Rituals come alive and have power to the extent that participants are willing and ready to undergo transformation. Authentic rituals pitch you out of old ways into new ways of being. They support letting go when a project is completed; and they motivate people to take hold when a new project needs to be launched.

Ritual and ceremony reawaken sacred sensing, opening us to the holiness of nature. Rituals help us align ourselves with the spiritual dimensions of nature. According to Ralph Metzner, "Rituals of reconciliation, this religious (relinking) worship . . . involves a kind of alignment or balancing, an establishment of right relationship, between self and other humans, animals, plants, the mineral kingdom, the elemental energies of the environment, and the creator, spirit(s) animating all evolving life forms." (in Fredric Lehrman's *The Sacred Landscape*) Rituals can attune us to our connections with natural cycles of growth and decay, of birth and death, to the many dynamic patterns that make up this web of our universe. A sensuous immersion into the myth, symbol, poetry, song, and dance of ritual can awaken us to an embodied way of knowing and being in the world that is much deeper than mere intellectual insight.

For this to happen, more of our rituals need to be practiced out in nature. As beautiful and inspiring as some of our indoor churches can be, they are not adequate to the task of connecting us with the spiritual dimensions of the earth. We need to take our religious practices, whether they be yoga, meditation, or prayer, into the great outdoors.

Activity Seventy-Six ➤ Ritual Assessment

Defining rituals most broadly as formalized patterns of behavior, how well do your daily, weekly, and seasonal rituals serve you? Do they connect you with nature? Do they provide your life with depth and meaning? Do they support putting you in right relationship with your world? How might you change your rituals to better serve you?

Sacred ritual involves using sacred objects and entering into sacred places at sacred times. These dimensions of the sacred are explored in the next three sections.

Sacred Objects

> *"The contemplation of objects, the volatile image of dreams which they evoke, these make the song . . . The symbol is formed by the perfect use of this mystery: to select an object and to extract from it, by a series of decipherings, a mood."*
>
> **Mallarmé**, French poet

Some of the objects we find in nature may take on additional meaning and power for us. Whether a feather, bone, shell, or stone, their special shape, beauty, or other characteristics draw us to them. (See, for example, Chapter 9 presentation on the sacred dimensions of rocks) These special objects may be keepsakes, physical objects that we keep for the sake of remembering our special connections with people, places, and experiences. We use them for rituals of remembrance. Most everyone collects memorabilia of one kind or another. Sometimes we wear these symbols of connection around our necks, wrists, or fingers, or carry them around in wallets, purses, or pockets. Some we hang on walls, place on mantels, or store in special boxes and drawers. Most of you, I'll bet, have made and kept a scrapbook or stored photographs in photo albums, the most common modern form of these rites of preservation.

When crafted by special artisans of a culture, natural objects take on new value. Carving and finishing wood, and cutting and polishing stones bring out new aesthetic refinements. Adorning them with religious icons enhances their sacred value. Rituals can be performed to imbue these objects with additional sacred significance. Sacred objects, whether the Pope's ring or a medicine man's pipe, are no longer merely physical objects. They have an important role to play in the religious rites and ceremonies of a culture.

We all participate in these rituals whether or not we believe in voodoo, supernatural powers, sorcery, objects that ward off evil spirits, and other forms of sympathetic magic. Ritual objects persist in the form of rabbits' feet, lucky charm bracelets, wedding rings, crosses hung around the neck, mistletoe, wreaths hung on doors and walls, dangling objects hung on the rearview mirrors of our cars, or religious icons placed on the car dashboard. What are the sacred objects in your life? Do they work for you? Explore the role sacred objects can play in reconnecting you with nature.

Activity Seventy-Seven ➢ Sacred Object Meditation

Select from among the things you have collected over the years, a natural object whether feather, stone, bone, wood, or seashell that has special meaning for you. Pick a special time and place where you can meditate in solitude. For starters, you might want to allow anywhere from 15-60 minutes. Go to your special place with your natural object. Relax and settle in quietly. (You might start with one of the tuning your organism activities in Chapter 3.) Then, sit quietly with your special object. Look at it. Touch it. Then, close your eyes, sitting in meditation, with it cradled in your hands. See what comes to you out of this silence as you focus your meditation on your natural object. You may have special memories triggered, feelings may surface, and images may come to mind. What lessons, if any, emerge from this experience?

Sacred Places

"Human beings are invariably driven to ground their religious experience in the palpable reality of space."

Belden Lane

Sacred space is a place for religious experience, a place where the divine reveals itself to us. Clear of clutter and noise, a sacred space offers a creative void, a wide-open place that has plenty of room for the divine. In sacred places the earth's voice can be heard more clearly. These places carry an intensity that arouses powerful depth of feeling. They manifest a special numinous quality.

Sacred places offer sanctuary: a safe place where one can move freely, breathe freely, act freely. For example, a wildlife sanctuary is a tract of land where animals take refuge in safety from hunters. Likewise, immunity from prosecution is afforded humans who take refuge in a sacred place. Sacred places that provide sanctuary are especially holy.

Many cultures sanctify the local landscape. Ritual oftentimes involves consecrating a territory. Sacred ritual reveals to us a sacred space: the sacred pillar, the axis mundi, the center of the world, the navel of the earth. Mountains, for example may "re-present," not in just a symbolic but also in a physical way, the various gods of a culture. When sanctified, the landscape becomes the geographical localization and orientation for experiencing the community's myths, rituals, and traditions.

These special places in nature become the sites for a culture's seasonal celebrations which connect the people to our earth's cycles as it revolves around our sun. In these cultures, one's identity is rooted into the land, trees, and life within it. Our highly mobile culture uproots many of us numerous times in a single lifetime. In sharp contrast, many indigenous peoples hold a deep attachment to place that they've maintained for hundreds if not thousands of years.

We need to renew our understanding of the need for sacred places. In our highly secularized culture, land has lost this spiritual dimension. We view it primarily as a commodity, an economic resource, to be bought, developed and resold, hopefully at a profit. In our culture, sacred sites of worship typically are located indoors, inside the walls of churches or synagogues. The land they are built upon is not typically acclaimed as sacred.

In his book on sacred places, James Swan describes the many kinds of places commonly identified as sacred: burial grounds (graves, cemeteries), purification places (streams, waterfalls, hot springs, sweat lodges), healing sites, sacred plant and animal sites, rock quarries, astronomical observatories, shrines and temples, historical sites, places of spiritual renewal, mythic and legendary sites, vision questing and dreaming places, rock art places, fertility sites, and sunrise ceremonial sites. Countless sacred sites cover the earth. In the *Encyclopedia of Religion*, I looked for sacred places in Sweden, the home of my ancestors. Within the Kola Peninsula alone, traditional home of the Saami, I found that 507 traditional sacred places have been identified. These sites were categorized by type of place: 149 hills and mountains; 108 steep cliffs, springs, waterfalls, rapids, and lakes; 30 islands, peninsulas, meadows, and heaths; and 220 cliffs or venerated stones.

Sacred places oftentimes possess some significant natural feature. These features may also connect with the seasonal cycles of the earth. For example, there is a sacred spot in the Southwest United States where the rising sun first casts its light between two naturally occurring large vertical rocks on the summer solstice. In some cultures both eastern and western, the discovery of sacred places has been linked with the summer solstice, the longest day of the year. This linkage was surprisingly confirmed in my own personal experience when I found out, months after the fact, that the discovery of my personal power spot on my first vision quest took place at the time of the summer solstice. Stonehenge, a kind of prehistoric observatory, is an example of a ceremonial site that was constructed to correspond to the earth's celestial cycles.

Sacred places have an incredible autonomy and permanency, being passed on from tribe to tribe, from religion to religion from time immemorial. A Catholic monastery near where I live in Oregon is located on a hilltop called Mt. Angel. Anthropologists later discovered that this same hilltop also served as a sacred site for early Native Americans. The famous cathedral of Chartres was built on the site of an old sanctuary with a well where the worship of a virgin was celebrated, not the Virgin Mary, but a Celtic goddess that preceded her. (Jung, *Analytic Psychology,* p.129-132) Examples like these are common throughout the world. Some sites are sacred circles cast and uncast for a single ceremony, while others become sacred only at special times of the season.

Sacred space exists within as well as without. Internally, the body may be viewed as a temple. Purification rituals sanctify the body. In meditation you find your center, the core or source of your being. Some Yoga traditions view the spine as the body's axis mundi. For them, energy centers called chakras exist along the spine that carry spiritually significant meanings. At the external end of the continuum, many know the universe as God's creation, the heavens being the vaulted ceiling of God's most grand cathedral.

Anthropologists believe that our earliest human ancestors performed religious rites in the deep recesses of sacred caverns. Prehistoric pictographs, painted on these cave walls, provide us with examples of some of humankind's first religious icons. These enclosed spaces continue to serve as the mother womb of a person's spiritual life. Walk into a sacred cave, a pyramid, a temple, a cathedral, into mother church, and you move into a world of spiritual images, a landscape of the soul. Whether cave or cathedral, these circumscribed places are the sacred containers in which people practice their religious rites. Like bread cooking in the oven, people are transformed in these enclosed places. The mysterious chemistry of powerful religious experiences cause people to rise up and go forth renewed.

The belief that some places carry more spiritual power than others is more controversial. Does Mount Olympus carry more divinity than Blake's grain of sand? Is contact with the profoundly beautiful more conducive to religious experiences? Or is the experience of the sacred, something that can happen anywhere, anytime; an experience that is based on the receptiveness of the person rather than produced by external conditions? Is all of god's creation equally holy? Explore for yourself.

A sacred place is not arbitrarily chosen, but is sought after and reveals itself to us. We follow signs, manifestations of the divine, which lead us to a special power spot, a spot filled with mana, the energy of being. Land can be viewed as a fountain of energy flowing through circuits of soils, plants, and animals. In this way, the earth body is comparable to the human body.

The experience of place is something you sense. You feel drawn to a sacred place. It has allure. It calls you. When you connect with that special place, you sense a special feeling of well being. It energizes you. It gives off a special ambiance. When in such a place, you might notice your voice dropping to a whisper, a shiver going up your spine, or some other inner response indicative of the its powerful qualities. When drawn to special places, people frequently have strong and meaningful experiences, and go away transformed and renewed. And, in the words of Rabbi Shlomo Carlebach, "You know a place is holy because it is so hard to leave."

Retreats, pilgrimages, and vision quests all entail visiting sacred places. We retreat to a sacred place of refuge for renewal, for revitalization. We may go to a local place (an altar in one's own home) or travel afar. On a pilgrimage, we travel to an already established sacred place. On a quest, we seek to discover or rediscover a new or lost sacred place. (See Chapter 15 for more on pilgrimages and quests) Going to your own personal sacred place is a returning to your spiritual Home. To quote a well-known proverb, "home is where the heart is," the place that puts you in touch with your love energy.

To tap into sacred consciousness, visit an established sacred site, or venture into nature listening for mother earth to call to you. Hopefully you will receive signs that lead you to a special place where she will reveal her secrets to you. You may find a special place that speaks uniquely to you, a "personal power spot." If you are fortunate enough to find such a place, go there regularly, when called, or when the occasion calls for it. In any case, go to the places that call you, and be open to their influence.

In The Power of Myth, Bill Moyers asks Joseph Campbell, "What does it mean to have a sacred place?" Campbell replies, "This is an absolute necessity for anybody today. You must have a room or a certain hour or so a day, where you don't know what was in the newspapers that morning, you don't know who your friends are, you don't know what you owe anybody, you don't know what anybody owes you. This is a place where you can simply experience and bring forth what you are and what you might be. This is the place of creative incubation. At first you may find that nothing happens there. But if you have a sacred place and use it, something eventually will happen."

Repeated visits to special places help develop your sense of connection to nature. A special place, for you, might be in your backyard, your garden, a nearby park, a special tree, stream, hill or mountaintop. Use your sense of natural attractions developed from these activities to discover or reconnect with your special places. Ideally, you will find a place you can return to frequently so you will be able to experience it at various times of day and night, and throughout the seasons. You will develop a sense of familiarity and deep understanding that is earned through prolonged contact just like you experience with long-standing friendships. And special places can be as precious to you, in their own way, as longtime friends.

"It is essential to experience all the times and moods of one good place."
Thomas Merton

Activity Seventy-Eight ➤Your Special Places

Where are your favorite places? Ask yourself the following questions about each place: What are the salient natural features of this landscape? What is it about this place that makes it special? What draws you to it? Is there a story linked to this place? Select one of your special places to visit regularly for meditation and communing with nature.

"Living in place is something that takes practice. Practice . . . means doing it, and doing it a lot of times. There is no substitute for that . . . Getting intimate with nature and knowing our own wild nature is a matter of going face to face many times."
Gary Snyder, in *Talking on the Water*

Guidelines for exploring sacred places:

1. Become aware of the local landscape, the qualities of the local surroundings, the flora and fauna that live there.
2. Learn the stories of the place, the legends, myths, and local history.
3. Visit places already recognized as sacred.
4. Open yourself to the sacred sense of a place. The Exploring Attractions Activity in Chapter 7, p. 227 is most helpful. See if you can sense some of the qualities of sacred places mentioned in this chapter.
5. Meditate and pray there.
6. Visit places you are drawn to many times at different times of the year.

RESOURCES:

James Harper *The Atlas of Sacred Places* (Henry Holt & Co. 1994)
Covers 33 sites around the globe arranged according to five types: (1) places associated with saints, gurus, spiritual teachers, (2) burial places, (3) shrines that evoke images of distant or mythic past, (4) temples to the glory of God, and (5) sites of pilgrimage. Includes location maps, practical gazetteer with suggestions for visiting, color photographs, along with background and history of each site.

Martin Gray *Places of Peace and Power*
website: www.sacredsites.com

Sacred Time

Ritual opens the gates to sacred time, the time that touches on eternity. We leave ordinary clock time behind and enter into the eternal now. Sacred times are revealed through the rhythms of the cosmos. The sacred is most powerfully available to us during times of transition—sunrise, sunset, midday, phases of the moon, and solstices. These insertions of sacred time are linked together in cycles, repeated every day, every Sabbath, every season, every year.

Some people take exception to the idea that some times are more sacred than others. They believe that all times are equally sacred, equally pregnant with holiness. Religious experiences, if we open ourselves to them, can strike at any moment. The eternal now is forever present if we can but find the doorway and cross the threshold. On the other hand, epiphanies may function like lightning. Perhaps, at certain times and under certain conditions, nature is much more likely to strike us with an epiphany. What is your experience of sacred time?

All cultures have cyclical seasons, years and eras for demarking periods of time. Everyone experiences periods of time coming to an end followed by new beginnings. They're commonly linked to the longest and shortest days of the year, the midsummer and midwinter solstices, and the days of equal length, the Spring and Autumn equinoxes.

Seasonal festivals connect communities to the rhythms of the earth through common participation in ritual ceremonies linked to changes in weather and vegetation, such as times for planting and harvesting in agrarian societies, and animal migrations in herding societies. Cultures maintain meaning and significance for their people by providing a map for traveling in time. Communities orient themselves in time by linking decisive historical events, myths, religious traditions, and folk customs to the natural world and its seasons. The birth, life, death, and resurrection of the god(s) of a culture are associated with and observed during winter, spring, summer, and fall seasonal celebrations. Festivals act as lodgings for travelers making their way through the seasons of the year. They provide opportunities for both rest from daily toils and joyous celebration. The festival cycle answers the human need for periodic purifications, regeneration, creation, re-balancing, and renewal.

Rituals also link people to the past, their ancestors and their origins. They root people in time. By participating in ritual enactments of their creation myths people bring these original events into their present experience. They remember and embody these events through re-enactment. Rituals of remembrance help us revive and relive special times, they link us to our heritage, and to the stories that put our lives in a context that make them meaningful and significant. In order to continue to play a meaningful role in guiding our lives, these traditional myths and stories must relate to the realities of our current circumstances.

In addition to connecting us to the past, meaningful rituals point the way for us as we navigate into the future. They provide us with a role to play, a mission in life. Orienting us in time and place, they give our lives meaning and purpose.

When the old beliefs and ways make no sense in the modern world of today, when the map no longer fits the territory, rituals lose their power and significance. To be alive and relevant, myths and rituals must be experienced by participants as meaningful. They must link their ancient traditions with creative visions for the future that intersect through the current lives of the people in their community. These common myths and rituals provide communities with a common mission, creating the glue which holds a community together.

Do your current rituals anchor you in time in ways that give you meaning and purpose? Do they connect you with the daily and seasonal rhythms of the earth? Do they provide you with periodic rejuvenation and renewal? The following guidelines will help you explore and enhance your participation in the sacred dimension of time.

Guidelines for Exploring Sacred Time:

1. Become aware of the seasonal cycles of your place. Explore what changes in weather, flora and fauna signal the changing of the seasons.
2. Learn about the customary seasonal celebrations that have been traditionally practiced in your area.
3. Set aside time to explore your experience and to practice sacred ritual at the times commonly considered as sacred: sunrise, sunset, solstices, etc.
4. Open yourself to the sacred sensing of time. Seize the moment by praying and meditating when you sense the time is ripe, no matter what the time of day or year.
5. Visit a sacred place regularly at different times of day, month, and year to develop a sense of how these different times tend to evoke different kinds of experiences. See how the living conditions of a habitat change along with these natural cycles of nature.

Ceremonial Rituals in Nature

For the religious person nature is never reduced to the merely physical, it has symbolic meaning as well. A ritual is a chain of symbolic acts performed in a setting of symbolic conditions. These ceremonial behaviors function to make concrete and experiential the mythic values of a society. Ritual is the enactment of myth. Ritual is the wellspring; myth, the container. Our daily lives are informed, infused with ultimate meaning and significance by linking the stories of our personal lives with our most grand living myth, the greatest story ever told. Our great stories and myths are filled with wisdom, in which the ageless mysteries of beauty, truth, and goodness are penetrated and revealed. They provide a "sublime frame" to the great events of human life such as birth, marriage, and death.

Living myths breath new life into us by connecting us with the Source of Life. They create religious experience, communing with the divine. Creation myths help us remember our origins. They penetrate the mystery of why anything exists at all.

All ritual is communication speaking to us in mind, body, and spirit by means of words, sights, sounds, smells, gestures, movement, and touch. Rituals are formed by weaving together these ingredients:

Special words: prayers, special poems, readings from sacred texts, responsive readings, mantras, mythic stories.

Special sounds: music, songs, chants, rhythms of drums & rattles, entering
  into silence for meditation.

Special postures and gestures: kneeling, yoga postures, mudras (symbolic
  positioning of the hands), sitting or walking meditation, counting prayers
  with rosary beads, making the sign of the cross.

Special acts: dancing, lighting candles, prostrations, communion, feasting,
  fasting, cleansings and purifications.

Special sights: icons, paintings, sand paintings, sculptures, mandalas.

Special smells: incense, flowers.

Let's probe the nighttime shadows and echoes from rituals past that linked
our ancestors to their natural surroundings. Imagine yourself a member of a small
tribal group gathered in a circle around a campfire sharing a meal. For awhile,
people simply sit in silence and gaze into the dancing flames of the fire. The
night sky fills with stars and the air with smells of burning wood. Out of the
surrounding darkness come the sounds of the night. Crickets, wolves, coyotes,
and frogs provide nature's familiar background music, punctuated by the
crackling of the fire at the center. You draw close to the fire and other warm
bodies for protection from the cold. You share with each other the stories of the
day. Reminded by today's current events, your respected elders weave in the
heroic legendary tales of your ancestors and stories of your gods and nature
spirits. Your story, today's stories, your group's favorite stories from yesterday
and days gone by, make you a witness to the living history of an oral tradition
that links your group's today with the mythic origins of their very first day.
These stories tell of your group's special relationship to the mountains, streams,
and animals that are part of your daily lives. A talking stick is passed around,
held by each person desiring to speak uninterrupted from the heart. You join in
the singing of songs. If this is a ceremonial night, there will be drumming,
chanting and dancing long into the night. And if this is a very special occasion,
the gods themselves, some in the form of animals, will make their appearances,
speaking out from behind the sacred masks of your tribe.

This idealized characterization is not far removed from what anthropologists
describe as our common heritage, from our not-so-distant indigenous past. Yet
many of these traditional practices will become lost to us forever when the last of
the tradition-holding elders pass on. What remains for most of us? The
occasional modern day campout rituals of weenie and marshmallow roasts with
singing around the campfire. Enjoyed by many, campfires have become so
tangential to our daily lives, especially when compared to the community
bonding maintained around them night after night for the vast majority of human
existence. Most of our nights are spent indoors. Instead of gazing into the fire, we
look at television screens. Television programming replaces the myths and

stories of our elders. Instead of group singing and chanting, we listen to the stereo. Instead of actively participating, we are passively entertained. Dancing has been moved from the hearth to urban nightspots, hardly natural settings. Are these modern nighttime rituals serving us well?

Replicating these rituals of indigenous oral traditions is neither feasible nor desirable. By creatively reincorporating what is essentially worth salvaging, we can establish rituals that once again reconnect us with nature. For example, people are creating group ceremonies to celebrate the solstices and equinoxes.

A tremendous wealth of knowledge from a variety of religious traditions is available for developing sacred ceremonies. We have a much broader knowledge base than ever before to guide us in the cultivation of our ritual gardens. The ideas and guidelines that follow will help you. Ceremonies involve moving through stages which call for different kinds of rituals.

Rituals for the Stages of Ceremony

Preparatory Rituals: Cleansing which may involve both the participants and the ritual site: smudging (in smoke) or baptising (in water), fasting, putting on special clothes, preparing the altar.

Rituals of Approach: Crossing the threshold(s) into the sacred. Through "gestures of approach" preparing to pass through a door from the profane to the sacred, such as bowing, prostrating, removing shoes, processional entry.

Invocation Rituals: Beginning. Entering sacred time and sacred space. For connecting with nature, the place of worship might be taking your place in a cathedral of old growth trees, on a mountain peak, or other special natural setting. The call to worship might be signaled by the sounding of bell, gong, shofar, conch shell, or the lighting of candles.

Enactment Rituals: Middle. Content & Substance. The main theme, story or event that forms the juicy content. The focus of the ritual celebration. What is to be re-membered.

Benediction Rituals: Ending. The closing of the ritual event which signals the return from sacred time and space. Putting out of candles for example.

Return Rituals: Crossing the threshold(s) in reverse from the sacred back into the profane. For example, putting your shoes back on, a recessional leaving of the sacred space.

Having likened this book to a cookbook already, using a bread-baking analogy seems only fitting: Preparation: cleaning & organizing of the kitchen, utensils, recipe, etc. Approach: Moving to the kitchen doorway with apron on and clean hands, ready to go when it's time to cook. Beginning Invocations:

Activating the yeast that enables the bread to rise. Middle: Kneading the ingredients together and baking. Ending: Taking the bread out of the oven. Turning off the oven. Return: leaving the kitchen. If the ritual service was good, you leave with some great soul food to nourish you until it's time to cook again. I know a local minister who made his weekly baking of bread into a ritual enactment of his spiritual practice, a living metaphor, yielding much more than just food for his family.

Guidelines for Creating Personally Meaningful Rituals

1. Probe your personal depths. Seek clarity in posing the question or identifying the issues that are centrally active in your current life situation.
2. Come up with the imagery and symbols that capture the issues, questions, a unifying theme. This central metaphor serves as the guiding form for the creation of the ritual. A clear metaphor that comes out of your gut helps ensure a personally meaningful and juicy ritual with transforming power.
3. Start making connections with how you might best express what this metaphor is about in action.
4. Weave together a series of interrelated ritual acts with a beginning, middle, and end.

To continue the bread-baking analogy, the steps outlined above are to help you develop your own recipe for creating a nutritious and delicious loaf of bread that would best feed your spiritual appetite. The guidelines below may give you some sense of what kinds of recipes are available or might be created that would best meet your needs.

Guidelines for Tailoring Your Ritual

1. **Simple vs. Complex:** You may prefer a Quaker type service with no icons or liturgy, what Quakers call an "absence of forms" except for "a few adventitious aids to devotion." This minimalist approach helps ensure that every outward word and act is a genuine expression of an inward state. You simply enter into sacred silence, opening yourself to the direct spontaneous expression of Life within. Little or no ritual may be your preference. On the other hand rituals can be elaborate, aesthetically rich experiences bringing together music, dance, drama, special dress, mask-making, incorporating the best of the decorative and performing arts. You can create a context of refulgent beauty, artistic inspiration at its best, a rich plethora of devotional aids: incense, icons,

sacred objects, inspirational words, group prayer, chanting, singing, responsive readings, dance, telling of sacred myths, and so on. Your preference for simple or complex may vary depending on the kind of celebration, people participating, and setting.

2. **Private Devotions vs. Public Worship:** Are you seeking individual inspiration (fasting, private prayer, meditation) or the creation of a communal experience which bonds people together (communion, baptism, circle dancing, marriage, induction, initiation). Healthy group ritual affirms the common patterns, values, shared joys, risks, sorrows, and changes that bind a community together. Private devotions clarify your unique mission and path and strengthen your personal inspiration and resolve to actualize what you have been called to do. Ritual events may include both, shifting back and forth between individual and collective forms of worship.

3. **Rejuvenation vs. Challenge:** Are you being called to rest in the valley or climb a mountain? Are you seeking rejuvenation and nurturance or the strengthening of your character through the discipline of meeting a challenge? Tailoring your rituals for the right amount of challenge parallels tailoring the nature activities in this book (which are little rituals in themselves). Failure to tailor rituals appropriately can cause rituals to misfire in two ways: (1) When the power of the ritual and nature's energy overwhelm the participants. The safe container provided by the structured events breaks. In its most extreme form, ecstatic celebration spills over into individual or group psychosis. (2) When the rite fails to capture the needed forces of nature to revitalize the participants. The container remains empty and the ritual is a flop. In designing a ritual occasion, seek the balance of rejuvenation and challenge that is right for you and your circumstance, neither empty nor overwhelming.

4. **Ecstasy vs. Serenity.** Is your inner feeling tone intensely directed outward towards a passionate expressive release? To what larger than myself may I surrender? Or is your direction inwardly moving to a deep peaceful sense of wholeness? Are you merging outwardly into nature or are you feeling the wholeness of your inner nature which contains and radiates with great light from the center of your being. Is your approach towards the excitement and stimulation, stoking up the fires of the body by singing, drumming, dancing, feasting, clapping, shouting? Or is it towards the soothing, slowing down of the nervous system through fasting, silent meditation, soft chanting, which leads you to the stillpoint

at the center of your being? Tailor your ritual to reflect your emerging inner state. Your ongoing ritual may have its own ebb and flow between these two poles of ecstatic release and inner peace.

Periodically, I go to a special place for rejuvenation. It's a day-trip, about a 1 1/2 hour drive each way. I usually arrive at midmorning and leave in the mid afternoon. Coincidentally, the sun shines in the river gorge where I go during these hours. Minimal preparation involves putting a towel, some sunscreen, journal, and lunch in a small knapsack. Sometimes I'll pick out a tape of some special music for the pilgrimage there and back.

The first threshold is a bridge over the stream, less than fifty yards from the trailhead. The solitude begins there. I often pause halfway across. From the bridge the trail becomes lush and green with a canopy of branches overhead. It's somewhat like entering a tunnel. I feel immersed in freshness, and I usually experience a magical luminescence to the many shades of green. Down the path a ways is a shallow cave nestled under a huge rock the size of a two-story building. One time I stopped there to grieve the death of one of my teachers. Further down the trail is the granddaddy tree. I stop to greet this wise elder with a pat or hug, pausing to admire his great height and girth.

The next transition occurs when the trail ends and the gorge begins. I begin to clamber over rocks and fallen trees as I move upstream. Big rocks abound and small waterfalls cascade into pools. I've visited when the water is a raging torrent in Spring and when the water gently cascades through a series of pools in the Fall.

My traditional destination is a special large flat rock, a perch that places me about ten feet above the flowing waters. From this vantage point, I can view the first fifty yards below where the stream enters the gorge. Upon arrival, if the weather is conducive to sun worshipping, I remove much more than my shoes. Each trip is different and the rituals unfold spontaneously. They often include, meditating, yoga, cleansing in the pools, journal writing, and most importantly taking in my surroundings: feeling the breeze on my skin, watching the leaves dance on the trees or spiral down in the Fall, listening to the splashing sounds of the stream, watching clouds drift overhead. Each visit brings encounters with a variety of wildlife: butterfly, water ouzel, osprey, red-tailed hawk, crow, duck, bumblebee, trout, river otter, centipede, spider, beetle, and ant. Then there are the ferns, mushrooms, lichens, mosses, and wildflowers. These co-participants mysteriously weave themselves into my outdoor service for rejuvenation. Much of the time, I feel like nature is the one putting on the service, and I am grateful to be able to attend.

These trips are usually simple rather than complex, for my private devotions, rejuvenation, and serenity. I keep them flexible and allow them to spontaneously unfold, instead of adopting a tight or formal structure. I've visited my special place in Spring, Summer, and Fall. Each time it's different with surprises I could never have anticipated. And each time I return feeling revitalized and deeply blessed.

Spontaneous Ritual

"There is something in us that transcends us. This is the same something that beckons to us from nature. It is the call of the wild to spiritual wholeness. The Self calls the ego through nature."
David Richo, *Unexpected Miracles*

Sometimes we are called unannounced into the sacred. The moment seizes us, and we are blessed with an epiphany. On other occasions, with minimal preplanning, we easily drop into the sacred by simply showing up for a sunrise, by saying the prayers and songs that come to mind at the time, and finishing when we feel complete. Sometimes, by the grace of God, we are delivered up an unexpected surprise, like coming around a bend on the path and finding wild berries ripe and ready for picking. When we recognize a good opportunity, we can seize the moment. I find it challenging to be open to life's sacred moments, to restrain from filling my life up with busyness that leaves no room for these gifts of grace. The next chapter explores the nature of these religious experiences and how to cultivate them.

14

Opening to Peak Experiences

"I remember the night, and almost the very spot on the hilltop, where my soul opened out into the Infinite, and there was a rushing together of the two worlds, the inner and the outer. It was deep calling unto deep— the deep that my own struggle had opened up within being answered by the unfathomable deep without, reaching beyond the stars. I stood alone with Him who had made me, and all the beauty of the world, and love, and sorrow, and even temptation. I did not seek Him, but felt the perfect unison of my spirit with His. The ordinary sense of things around me faded. For the moment nothing but an ineffable joy and exultation remained. It is impossible fully to describe the experience. It was like the effect of some great orchestra when all the separate notes have melted into one swelling harmony that leaves the listener conscious of nothing save that his soul is being wafted upwards, and almost bursting with its own emotion. The perfect stillness of the night was thrilled by a more solemn silence. The darkness held a presence that was all the more felt because it was not seen. I could not anymore have doubted that He was there than that I was. Indeed, I felt myself to be, if possible, the less real of the two."

from **William James**, *The Varieties of Religious Experience.* (p.66)

People throughout the ages have broken through their everyday mundane experience of the world to experience the underlying unity between themselves and nature-as-a-whole. Jung's description of his experiences of merging with nature is a case in point, "At times I feel as if I am spread out over the landscape and inside things, and am myself living in every tree, in the splashing of the waves, in the clouds and the animals that come and go, in the procession of the seasons." A mystical "oceanic feeling" accompanies the flowing together of the person and the world into a single unbounded whole. This merging of self and other, gestaltists call *confluence*.   And, depending on the person and the circumstances, it can be the source of an authentic revelation, a pathological disturbance, or both. Anthropologist Levi Bruhl called this sense of belonging to the underlying and animating energy of all finite things—whether it be trees, birds, animals, grass, sky, or insects—*participation mystique*. Ecstasy literally means the state of being outside oneself, a sense of being a part of a moving reality that is greater than the self. Ecstatic identification involves an extension of the ego boundaries, a dissolving or birth into a wider consciousness of the great oneness of all life.

This empathic extension of the boundaries of self is the path of love. Ultimately, in their most ecstatic form, these experiences involve mystical identification with God, with the sacred, with what abides. Every festival of rejoicing and thanksgiving includes elements of the ecstatic.

Here are some common characteristics of peak experiences:

- A feeling of merging, belonging, unity or oneness with one's surroundings or even all of creation.
- A sense of some ultimate meaning, reality, or truth being revealed.
- Ordinary time and space seem to dissolve as one becomes so fully present in the moment that one seems to touch the eternal.
- A sense of sacredness or divine presence.
- The impossibility of describing the experience in words.
- Resolution or understanding of opposites or paradoxes.
- Feelings of blessedness, joy, ecstasy, serenity.

"As we go through life, we tune ourselves to our surroundings in a modulating flow of focus. Sometimes we are completely wrapped up in our inner world of thoughts. Later we may be directed outwards, unthinkingly absorbed in fascinated observation of external events.

The mode which we call sacred is one where inner focus and outer focus are balanced and blended, where there is a reciprocal mirroring of idea and sentiment from within and imagery and sensation from without.

It is a waking trance state, ripe with knowledge. This knowledge seems to come to us from a wise source which calls us home."

Fredric Lehrman, *Sacred Landscape*

The rediscovery of the spiritual, the "holy" in nature involves an opening out to that which is beyond us. Buber called this opening out hallowing. I'm continually amazed by how easily we become preoccupied, closed down in ways that keep us oblivious to some of the most dramatic grandeur that nature has to offer, not to mention the ordinary miracles of daily life. Tragically, many a fantastic sunset or rainbow goes unnoticed. Or we get so concerned with taking a good photograph that we forget to really experience the power and beauty of nature's spectacular sites. I remember a rushing parent dragging a child away from one of the spectacular viewpoints at Crater Lake National Park saying, "We'll be able to see it on our slides when we get home." Another opportunity for intimate dialogue with nature missed. The picture of Crater Lake on the menu replaces the meal.

Yet, most of you, on at least a few occasions, have experienced those special times when you lose your self-consciousness and become completely absorbed in experiencing your natural surroundings. This letting go of self-absorption, of dropping barriers of self-interest, this self-forgetting leads you to entering into your experiences so fully that you gain the sense of becoming one with what you are experiencing.

Most often, however, our frame of mind is the barrier that keeps us from noticing nature's epiphanies. We easily slip into a frame of mind that makes for dullness rather than for vibrancy. Nature is not dull. It is overflowing with wonderful opportunities. The ordinary is more sensational than what we imagine it to be. Ralph Waldo Emerson reminds us of how we take life for granted, losing our sense for the tremendous mystery before us, "If the stars should appear one night in a thousand years, how would men believe and adore!"

The activities throughout this book serve as gateways for us to leave our habitually dull modes of consciousness and enter into a more open and receptive state for discovering nature's inspirational gifts of wisdom and beauty. The activities in this chapter will help you cultivate peak experiences in nature.

Barriers to Peak Experiences

Why are these experiences so rare? The gates for entering into these ecstatic experiences may be concealed by dark shadows. In these dark shadows often lurk the monsters of our deepest fears.

In a world emphasizing rational self-control, people fear entering into the "wilder-ness" of powerful emotions. Things might get out of hand, too wild. On the verge of powerful feelings, clients will often say to me, "I don't want to lose it." At a local engineering firm they call it "going non-linear." Surrendering to the emerging experience and letting go of any attempt to control what will happen is a barrier for many. People fear being overwhelmed with feelings and developed strategies to avoid it. As a spiritual teacher of mine, Rabbi Shlomo Carlebach once told me, "One way to avoid the flood of feeling is to structure our time." Passion is both desired and feared.

For the passionate, there is agony as well as ecstasy. Life has not been arranged so that we can choose to have only pleasurable feelings. To reach joy, a price of admission must sometimes be paid. People may first have to plunge into the depths of their fear, guilt, and remorse, bottoming out before rising up into feelings of joy and ecstasy. Widespread suffering is a reality that must be faced by all seekers regardless of creed. The good news is that there is a gateway to heaven. The bad news is there is sometimes a kind of hell to pay as part of the price of admission. One may indeed have to pass through the valley of the shadow of death in order to dwell in the house of the Lord.

How do we gain the courage to face these fears, our fears of loss of control, of being overwhelmed by feeling, of facing our pain and the sufferings of the world? Rabbi Shlomo Carlebach would say, "It is the smell of paradise that gives us strength." I believe that inside each of us is a deep longing and desire to re-member our paradise lost.

Remembering peak experiences, past tastes of paradise, can activate our hunger for more. An internal state of readiness is created that is otherwise lacking when our peak experiences remain forgotten relics of the past.

Activity Seventy-Nine ➤ Remembering Peak Experiences

Begin with a tuning your organism activity from Chapter 3. As you relax and settle in, briefly remember just enough to identify some of your most joyful experiences in nature. Which ones were especially powerful or profound for you? Select one that you are drawn to at this moment. Then bring it to mind. Close your eyes and recall the particulars of your experience, bringing them into your imagination, your mind's eye. Where are you? What are you wearing? What is the weather like? The colors in the sky and surroundings? Remember particular smells . . . , sights . . . , feelings you are having . . . As you recall these details, enter into a scene from this experience as if it were happening now, reliving it as best you can as a vivid daydream. When you finish your reliving experience, examine what messages this experience has for you today.

Nature as Catalyst for Peak Experiences

"For those who have a religious experience all nature is capable of revealing itself as cosmic sacrality."
Mircea Eliade, *The Sacred and the Profane*

Nature is a powerful catalyst for peak experiences. When we let in nature's primal vitality, we cannot help but be moved. Research studies of accounts of peak experiences consistently find nature to be the most common setting. (Alister Hardy in *The Spiritual Nature of Man: A Study of Contemporary Religious Experience*, Oxford Univ. Press 1979, p.1, cites studies by Wuthnow 1978; Greeley 1974; Keutzer 1978) What are these nature-induced peak experiences like?

"One day, in youth, at sunrise, sitting in the ruins of a castle and again in the mountains, under the noonday sun, lying at the toot of a tree and visited by three butterflies; one more at night upon the shigly shore of the ocean, my back upon the sand and my vision ranging through the milky way;—such grand and spacious, immortal, cosmogenic reveries, when one reaches to the stars! Moments divine, ecstatic hours; in which our thought flies from world to world, pierces the great enigma, breathes with a respiration broad, tranquil, and deep as the respiration of the ocean, serene and limitless as the blue firmament; . . . instants of irresistible intuition in which one feels one's self great as the universe, and calm as a god . . . What hours, what memories! The vestiges they leave behind are enough to fill us with belief and enthusiasm, as if they were visits of the Holy Ghost."
from **William James,** *The Varieties of Religious Experience.*

We may feel dwarfed in the presence of whales, giant redwoods, and the starry skies. These are important experience for us to have at the hands of nature, to help us recognize that we're not the sole stars of the show. Humbling experiences break us out of the egocentric and anthropocentric self-preoccupations that isolate us. They enlarge our perspective. Most importantly they introduce awe and wonder into our lives which are primary generators of spiritual and religious experiences. The powers of nature can cause feelings of ecstasy that we'll never get watching television. Nature's powers command our attention and respect. These experiences of nature can take hold of us in ways that cause us to change our ways, sometimes subtly, sometimes dramatically.

The most grand and magnificent in nature is not always what breaks through to touch us in powerful ways. Author J. Welwood explains how the ordinary can become the occasion for a peak experience, "In such moments, we may become aware of a sharpness or luminosity in our experience of the world—a leaf stands out as bright, green, 'leafy,' in a new way which is, at the same time, 'nothing new,' completely ordinary. Obviously a leaf is still a leaf, as it always has been, but the depth of our openness to experience has changed. In these 'little awakenings' we catch a fleeting glimpse of how we are fundamentally not separate from the whole of life. We discover the world in ourselves, and ourselves in the world." J. Welwood (Ed) *The Meeting of the ways: Explorations in East/West Psychology* (Schocken Books 1979) In the words of Martin Buber, "Every particular *thou* is a glimpse through to the eternal *Thou*."

Contacting Spirit

> *"God is the breath inside the breath."*
> **Kabir**

Spirit is the animating or vital principle, that which gives life to the physical organism in contrast to its purely material elements. To be born is to begin to breathe on your own. To be alive is to breathe. To expire, to cease breathing, is to die. The mysteries of life and death can be directly experienced through contact with your own breathing. To be inspired is to take in the breath of life. For centuries, meditation, yoga, and religious practices throughout the world, have focused on breathing as a spiritual discipline, as a vehicle for religious experience. Your breath tells you that you are filled with the spirit of life. The rhythm of inspiration and expiration can be used to open the boundaries of the self and one's compassion for life.

Activity Eighty ➤ Inspirational Breathing

Sit quietly in a quiet place. Relax and slow down. Begin by paying attention to your breathing. Follow the air as it flows in and out of your body, in and out through your nostrils. Feel the temperature of the air. Listen to the sounds of your breathing. Pay attention to each inhalation and exhalation. When your mind wanders, simply bring your attention back to your breathing. After settling in comfortably to the rhythm of your breathing, add this simple private liturgy. As you inhale, know that you are taking in the gift of life. You are taking in the life-giving energies of the world into yourself. With gratitude, receive the life-giving oxygen into every cell of your body. As you exhale, give your care back into the world. Allowing, surrendering, letting go. With compassion, you are giving back to the world. Allow yourself to experience this rhythm of give and take that moves through you. As you continue to focus on your breathing, say to yourself as you breathe in, "I receive with gratitude." and as you breathe out, "I give back with compassion." Taking in and giving back. Inhale with gratitude. Exhale with compassion. This is your life-giving exchange with the world. Continue this silent mantra for the period of meditation that seems right for you on this particular occasion.*

> *"A human being is part of a whole, called by us the 'Universe,' a part limited in time and space. He experiences himself, his thoughts and feelings, as something separated from the rest—a kind of optical delusion of his consciousness. This delusion is a kind of prison for us, restricting us to our personal desires and to affection for a few persons nearest us. Our task must be to free ourselves from this prison by widening our circle of compassion to embrace all living creatures and the whole of nature in its beauty."*

> **Albert Einstein**

When in dialogue with nature, we can have powerful moments of insight and illumination. This happens when the I-Thou mode of being becomes so dominant that we become totally immersed in the experience. These consummate moments are powerful confirmations of our faith in the possibility of integration and wholeness, a confirmation of the healing process by which one can restore one's relation to the world. The meaning of human existence is revealed, even if it's

---

* Adapted from Sam Keen *Hymns to An Unknown God* pp. 144-45

only a glimpse. In these moments of being totally absorbed with another, we are put in profound contact with our own basic humanity and the nature of *Being*. We experience being part of the whole. Our *being* merges with *Being*.

The I-Boundary Expansion Activity below invites this "widening of our circle of compassion" experience.

Activity Eighty-One ➢ I-Boundary Expansion

This activity invites you to expand your I-boundaries. First you need to find a special place in nature; one that has some beautiful attractions for you over a wide range of distances, from the close-in, at-your-feet distance, to the middle range distances, and continuing out to a far-reaching panoramic view. Find the particular spot within this special place that attracts you most and where you can sit comfortably for this nature meditation activity. Either sitting or standing erect, ground yourself to your spot. Sense the ground firmly supporting you. Next, do the Centering Activity on page. When you feel calm, relaxed, centered, and alert, then extend your awareness just beyond your body to your most immediate surroundings. You might begin by silently repeating to yourself the "Now, I'm aware of . . . " phrase to help you focus. Notice the nearby rocks, grass, flowers, insects, and nature's activities at close range. Let your awareness freely drift until you notice something standing out strongly in your awareness or something that you return to again, something to which your awareness is especially drawn. Continue to focus your awareness and become more fully aware of the many aspects of this object. What is it like? . . . What are its characteristics? . . . What does it do? . . . Take time to discover more details about it. What is its color? texture? smell? motion? sound? size? How does it fit in with its surroundings? As you continue to explore more deeply see if you can allow yourself to become empathically attuned and identify with it in such a way that you feel yourself closing the distance, resonating with, even melting into it. Explore how intimately connected you can feel with it. See if you can experience yourself entering into what you see and sense. Do not judge yourself if you don't think you are getting very far. Any relaxed sense of expansion and connection is progress to celebrate and build on. When your mind wanders, gently bring it back to what's before you.

Let your awareness naturally move on to the next object of attraction that is a little further away. Again explore and allow yourself to empathically identify with what you are experiencing. Feel yourself in the trees. Feel yourself in the birds. Feel yourself in every sound, and movement of nature. Continue to stay with your present awareness as it moves to natural attractions at gradually increasing distances until you reach the panoramic view and the sky on the distant horizon. See if your identifications can build on one another so you continue to feel connected with everything from the most close to the most distant. See how much you can experience yourself in nature and nature in you. Continue to explore and drink it all in until you feel full and complete. Then gently close your eyes and savor the afterglow of this experience. To what extent are you feeling oneness with life?

Peak experiences occur in a great diversity of forms. Your peak experiences are uniquely yours and may differ greatly from mine. I conclude this chapter with an attempt to describe one of my own, adapted from my journal.

Friday morning, May 23, 1995. I'm up to greet the sunrise, sitting in meditation atop a big rock at the peak of a granite rock pile. I'm facing East looking over a wide expansive vista across the Owens Valley, 3000 feet below, toward the rising sun. The beautiful snow-covered peaks of the Sierra Nevada rise behind me.

Ever changing, without interruption, gradually shifting shades, hues, forms, tones, colors, shapes, patterns, I become entranced by the beauty of a sunrise in motion. I am drawn further and further into the sunrise as I continue to absorb one of nature's glorious displays. A grand symphony for all my senses penetrates inward to my core. I slowly inhale the cool, fresh life-giving air in one marvelously smooth inhalation. As sensations flow in through every pore, the depths "within me" flood with feeling.

With my next breath, this beautiful panoramic scene transforms into an even more glorious display. The wind stirs up little droplets of morning dew which, reflecting the light of the newly rising sun, appear as dancing diamonds. Dozens become hundreds . . . become thousands . . . Up close, they streak across my field of vision like subatomic particles, little comets of cosmic energy wildly swirling about.

I feel like a sponge mysteriously filling simultaneously from inside-out and outside-in with countless dancing sparkling dewdrops of energy. This implosion of the ever-increasing intensity of uncontainable excitement rebounds outward. I am brought to me feet, arms outstretched to receive. My sponge runneth over with gratitude. Like a gently exploding star of flowing expansiveness I am catapulted into the beyond. Sparkling. Sparkling World. Sparkling me. Sparkling Dance. Sparkling. Dispersion enfolds into immersion. As I exhale, I float into a kind of suspended animation, slipping into a stillpoint amidst this whirling ecstatic dance. Enveloped, held in nature's sublime embrace, I rest in a most vibrant peace. Stillness in sparkling.

Gradually, as the silver dance dissipates, like waking up from a dream, I am drawn back into the particulars of this beautiful place in their more familiar form. A bird singing, the chill of the cold on my face, . . . The passing of time returns as my attention wanders across the landscape, landing here, then there. Joyfully, gratefully, I emerge back into this worldly dance with an overflowing heart, still reverberating in my connection with the oneness of it all. I feel incredibly alive, every cell of my body pulsating with this energy. I must have a special sparkle in my eye.

15

Retreats, Walkabouts, Pilgrimages, and Vision Quests

"If people are willing to give themselves the gift of some improvement in their life, there is nothing that can beat having a deep and prolonged contact with nature."

Roger Payne, in *Talking on the Water*

"At the gates of the forest, the surprised man of the world is forced to leave his city estimates of great and small, wise and foolish. The knapsack of custom falls off his back . . . Here we find Nature to be the circumstances which dwarfs every other circumstance, and judges like a god all men that come to her. We have crept out of our close and crowded houses into the night and morning, and we see what majestic beauties daily wrap us in their bosom . . . The anciently reported spells of these places creep on us."

Raph Waldo Emerson, *Nature*

This chapter covers the prescribing and ingesting of large doses of nature over extended periods of time. When we're immersed in the natural world, the clutter and complexities, the demands and interruptions, the noise and distractions of a landscape dominated by modern culture are left behind. The indoor world of artificial light, the air conditioning, and the glass and cement that separate you from nature are out of the way. Instead of gardens, you encounter wildflowers. You enter the territory not of neighborhood cats and dogs, caged parakeets, nor the fenced in fields where sheep and cattle graze, but the territory of deer, bear, mountain lion, and eagle. You enter the outdoor world that inspired Thoreau and Muir. Exposure to nature in these wilder places provides a special chemistry for experiencing. Extended stays in nature offer great opportunities to simplify, to leave the cultural baggage behind; no phones, no jobs, no house maintenance, no schedules. These extended stays in nature come in many forms including retreats, walkabouts, pilgrimages, and vision quests.

Retreats

> *"In actualizing one's self, one's aspirations, ideals, and interests, it is often necessary to retreat from the world."*
> **Clark Moustakas**

A retreat helps us let go because of distance, because out-of-sight supports out-of-mind. Also, nature's rhythms are much more soothing than downtown megalopolis. Nature often invites solitude and serenity. We take ourselves out of the pressure and strain of our daily lives. Who are you when stripped of your cultural roles? When there is no one around to please but you? When there are no schedules to follow? No money to make? From a distance, we can examine the family and cultural forces that shape us. We can discover and examine previously unquestioned cultural rules and practices that cause us inner conflict and pain. What natural parts of yourself were squelched in your training to adapt to the culture? From outside the rat-race mazes of our daily lives, we can stop and get an overview. Retreats are not for sticking our heads in the sand, but for looking down on our lives from the mountaintop. By distancing ourselves from the particular urgencies of our lives, we gain perspective. We are not simply running away from our responsibilities in the so-called real world. This is not a cowardly retreat from the battlefields of life, but rather a purposeful disengagement. It takes courage to face honestly the big picture of our lives.

Retreats often involve taking refuge, going to a place of shelter and comfort for restoration and rejuvenation. Unlike a call to action, taking refuge is a call to rest and being. When tired, frightened, lonely, or stressed, we naturally seek out something that promises us comfort and renewed strength. Some of the things we commonly attempt to take refuge in can be misguided and unhealthy. We take refuge in mindless zoning out in front of the television, snacking on junk food, numbing out with drugs, and other forms of escape. Healthy forms of taking refuge are not to be confused with these avoidance tactics. Healthy retreats reconnect us with the positive resources within and without. They involve saying "yes" not "no" to life.

The wide open spaces of the outdoors, rather than the tight space of office or apartment, and the wide expanse of time created by not having to adhere to a tight schedule nor cope with a myriad of phonecalls and other interruptions, set us free. An open environment opens us up.

On the other hand, when healing is your primary concern, a nurturing nestlike setting might be best, a retreat center which provides food, lodging, hot springs, massages, creature comforts, and lots of tender loving care. Keep your unique needs in mind when choosing your destination, whether a retreat center, campground, or more remote wilderness setting.

Activity Eighty-Two ➤ Knowing Your Place of Refuge

When you were a child, did you have a special place in your backyard, nearby park or woods, perhaps a treehouse, hideout, or a spot by the creek where you would go when you needed relief from your life struggles? Did you have a secluded place to go to when you wanted to be alone? What was your childhood refuge like? What made it special for you? What did you do there? Do you have a place like that now? If not, imagine a refuge that would be ideal for you at this point in your life. Why not seek out such a place to have as a resource when you need a time out from life's activities?

Unburdening

On these excursions, you can find out how little cultural baggage you really need. Unburdening physically supports unburdening psychologically. Beware of the tendency to carry too much stuff. With so many gadgets and gear available these days, it's feasible to pack in showers, computers, TV's, kitchen sink, and almost everything else imaginable. I've seen people, without the aid of pack animals, head down the trail for a weekend excursion looking like they were planning to spend a year or two, a thousand miles or more from civilization. I still remember a cartoon from childhood that shows a family with their car crammed full of gear getting ready to leave for a family camping trip. The husband is saying to the wife, "We're not getting away from it all, dear. We're taking it all with us."

Some excursions are designed to expose us to the elements and others are designed to provide sufficient creature comforts so that unnecessary suffering and distress do not dominate the experience. You can have gourmet meals or you can fast. This important planning decision of how much baggage to carry depends on you, your circumstances, and what you want from your excursion into nature. When you pack for an extended stay in nature, consider your decisions of what to take in the light of them being a metaphor for unburdening, simplifying, letting go of security blankets, for finding out about your own attachments to things.

RESOURCE:

Roger Housden, *Retreat: Time Apart for Silence & Solitude* (HarperCollins 1995)

Outlines a wide range of methods and approaches to the practice of retreats from a variety of traditions. Includes a chapter on "The Way of the Wilderness." Appendix includes a listing of retreat centers and contacts.

Non-Doing

Doing nothing in our modern world is often equated with wasting time, with not getting anything accomplished. For starters, we need to challenge this prejudice. Laziness has nothing to do with this approach to nature. Active experiencing, mindfulness, living fully is in sharp contrast to the sin of sloth. Life is embraced with empathy, not apathy. For avoiding these negative connotations, I like the term, "non-doing."

Remember, you are not going camping, boating, or fishing. Not filling the time with recreational or other types of activities is a challenge. There are so many ways to fill up your time: catching up on reading, preparing meals, messing with your gear, and on and on.

Some activities are more tricky to evaluate. Journal writing may plunge us deeper into the meaning of our experiencing of ourselves and nature, or it may distract us from it. Are we going to experience heaven or write about it? Nature photography also works both ways. It may lead us into a deeper connection with nature. In other instances, we may distance ourselves behind the lens, especially when focusing on the technical aspects of the picture taking.

Outwardly, doing and being may look the same. The critical difference is not so much in what you are doing but in how you are doing it. The Doing and Being

Activity in Chapter 2 helped you explore this difference. A subtle shift in approach, in attitude, in effort can make all the difference. You can dutifully do your meditation or you can drop into a meditative state of being. Crossing the threshold from busy doing into the serene expanse of being is hard enough, but maintaining it can be as difficult as being relaxed while balancing on a tightrope. The tricksters of restlessness, boredom, anxiety, worries, fears, loneliness, and other personal demons will come along and twang the rope. Other times, you will drop into being like a child curling up in Mother Nature's arms. Whether easy or difficult, the challenge is to minimize doing and maximize being.

Walkabouts

"With birth at one end and death at the other, we wander about, trying to make sense of our lives. If we can accept the wanderer in us, we will learn to love the holy fool whose wisdom is so valued and appreciated in Russia and in India. Venturing into the psyche's vast spaces and daring to explore the world around us, we can enter into a spiritual freedom and maturity that is as vast and boundless as the tundra. Wandering, we finally will discern, is really wondering at the glories of existence."

Linda Leonard, *Creations Heartbeat*

Participating in the activities in Chapter 2 and 7, you learned some guidelines for exploring nature by wandering about following your natural attractions and repulsions. Extended nature wanderings are called walkabouts. They can take many forms. Dreamwalk is a term used for the Australian Aborigines' walkabouts, while medicine walk refers to the Native Americans version. Some Native American vision quests begin with a medicine walk as a way to discover one's power spot. Celtic monks, believing that their faith would be purified by placing themselves completely in the hands of God's mercy, used to row out into the North Atlantic in small wooden framed boats without destination or provisions, and drift. As a result of these oceanic "driftabouts" (sic), some of the great monasteries of the Celtic world were built on windswept, wild islands like Iona in the Hebrides. Alan Watts, popularizer of Eastern Philosophy, advocated the value of non goal-directed travel. "The Chinese poets speak of wandering in the forest of one's thoughts, wandering in the great Void, of going along with streams and clouds and birds and not being in search of anything; it is good just to drift."

These wanderings can be planned for minutes, hours, days, or even months at a time. I've included here a daylong version.

Activity Eighty-Three ➤ Medicine Walk

This is a daylong, sunrise-to-sunset wandering. Prepare your knapsack with necessary items for safety, weather conditions, and terrain. This is a solo experience so make sure someone knows where you are going and when you will return. You may go with other buddies arranging a system for safety checks that will also protect your solitude. Consider a daylong fast. Arrive at the starting place just before sunrise and plan your return for just after sunset. If you do not know map and compass orienteering skills, play it safe, staying on or very near trails and close to familiar landmarks. Follow a spontaneous, intuitive course paying attention to your moment-to-moment attractions. Minimize planning so you can create this experience as you go at your own pace. You can travel inches or miles. Let nature be your teacher. What does nature have to say to you today about you and your life? Pay attention to nature's signs and symbols communicating to you about your life purpose, values, concerns, fears, loved ones. Note special places, encounters with plants and animals, the interaction between the weather and your mood, and incorporate variations from the other activities that fit for you on this particular occasion. However, guard against filling the time with activities. Keep it simple.*

Pilgrimages

> *"Pilgrimage is extroverted mysticism just as mysticism is introverted pilgrimage."*
>
> **Edith Turner**

Like retreats and walkabouts, going on a pilgrimage involves moving out of your normal structured existence, voluntarily dislocating yourself from daily routines and relationships. Unlike the retreat and other forms of travel, the pilgrimage has a sacred dimension involving a ritual journey to a holy place, a place where the human and divine meet. Pilgrims seek out the divine both for receiving blessings and for giving thanks.

---

* For another version of the "medicine walk," see Foster & Little's *Book of the Vision Quest*.

The pilgrimage has both an outward and inward dimension which support each other. Just as the external pilgrimage invites an inner journey, the inner pilgrimage invites expression in the outer environment. Inwardly, the pilgrim journeys to the center of self and inevitably becomes lost in the labyrinth of the complexities of one's personality and character structure. Just as the North Star serves as a fixed point in the sky to orient the traveler outwardly, inwardly an insight or myth helps guide the process. Outwardly and inwardly, the destination provides a sense of focus and direction for the pilgrim. To reach your destination is to arrive at a holy place that promises healing and renewal. Your self journeys to your Self where one's inner essence merges with the divine essence. On the spiritual plane, the pilgrimage represents a journey toward ultimate truth, higher consciousness, or God.

On the external physical plane, pilgrimages involve going to a holy land, visiting a sage or saint, or returning to a place of origin. Pilgrimages have a destination, whether it be a religious shrine, sacred cave or mountain; and the experience of the journey and the return are as important as being there. Many cultures include pilgrimages to springs, mountains, and caves as part of the process of honoring the passing of the seasons. The outward journey also supports the goal of finding the place in this world where you can be of service. The pilgrimage combines the inner journey to union with God with the outer journey of service to the community which are as integral to living a spiritually guided life as inhaling and exhaling are to breathing.

The outward landscape activates and mirrors the inner landscape of the psyche. When pilgrimages provide the challenge of a difficult journey over rugged terrain, they become ascetic in nature. Meeting this challenge promotes your spiritual ardor. The difficulty of the journey may be linked to the spiritual testing and achievement of merit for the pilgrims.

Pilgrimages may last as long as a typical vacation, for several months, or even an entire year. They may involve stopping at a number of way stations along the way. Pilgrimages may take the form of traveling around and toward a sacred center. This circumambulatory form, or *pradaksina*, is the characteristic form of Tibetan pilgrimage. (See Mountain Circumambulation Activity, p. 204)

Many tourist sites have a prehistory as sacred destinations for pilgrimages. Tourism may have its roots in pilgrimage, tourism being the secularized form that remains when the conscious spiritual intent of the journey has been lost. Pilgrims visit as an act of devotion. Tourists visit as spectators. While insensitive tourists detract from the sacred atmosphere of a place, sensitive tourists may be filled with a sense of awe even though the place visited is unrelated to their personal history, culture, or religious traditions.

While tourism now outstrips pilgrimage in worldwide popularity, pilgrimages remain very common throughout the world. For example, many thousands of Shintoist and Buddhist pilgrims climb Japan's Mt. Fuji each year. A small natural grotto with a spring located in Lourdes, France is currently the world's most frequently visited sacred site. Every year, millions upon millions of people all over the globe from many differing religious orientations travel to places like Mecca in the Middle East (Muslim), Ise in Japan (Shinto), Banaras in India (Hindu), Jerusalem in Israel (Christian, Jewish, and Muslim) and countless other less famous sacred sites. A 1957 compilation lists more than 1800 pilgrimage sites for the Hindu tradition alone.

Since antiquity, people have been drawn to riverbanks, mountain peaks, and desert shrines. Pilgrimages, Vision quests, and Rites of Passages have existed from time immemorial. Anthropologists speculate that these activities go back at least to the period of Paleolithic cave paintings over 17,000 years ago. These rites continue to exist today in a dazzling variety of forms in cultures all over the globe. They're so pervasively connected with our evolutionary history that some Jungian scholars claim that we're hard wired for these forms of activity just as we are for language. Allowing for the powerful influence of cultural conditioning which can support or repress it, pilgrimage may be a part of our evolutionary heritage much like migration is imprinted in other species.

As I write these words, I'm looking out over the Pacific Ocean watching a group of whales spouting off the coast at Newport, Oregon. Over the last decade, a number of migratory whales have decided to make this area their year-round home. The group has grown in size to over 250. Marine scientists are now trying to explain this change in behavior. While scientists study the mysteries of species moving about the earth, begin to explore your own experience of journeying and homecoming.

Guidelines for planning a pilgrimage

1. **Identify the theme(s) for your journey**. What is the reason for your journey? Are you seeking blessings or healing to handle suffering? Is thankfulness and celebration called for? How can the journey be an outward manifestation of your inward journey to the center of yourself?

2. **Identify your needs for traditional structures for support.** Do you want to go on a preplanned pilgrimage with a group of fellow pilgrims with a guide to lead the way? Will your pilgrimage be supported and enhanced by taking place within the forms and traditions of an established religious practice? Or is it important to create a pilgrimage that is unique to your personal situation and circumstances rather than fitting in to a traditional form?

3. **Choose where to go.** Pick a place that is a good outward representation of the theme of your inward journey. Consider these possibilities: A place of origin: your birthplace, land of your ancestors. A sacred place out of your religious tradition. A place you are mysteriously drawn to. A place that reflects the images and themes of your current inner journey.

4. **Select a time for your pilgrimage.** Is the season important? What length of time is called for?

5. **Decide on the amount of challenge or difficulty that is appropriate for your pilgrimage.** Does your pilgrimage theme have an ascetic quality that could be reflected in the ruggedness of terrain, mode of transportation, and kinds of rituals selected?

6. **Choose the form and route of your pilgrimage.** Will there be way stations along the way to the destination that add meaning to the journey? Would your journey better be designed as a circling around from place to place (circumambulation form) or a journey to a sacred place and back?

7. **Create some ritual observances that support and enhance the theme and purpose of your pilgrimage.** See Chapter 13 for ideas.

Circling the Mountain

When I was a young college student at San Jose State, a fellow student invited me to go on an interesting adventure. He drove me to a state park North of San Francisco where we "circumambulated" Mt. Tamalpias in celebration of Buddha's birthday with a group led by poet Allen Ginsberg. We began at sunrise at the base of the mountain, winding our way up paths in a clockwise direction, arriving at the summit at noon, continuing on around and down, and concluding back at the base of the mountain at sunset. The group stopped regularly for ritual chanting and readings at various points along the way. While much of the details have slipped from memory over the years, I remember how solid and energized I felt at the end of the day.

Circumambulation is the ritual of walking around a sacred center. In Buddhist and most other traditions, this is done in a sunwise or clockwise direction. In others, such as Muslim or the indigenous Bon of Tibet, counterclockwise. In Tibet, a thirty-two mile path circles the snowcapped summit of Mt. Kailas. This mountain attracts Buddhist, Hindu, Jain, Bon-po and other worshipers from every corner of the globe, and is the most well-known site in the world for the circumambulation ritual. You can adapt the next mountain activity to fit the accessible geography of your own area and the occasion you wish to observe.

Activity Eighty-Four ➤ Mountain Circumambulation

Select a hill or mountaintop that can be easily hiked in a single day. Begin at sunrise. Time your ascent so you reach the summit at noon. Time your descent so you return at sunset. Circumambulate means to go around. If circumstances allow, see if you can ascend by circling the mountain in a clockwise direction so that you cover all 360 degrees during your hike. Select some rituals, meditation time, or brief nature activities to do at sunrise, noon at the summit, sunset, and at various points along the way. The pace should not be rushed, but steady like the path of the sun across the sky. Unless loose approximations and adaptations are acceptable, scout the practicality of the place in advance. This is especially important if you want to go a particular direction, complete a full 360 degrees around the mountain, or meet other requirements.

Vision Quests

"Where there is no vision, the people perish."
Proverbs 30:18.

The archetypal myth of the heroic journey underlies the vision quest nature experience. This journey requires the hero or heroine to leave all that they love and own behind and venture out alone into the wilderness. In this wild and uncharted territory, the hero seeks a sacred place where there's hidden treasure: a vision for the renewal of both the self and the world. Dragons must be faced with courage and perseverance before nature will give up her treasure. After receiving a vision, the hero is challenged to return to the world of daily living to share and implement the vision in order to help sustain and regenerate the world.

By going on a vision quest, you put yourself in the role of the heroic protagonist. You become engaged in your own unique personal myth creation. You attempt to render your world spiritually significant through your own active participation in a ritualized drama. The end result, ideally, is the sacred gift of a vision by which you can transform yourself and the world around you.

Vision quests, especially those involving rites of passage, are typically the most rigorous and challenging ways of encountering nature. They are most often constructed in the spirit of an ordeal. The choice of desert landscape or other rugged terrain supports an intentionally ascetic dimension. Vision quests typically involve a solitary journey and may include several days of fasting.

The hardships involved teach important lessons. Fasting, in addition to fueling our hunger for a vision, can teach us about managing our desires. When a people turn into rampant pleasure seekers, living lives constricted by fearful avoidance of pain and suffering, then a revisiting of asceticism may help bring it back into balance. As stated in the *Tao Teh Ching*, sacred text of Taoism, "When the desires of men are curbed, there will be peace and the world will settle down of its own accord."

Vision quests follow the classic three-stage form for rites of passage. The first stage is called severance. In this stage you are stripped of all cultural and social supports, cut off from family, friends, work, daily routines and roles, responsibilities and privileges. You achieve severance by the geographical act of leaving home, by entering into the wilderness, and by leaving the company of others. Rituals and other ceremonial activities mark and accentuate the act of severance. Contemporary outward bound programs call these alone times solos. Modern versions help ensure your safety by setting up a fully supplied base camp, providing guides as overseers who are trained in emergency wilderness first aid, establishing a buddy system, and designating a pile of stones as a daily message center.

Exposure, not shelter, from nature is emphasized. In some Native American traditions, questers left their tribe with nothing but a blanket. They were required to spend days sitting within the confines of a sacred circle of stones exposed to the cold, hot sun, wind, and rain. Preparing for severance involves the ritual act of choosing what is absolutely necessary for safety and security, and letting go of all of the nonessentials you dare to leave behind.

The second "threshold" stage is the "liminal" period of incubation, the transitional phase of personal change. The word, "liminality" comes from the Latin root *limin*, meaning the centerline of the doorway. This stage is the time and place of crossing over the threshold. You cross the threshold into the wilderness, which symbolizes entering into the wild unknown place of change. This is the passage between the old and the new, the time when the old vision becomes obsolete and the new vision is not yet.

The selection of a landscape with the right ambiance is important since it is the staging ground for your transformational experience. You seek out a sacred personal "power spot" within this wild landscape where you will spend your alone time. You are called to this particular spot because it has a special resonance that mirrors and sends message to the your psyche. Sometimes arranged in the form of a sacred circle, your sacred space serves as the safe container in which your incubation takes place.

The rites of passage from the old to the new may take the form of a ritually enacted death-rebirth experience. You typically enact this phase by staying awake for an all-night vigil, from sunset to sunrise, in a ritually constructed circle of stones. This sacred circle serves as both the tomb and womb for your death and rebirth. A longer version extends for one full day, from sunrise to sunrise. The day and night of the earth, its daily death and rebirth, provide the context for your personal death-rebirth experience. You incorporate ritual to demarcate and intensify this transition. You might chose to make a small fire and burn an object that symbolizes your old self that is dying.

During this liminal time you cry out for your new vision, and then listen for nature's response. Nature answers with signs and symbols that carry the messages and teachings that you're seeking. During this stage, nature is both the testing ground in which your life and death drama is played out, and the regenerative wellspring for your spiritual wisdom and strength.

In the womb of Mother Nature, you experience the death of the old stage of life and the rebirth of receiving a new vision for the next stage in your life. Your sense of "who I am" is renewed. You gain a renewed sense of your mission in life. You obtain a clearer vision of the way you can apply your unique gifts to sustaining and regenerating the world.

Activity Eighty-Five ➤ Circle of Stones

Select a personal power spot where you will spend one full day, from sunrise to sunrise. Make a sacred circle of stones, 8-10 feet in diameter. Remain inside this circle the entire time, except when relieving yourself nearby. The stones you select can carry special symbolic meaning for you. Casting the circle to pinpoint and honor the four directions is also an option. Consider fasting.

Let your physical hunger fuel your spiritual hunger for a vision. From within your circle, call out for your vision and pay attention to nature's response. If it is safe, you might build a small fire during the night. You might also burn a ritual object in the fire to symbolize the death of the old self (old habits, old lifestyle, old beliefs) to make way for your newly emerging self.

Vision quests challenge you to face your personal dragons. Dragons common to this territory include loneliness, anxiety, boredom, emptiness, impatience, self-doubt, lack of faith, and primordial fear. We give away our power to that which we fear. Self-mastery involves facing these fears. Fear then can be viewed, not as a weakness, but as a teacher. Passing through our fears, we enter the gateway to new power and wisdom. Confronting the fear of death is an essential component of rites of passage that confers the courage needed to maintain integrity in the living of one's life.

The most difficult part of vision questing, however, does not involve facing your fear of death or enduring the physical hardships of the quest. The greatest challenge is keeping your vision alive. When you return to your people, you must find ways to manifest your vision in daily life. This third and final stage of the vision quest is called incorporation.

If this essential link between your quest experience and your home community is aborted, you may become increasingly split, creating more inner conflict than before the quest. For your quest to be complete, you must share and implement your vision back home in your community. It's not over when it's over. Did anyone tell you that "following your bliss" is easy? Think again.

The day-to-day implementing of your vision may challenge you to make significant changes in your lifestyle. Your new wings will be tested, your habits changed, and your talents developed. You may take on a new role or leadership position in your community.

Unfortunately, returning questers may meet with hostile resistance to implementing their vision. An enthusiastic welcome for returning vision questers by a community lovingly ready to receive their new visions and changes in lifestyle is not part of modern culture. Therefore, providing support for your re-entry is especially important.

Anticipate your homecoming before you leave your vision quest site. Meditate on insights gained, your gifts for the community, and how your life will be different upon return. Your gifts might include poetry, song, good deeds, drawings, arts, crafts or other contributions related to your vision. Ask yourself: "What am I leaving behind, and what am I bringing out with me? What parts of my experience are meant to be private and what parts am I to share?"

Developing your personal vision quest story and integrating it into your life story supports this transition. Share this story with your guides who can help you bring it altogether, with loved ones who can understand and support your new life tasks, and with fellow questers who can relate to your experience because of their own. Some vision quest programs offer little or no re-entry support. Others arrange for gatherings of loved ones to receive the returning questers or for follow-up meetings with fellow questers to help with this difficult transition. Be prepared to meet the challenges of re-entry into the culture.

Our culture, like all others, contains transition rituals such as graduation ceremonies, weddings, retirement parties, and funerals. However, in general, we do not have cultural supports that prepare us for these rigorous vision quest type experiences. These rituals stress participants both physically and psychologically. This is no picnic. Even if you are a rugged outdoorsman with wilderness experience, I strongly recommend that you obtain a guide. (See "Resources") These experiences are not for everyone.

Why put yourself through something like this? The vision quest is a powerful ritual form that, throughout the ages, has given questers meaningful responses to their deepest life questions, supported transitions to new life stages, clarified who they are by putting them in touch with their depths, and directly connected them with the teaching and healing powers of nature. When a person becomes disoriented and burned out, a vision quest offers a powerful way to reset one's life compass. This experience rejuvenates and inspires a renewed sense of purpose in life. Ideally, you return with a better sense of your gifts for your people and a vision of how you will share them.

Ask yourself, "Is a vision quest right for me?" Choosing this experience begins with a period of introspection in which you examines your reasons for questing. Re-examine and clarify these reasons during this initial preparation period, share with your group of guides and fellow questers, or special family and friends. Ask yourself, "What is being sought? What transition in life am I facing?" The questions of your quest remain an important focus throughout the experience. Since these adventures should begin with careful preparation and planning, most contemporary vision quest programs require attending a series of pre-trip meetings. Preparation also includes the logistics, equipment, first aid, and safety considerations for the trip.

Traditionally, the most rigorous and ongoing experiences are reserved for a select group of individuals, the shamans, mystics, healers; those responsible for carrying the wisdom, rituals and teachings of a culture. While all forms of vision quest are meant to be challenging, these experiences can be designed with a wide range of difficulty, allowing for varying degrees of food and shelter, ruggedness of terrain, length of stay, etc. For example, most Outward Bound solo experiences require little or no fasting. Solos can last for minutes or months. Vision quests also vary in the amount of preparation, group support, and follow-up debriefing after the experience. As with the other activities, remember to tailor your extended experiences in nature to match your own readiness.

"The meanings of a wilderness trip, and especially of a long one, will often surface slowly, layer by layer. You probably grasp the obvious lessons while you are still out there. Days or weeks or months later, more layers may unfold, one by one. But the deepest meanings can linger

for years in a kind of twilight; you know they lurk there, somewhere, but that is about all."

Colin Fletcher, *The Secret Worlds of Colin Fletcher*

RESOURCES:

Steven Foster & Meredith Little *The Book of the Vision Quest* (NY: Prentice Hall 1988)

School of Lost Borders, P.O. Box 55; Big Pine, CA 93513; Website: www.schooloflostborders.com/
A great resource for guided quests, books & materials, etc.

Animus Valley Institute, 54 Ute Pass Trail; Durango, CO 81301. Website: www.animas.org
Offers programs and guided quests.

Concluding Comments

RETURNING HOME

"One of the highest and best things that man can conceive is a human life nobly and beautifully lived—therefore our loyalties and energies should be devoted to the arrangement of conditions which make this possible. Our challenge is to discover how to make this world a place conducive to the living of a noble human life, and then to help people in every possible way to live such lives."

John H. Dietrich

Vision quests, pilgrimages, walkabouts, and retreats presuppose a home from which we leave and to which we return. Guarding against the tendency to over-compartmentalize our lives, we must not reserve communing with nature for special occasions only. We need to cultivate a sense of place in our everyday lives, in our own backyards.

How can we creatively design our homes and communities to live in harmony with the natural landscape and ecology? The fields of architecture, landscape architecture, gardening and agriculture, urban planning, environmental psychology, and many other areas of expertise can all play an important role in meeting this challenge by including the ecological perspective in the creation, development, renovation, and renewal of our living spaces.

However, technical manipulations of the landscape, no matter how knowledgeable, do not reach the deepest roots of the problem which are psychological and religious. Solutions based solely on legal, economic, and ecological principals, I believe, are destined to fall short. If the boat is off course and sinking, re-arranging the deck chairs won't help. We need changes in consciousness that reconnect us with nature, with our own nature and Nature-as-a-whole. Our knowledge and technical expertise will be successful to the extent that they are put into the service of realizing a new ecological vision for humanity. This deep inner change must become widespread enough to permeate our entire culture so that once again we, as a people, will walk together on sacred ground.

This change in consciousness will enable us to change our lives and our culture to live in accord with nature's way. In the words of Wendell Barry, "In nature all that grows is finally made to augment the possibility of growth, and so nothing is wasted. This year's leaves decay and enter the intricate life of the soil, which assures that there will be more leaves another year. It is this pattern and only this—not any that we may conceivably invent—that we must imitate and enter into if we are to live in the world without destroying it."

When people listen to the land, their cities will seem to grow out of the earth itself. Everything will be in proportion and balance. The angles, colors, orientations of streets and vistas will welcome and include the landscape at every turning. Nature, dwellings, and people will be in harmony and the combination will be aesthetically pleasing to the senses. Communities will support and encourage their members to live a life in resonant participation with the rhythms of nature. Being familiar with one's bioregion will be as important as knowing one's way around the local streets and highways. The customs and mores, the political, economic, educational and religious institutions will support a diversity of lifestyles and occupations, all of which exemplify and extol this fundamental understanding of our place in the grand scheme of things.

Movement towards the fulfillment of this idyllic vision begins with changes in human consciousness. We can learn to creatively dwell in harmony with our local ecosystems so that life flourishes. Ending generations of transience, displacement, and exile, we can become inhabitants who intimately know and honor the land. We can learn to appreciate and be nurtured by the land on all levels: its nurturance of our basic needs for food and shelter; its psychological supports; its community supports of belonging to kin, both human and nonhuman; its nurturance of the human imagination; its providing us with beauty and solitude; and its inspiration of our souls on the spiritual level. In the words of Scott Sanders, we can learn to "fashion a life that is firmly grounded—in household and community, in knowledge of place, in awareness of nature, and in contact with that source from which all things rise."

What will motivate us to transform our living environments from urban jungles (a term exposing our prejudices against jungles!) into communities living in harmony with nature? As stated before, it begins with a change in perception. We need to get a taste for what it is like to live in healthy communion with nature. Simultaneously we will uncover the painful loss of our alienation, and develop a growing hunger to find home. We must end our restless misplaced efforts to find fulfillment via the geographical cure. Pulling up roots to seek the land of our dreams is not the solution. Rather, it resides in its opposite, in sinking in our roots, in making a commitment to place. An environmental ethic flows naturally out of this commitment to homeland. Rooted in place, we will make decisions based on our vision of homeland as a beautiful place that will best nurture not only ourselves and our children, but also our children's children and the many generations to come. Our hope for the future lies in our willingness to say yes to this kind of belonging.

In the words of David Steindl-Rast, "Love is saying yes to belonging. Anything that we call love is in some way related to this yes. What ties all the various notions of love together, from sexual love to love of your pets, to love of your country and love of the world and love of the environment, is that we are saying yes to belonging. And that saying yes is not just an intellectual assent; it has profound moral implications. It means acting the way people act when they belong together."

On the wall over one of my best friend's toilets hangs a poster with a picture of Mt. St. Helens with her top blown. Below the picture is a quotation by the Greek philosopher Heraclitus. "There is nothing permanent except change." A paradise of harmony between man and nature is not a fixed state of grace that we will ever achieve once and for all. Rather, this harmony is co-created in an ongoing communal dance that must be continuously re-choreographed as individuals develop, cultures change, and ecosystems evolve. The goal is the way. At any given moment, our salvation hangs in the balance. Greta Sibley, in her book *Being Home,* puts it this way, "There isn't living and Living. The only difference is how completely we give ourselves to living, how we let ourselves be part of the cosmos and be lived. There is no alternative utopia running parallel to this life. This is it." Whether or not we enter into this dance of life with nature in reverence and loving kindness is up to you and me, here and now. Good journey and welcome Home!

Activities Index

BIBLIOGRAPHY

Abram, David *The Spell of the Sensuous* (Pantheon Books 1996)

Aisenberg, Nadya (ed) *We Animals* (Sierra Club Books 1989)

Altman, Nathaniel *Sacred Trees* (Sierra Club Books 1994)

Badiner, Allen Hunt (ed) *Dharma Gaia: A Harvest of Essays on Buddhism and Ecology* (Parallax Press 1990)

Barry, Wendell *Unsettling of America* (Sierra Club 1977)

Berry, Thomas *The Dream of the Earth* (Sierra Club Books 1988)

Berry, Thomas & Brianne Swimme *The Universe Story* (Harper 1992)

Berry, Wendell *The Unforseen Wilderness* (Univ. Press of Kentucky 1972)

Bassoff, Evelyn S. *Mothering Ourselves* (Penguin Books 1992)

Bates, William H. *Better Eyesight Without Glasses* (Holt & Co. 1981, c.1943)

Binswanger, Ludwig *Being-in-the-World* (Harper & Row 1967) Jacob Needleman (translator)

Bodian, Stephan (ed) *Timeless Visions, Healing Voices* (Crossing Press 1991)

Briggs, John *Fractals: The Patterns of Chaos* (Simon & Schuster 1992)

Brooks, Charles *Sensory Awareness: The Rediscovery of Experiencing* (Viking Press 1974)

Brown Jr., Tom *Tom Brown's Field Guide to Nature Observation and Tracking* (Berkley Books 1983)

Buber, Martin *I and Thou, 2nd Ed,* (Charles Scribners Sons 1958)

Burton, L. 1981. A critical analysis and review of the research on Outward Bound and related programs. Ph.D. diss., Rutgers University, New Brunswick, New Jersy.

Cialdini, Robert B. *Influence: The Psychology of Persuasion* (William Morrow 1993)

Clinebell, Howard *Ecotherapy: Healing Ourselves, Healing the Earth* (Fortress Press 1996)

Cohen, Michael J. *Well Mind, Well Earth* (World University Press 1994)

Cornell, Joseph *Listening to Nature* (Dawn Publications 1987)

Cross Currents: The Journal of the Association for Religion and Intellectual Life (Summer '94) Vol. 44, No. 2. Cover theme "Nature as Thou"

Cumes, David *Inner Passages, Outer Journeys: Wilderness, Healing, and the Discovery of Self* (Llewellyn Publications 1998)

Diagnositic and Statistical Manual of Mental Disorders, Fourth Edition (American Psychiatric Association 1994)

de Waal, Esther *A Seven Day Journey with Thomas Merton* (Servant Publications 1992)

Duensing, Edward and A. B. Millmoss *Backyard and Beyond: A Guide for Discovering the Outdoors* (Fulcrum Publishing 1992)

Edwards, Tilden *Living Simply through the Day: Spiritual Survival in a Complex Age* (Paulist Press 1998)

Ehrlich, Gretel in *Talking on the Water* Jonathan White (ed.) (Sierra Club 1994)

Elkins, James *The Object Stares Back: On the Nature of Seeing* (Simon & Schuster 1996)

Fletcher, Colin *The Complete Walker III* (Alfred A. Knopf 1987)

Foster, Steven and Little, Meredith *The Book of the Vision Quest: Personal Transformation in the Wilderness* (Simon & Schuster 1988)

Fouts, Roger *Next of Kin* (William Morrow 1997)

Fromm, Erich *Man for Himself* (Holt, Rinehart & Winston 1947)

Fulghum, Robert *From Beginning To End: The Rituals of Our Lives* (Villard Books 1995)

Gallagher, Winifred *The Power of Place* (Poseidon Press 1993)

Gleick, James *Nature's Chaos* (Viking 1990)

Glendinning, Chellis *My Name is Chellis:And I'm in Recovery from Western Civilization* (Random House 1994)

Gore, Al *Earth in the Balance* (Houghton Mifflin 1992)

Grigg, Ray *The Tao of Relationships* (Bantom Books 1988)

Gunther, Bernard *Sense Relaxation* (Collier Books 1968)

Hanh, Thich Nhat *The Art of Mindful Living* (Sounds True Recordings 1991) Audiotape

Harper, James *The Atlas of Sacred Places* (Henry Holt & Co. 1994)

Hendee, John C. & Randall Pitstick "The Use of Wilderness for Personal Growth and Inspiration" Presentation to the 5th World Wilderness Congress, Tromso, Norway, September 1993.

Hinchman, Hannah *A Trail Through Leaves: The Journal as a Path to Place* (W. W. Norton & Co. 1997)

Housden, Roger *Retreat: Time Apart for Silence and Solitude* (HarperCollins 1995)

Hull, Fritz (ed) *Earth and Spirit* (Continuum 1993)

Hycner, Richard *Between Person and Person: Toward a Dialogical Psychotherapy* (The Gestalt Journal 1991)

Jung, C. G. *Memories, Dreams, Reflections* (Vintage 1989)

Keen, Sam *Hymns to an Unknown God: Awakening the Spirit in Everyday Life*
(Bantam, 1994)

Ives, Jack D. (ed) *Mountains: The Illustrated Library of the Earth* (Rodale Press
1994)

James, William *The Varieties of Religious Experience* (Modern Library 1929)

Jastrab, Joseph *Sacred Manhood, Sacred Earth: A Vison Quest Into the
Wilderness of a Man's Heart* (Harper Collins 1994)

Kabat-Zin, Jon *Wherever You Go There You Are* (Hyperion, 1994)

Kellert, Stephen R. *Kinship to Mastery: Biophilia in Human Evolution and
Development* (Shearwater Books 1997)

Kepner, James I. *Body Process* (Gestalt Institute of Cleveland Press 1987)

Keutzer, C. (1978) Whatever turns you on: Triggers to transcendent experiences.
Journal of Humanistic Psychology, 18(3), 77-80.

Kockelmans, Joseph J. (ed) *Phenomenology* (Doubleday & Co. 1967)

LaChapelle, Dolores *Earth Wisdom* (International College 1978)

LaChapelle, Dolores *Sacred Land, Sacred Sex, Rapture of the Deep* (Kivaki
Press 1988)

Lamberg, Lynne *Bodyrhythms* (William Morrow & Co. 1994)

Lane, Belden C. "Desert Attentiveness, Desert Indifference" *Cross Currents*
Summer 1994, pp. 193-205.

Lasher, Margot *And the Animals Will Teach You: Discovering Ourselves
Through Our Relationships with Animals* (Berkeley Books 1996)

Lawlor, Elizabeth P. *Discover Nature at Sundown* (Stackpole Books 1995) le Guerer, Annick *Scent: The Mysterious and Essential Powers of Smell* (Random House 1992)

Lehrman, Fredric *The Sacred Landscape* (Celestial Arts 1988)

Lieberman, Susan Abel *New Traditions* (HarperCollins 1991)

Linn, Denise *Quest: A Guide for Creating Your Own Vision Quest* (Ballantine 1997)

Leonard, Linda Schierse *Creation's Heartbeat: Following the Reindeer Spirit* (Bantam Books 1995)

Manes, Christopher *Other Creations: Redicsovering the Spirituality of Animals* (Doubleday 1997)

Marshall, Peter *Rethinking Our Place on Earth* (Paragon House 1994)

Maslow, Abraham *Toward a Psychology of Being* (Van Nostrand 1962)

May, Rollo *Man's Search for Himself* (W.W. Norton & Co. 1953)

McHarg, Ian L. *Design with Nature* (John Wiley 1992)

McLuhan, T.C. *The Way of the Earth: Encounters with Nature in Ancient and Contemporary Thought* (Touchstone 1994)

Merleau-Ponty, Maurice *The Essential Writings of Merleau-Ponty*, Alden Fisher (ed), (Harcourt, Brace & World 1969)

Metzner, Ralph in *Sacred Landscape* Fredric Lehrman(ed.) (Celestial Arts 1988)

Mohrardt, David and Richard Schinkel *Suburban Nature Guide: How to Discover and Identify the Wildlife in Your Backyard* (Stackpole Books 1991)

Mood, John (translator) *Rilke on Love and Other Difficulties* (WW Norton 1975)

Moore, Thomas *The Re-enchantment of Everyday Life* (HarperCollins 1996)

Moustakas, Clark E. *Loneliness* (Prentice-Hall 1961)

Munro, Eleanor *On Glory Roads: A Pilgrim's Book about Pilgrimage* (Thames and Hudson Inc. 1987)

Nabhan, Gary Paul & Stephen Nimble *The Geography of Children: Why Children Need Wild Places* (Beacon Press 1994)

Nash, Roderick *American Environmentalism* (McGraw-Hill 1990)

Oates, David *Earth Rising* (Oregon State University Press 1989)

Pack, Robert *Poems for a Small Planet* (Middleburg College Press 1993)

Pappenheim, Fritz *The Alienation of Modern Man* (Monthly Reveiw Press 1959)

Perls, Frederick 1959 paper, published in *Gestalt Is* John O. Stevens (ed.) (Bantam 1977)

Perls, F. et. al. *Gestalt Therapy* (Julian 1951)

Perls, Frederick "A Life Chronology" *The Gestalt Jnl.* Fall 1993, Vol XVI, no. 2, p.5-9.

Pipher, Mary *The Shelter of Each Other: Rebuilding Our Families* (Ballantine Books 1997)

Polster, Erving & Miriam *Gestalt Therapy Integrated* (Vintage Books 1974)

Poole, Robert (ed) *The Incredible Machine* (National Geographic 1986)

Rader, Dotson "I Can Sing Of Death, But I'm Obsessed With Life" *Parade Magazine* June 11, 1995, pp. 4-5.

Rechtschaffen, Stephan "Timeshifting: How to Pace Your Life to Natural Rhythms" *Noetic Sciences Review* Summer 1997, No. 42, pp. 16-20.

Regenstein, Lewis G. *Replenish the Earth* (Crossroad Publishing Co. 1991)

Reid, Robert Leonard *Moountains of the Great Blue Dream* (North Point Press 1991)

Reisman, David *The Lonely Crowd* (Yale University Press 1961)

Reynolds, Rebecca A. *Bring Me the Ocean: Nature as Teacher, Messenger, and Intermediary* (VanderWyk & Burnham 1995)

Richo, David *Unexpected Miracles: The Gift of Synchronicity and How to Open It* (Crossroad 1998)

Roberts, Elizabeth and Elias Amidon (eds.) *Earth Prayers* (Harpers San Francisco 1991)

Rogers, Carl *Person to Person* (Real People Press 1967)

Rogers, Pattiann *Firekeeper: New and Selected Poems* (Milkweed Editions 1994)

Roszak, Theodore *Voice of the Earth* (Simon & Schuster 1992)

Roszak, Theodore "Beyond the Reality Principle" *Sierra,* March/April 1993, pp.59-62, 80.

Ruitenbeek, Hendrik M. *The Individual and the Crowd: A Study of Identity in America* (New American Library 1964)

Sams, Jamie and David Carson *Medicine Cards: The Discovery of Power Through the Ways of Animals* (Bear & Company 1988)

Sanders, Scott Russell *Staying Put: Making Home in a Restless World* (Beacon Press 1993)

Sauer, Peter (ed) *Finding Home: Writing on Nautre and Culture from Orion Magazine* (Beacon Press 1992)

Saunders. Nicholas J. *Animal Spirits* (Little, Brown and Company 1995)

Scott, Neil R. "Toward a Psychology of Wilderness Experience" *Natural Resources Journal,* Vol. 14, April 1974, pp. 231-237.

Spretnak, Charlene *States of Grace* (Harper Collins 1991)

Suzuki, David and Knudtson, Peter   *Wisdom of the Elders: Honoring Sacred Native Visions of Nature* (Bantam Books 1992)

Swan, James *Nature as Teacher and Healer* (Random House 1992)

Swan, James *Sacred Places: How the Living Earth Seeks Our Friendship* (Bear & Co. 1990)

Thorne-Miller, Boyce *Ocean* (Collins 1993)

Torrey, E. *Schizophrenia and Civilization* (Jason Aranson 1980)

Ulrich, Roger   View through a window may influence recovery from surgery. *Science* 1984; 224: 420-421.

van der Post, Laurens *The Heart of the Hunter* (William Morrow 1961)

Van Matre, Steve & Bill Weiler *The Earth Speaks* (Institute for Earth Education 1983)

von Eckartsberg, Rolf   "Toward an Ecological Social Psychology of the Individual and the Idea of Lifestyle" *Duquesne Studies in Phenomenological Psychology* (Duquesne Univ. Press 1971) pp.373-384.

Vroon, Piet *Smell: The Secret Seducer* (Farrar, Straus and Giroux 1994)

Watts, Alan *Cloud-Hidden: Whereabouts Unknown* (Random House 1968)

Welch, John *Spiritual Pilgrims* (Paulist Press 1982)

Welwood, J. (ed)   *The Meeting of the Ways: Explorations in East/West Psychology* (Schochen Books 1979)

Wheelwright, Jane Hollister & Lynda Wheelwright Schmidt *The Long Shore: A Psychological Experience of the Wilderness* (Sierra Club Books 1991)

White, Jonathan   *Talking on the Water: Conversations about Nature and Creativity* (Sierra Club 1994)

Williams, Terry Tempest *Refuge* (Random House 1991)

Wuthnow, R. (1978). Peak experiences: Some empirical tests. *Journal of Humanistic Psychology*, 18(3), 59-75.

From the Author

Dear Reader,

My love of nature goes back as long as I can remember. However, my experiences in nature, as wonderful as they were, remained limited by the blinders of our culture's commonly held assumptions about nature. This changed in 1987 at age 42 when I planned a five-day backpack for personal rejuvenation. Through a series of amazing coincidences, this trip evolved into a self-styled vision quest experience, the first of my annual pilgrimages into the woods that have had an unexpectedly powerful transforming effect on my life.

Before my quest, outdoors was for recreating, especially for fishing. After the quest, I became hooked on "cosmic fishing," a metaphor that emerged for catching epiphanies in nature. Being in nature became the primary focus. An ever-deepening commitment grew as I consciously explored and cultivated my relationship with nature. Now, nature speaks to me and I listen. I enter into relationship with nature, a relationship so intimate that I experience her as the very ground of my being. My nature experiences now serve as primary guiding forces in the way I live my life.

As a mental health counselor and counselor educator I have devoted all of my adult years to mastering relationship skills to help people heal and grow. My two greatest passions, being with clients in my office and being with nature in the great outdoors, remained separate until my vision quest experiences challenged me to bring them together. I began wondering how these kinds of nature experiences, which had been so powerfully transforming for me personally, might also apply to mental health practices in general.

This wondering resulted in my becoming involved in the newly emerging field of ecopsychology. I wrote a professional journal article in 1993, and in 1996 I participated in the "Ecopsychology, Mental Health, and Psychotherapy Symposium," the first national symposium to explore the implications of an ecological worldview for clinical theory and practice. Then I was invited to London to present a keynote paper "To Heal Ourselves and the Planet: Moving Towards an Ecological Worldview" at the "Changing Minds Towards the Millennium" Conference. I began offering "Nature and Psyche" presentations and workshops on rafting trips and at beautiful retreat centers.

Of my many involvements on this journey, completing *Communing with Nature* has been the greatest challenge. This labor of love to fulfill my commitment to offer to others what I've learned about the benefits of enhancing your relationship with nature began on the banks of the Breitenbush River in January of 1994. My hope is that many of you will be interested in finding out how much there is to be gained by improving your relationship with the living earth.

Wishing the best for you and the earth,

John Swanson